Anatolia Junction

# Anatolia Junction

A Journey into Hidden Turkey

Fred A. Reed

Talonbooks
1999

Copyright © 1999 Fred A. Reed

Talonbooks
#104—3100 Production Way
Burnaby, British Columbia, Canada V5A 4R4

Typeset in Adobe Caslon and printed and bound in Canada by Hignell Printing.

First Printing: October 1999

Talonbooks are distributed in Canada by General Distribution Services, 325 Humber College Blvd., Toronto, Ontario, Canada M9W 7C3; Tel.:(416) 213-1919; Fax:(416) 213-1917.

Talonbooks are distributed in the U.S.A. by General Distribution Services Inc., 4500 Witmer Industrial Estates, Niagara Falls, New York, U.S.A. 14305-1386; Tel.:1-800-805-1083; Fax:1-800-481-6207.

Canada

The publisher gratefully acknowledges the financial support of the Canada Council for the Arts; the Government of Canada through the Book Publishing Industry Development Program; and the Province of British Columbia through the British Columbia Arts Council for our publishing activities.

**Canadian Cataloguing in Publication Data**
Reed, Fred. A., 1939-
    Anatolia Junction

    Includes bibliographical references.
    ISBN 0-88922-426-9

    1. Reed, Fred A., 1939-  —Journeys—Turkey.   2. Turkey—Politics and government—1980-  3. Turkey—Social conditions—1960-   4. Turkey—Description and travel.  I. Title.
HN 656.5.A8R43 1999      956.1'039       C99-910807-7

# Contents

| | Map of Turkey | 6 |
| | Acknowledgements | 9 |
| | Map of Istanbul | 13 |
| | Introduction | 15 |
| I | The Grave Robbers | 29 |
| II | The Search for Said | 35 |
| III | The Journey to the East | 45 |
| IV | More Than Meets the Eye | 63 |
| V | The Secret Garden | 89 |
| VI | Galata Diary | 117 |
| VII | In the Shadow of the Citadel | 149 |
| VIII | The Hour of Remembrance | 167 |
| IX | City of Black | 183 |
| X | Rum Millet | 203 |
| XI | The Fish and the Fire | 229 |
| XII | Of Headscarves and Mystics | 241 |
| XIII | A Metallic Gold Chevrolet | 263 |
| XIV | Epilogue | 289 |
| | Notes | 303 |
| | Index | 313 |

GEORGIA

EA

amsun

ARMENIA

Erzurum

• Sivas

IRAN

Tatvan

URKEY

Bitlis⊙ ⊙ ⊙Van

Hizan

Diyarbakir ⊙ ⊙Nurs

KURDISTAN

Mardin ⊙

Urfa ⊙

IRAQ

Euphrates

Tigris

SYRIA

kms

0     200     400

rut

ON   • Damascus

Places visited in this book.

*Map by Anthony Reed*

# Transliteration

Arabic and Turkish words have been transliterated as follows:

For the convenience of the general reader, I have used standard English rather than Turkish orthography except for proper names such as Atatürk, Inönü, Beyazit Camii, Istiklal Caddesi. Arabic rather than Turkish transliteration has been used for common Islamic terms such as *Qur'an, shari'a, ulama*. The Turkish spelling has been retained for some common nouns, i.e., *medrese*.

# Acknowledgements

To Gilles Gougeon, David Homel, Jean-Daniel Lafond, Hossein Raghfar, Mustafa Rokhsefat and David Sherman who, in diverse but essential ways were prodigal in their support and assistance, I owe unconditional thanks. André Patry put at my disposal his substantial clipping file on Turkey—and his keen analytical eye. Jacques Bouchard, head of the Département d'Études Néohelléniques of l'Université de Montréal assiduously tracked down books that shed light on the darkest corners of Byzantine and Ottoman history, and made available to me many others from his rich personal library.

I must express my deep gratitude to Dr. Uner Turgay, head of McGill University's Institute of Islamic Studies, who was unstinting in his encouragement. "Turkey is not a country, it's a universe," he assured me one day over lunch at the McGill Faculty Club. Two years and many pages later, I can testify to the accuracy of his assertion.

In Greece, Nafsika Papanikolatou and Panayote Dimitras of Greek Helsinki Watch made key human rights documents available to me. And how could I ever forget their pugnacious defense, against hostile Greek opinion, of my previous book, *Salonica Terminus*? On my way from Macedonia to Istanbul, Thanasis Daskalakis welcomed me back to Kavalla with his inimitable wry humor and hospitality; and in Athens, Barbara Fields' wise and witty conversation provided nourishment for the spirit.

In Turkey, the task of thanking all those who came to my assistance, whether in Istanbul and Ankara, Konya and Erzurum, Diyarbakir, or in Mardin and Urfa, Isparta, Afyon and Emirdag is a happy but a delicate one. Readers will understand that the following list is not exhaustive, and that many of those named are not identified, a necessary precaution in that tension-charged land. Several, because of the sensitivity of their positions have not been named at all. I trust they will accept this anonymous expression of my gratitude for the hours of fruitful discussion, the introductions, and the counsel. I trust, too, that those individuals named in the text, even with pseudonyms, will accept my thanks for sharing their wisdom and their time with me.

Dr. Ahmet Davutoglu of the Foundation for Science and Arts demonstrated exemplary professional and human concern for my project. Dr. Ferhat Kentel of the Istanbul Social Research Center shared his erudition and passionate attachment to Turkey's past, present and future, as well as putting at my disposal a series of penetrating analyses of the country's Islamic movement. Dr. Numan Kurtulmus, of the Fazilet Partisi's Istanbul Branch, spared precious time for me on a rainy day during Ramadan. Professors Zafar Toprak, Ahmet Yasar Ocak, and Hasan Onat were generous with their both their time and insight.

I am grateful to Halit Eren, director of the Research Centre for Islamic History, Art and Culture of the Organization of the Islamic Conference, for granting me access to the library of his institution, which today occupies a portion of Sultan Abdülhamid's Yildiz Saray; likewise, to Dr. Azmi Özcan, president of the Centre for Islamic Studies of the Turkish Religious Foundation in Üsküdar, who arranged for me to use the Centre's rich resources.

Journalists Ali Bayramoglu, of *Yeni Yüzyil*, Aytun Altindal, Ahmet Tasgetiren of *Altinoluk*, and Hakan Aslaneli of the *Turkish Daily News* shared with me both their insight into and information about contemporary Turkish reality. And without the perceptive commentary and keen judgment of Akif Emre, editor of *Yeni Safak*, my grasp of the complexities of religious politics in Turkey would have been far poorer.

My stay in Istanbul owed much to the kindness and timely assistance of Mehmet Dukkanci, to the hospitality of Dr. Nuri and Neziha Karaman, and Sitki Çolak, transplanted Thracians all. Ercan Balci, Necip Fazil Kurt, Ismaïl Özdogan, Kenan Camurcu of the Istanbul Organization, philosopher Ali Bulaç and Mustafa Sen of the National Youth Organization, all helped sharpen my understanding of a fast-changing political and social environment. Dr. Ömer Bolat of the Independent Industrialists' and Businessmen's Association (MÜSIAD) and his colleague Mustafa Özel administered a capsule course on the Turkish economy from an Islamic perspective.

In Ankara, I spent memorable—and fruitful—hours with Mehmet Pacaci, Mehmet Said Rehber and Osman Tastan; in Konya, with Fatih Aygün and his family and friends.

No expression of gratitude would be complete without mention of Yorgos Benlisoï of the Ecumenical Patriarchate Library, who introduced me to Patriarch Bartholomeos I, and allowed me to use the venerable institution's unique collection.

And without the good-humored help of Asuman Dagistanli, I would probably still be looking for a proper hotel or the right bus line.

The research and writing of this book could not have been carried out without the assistance of the Canada Council for the Arts. Parts of it have previously appeared in a different form in the pages of *La Presse*, thanks to Marcel Desjardins, who trusted my hunches where lesser editors might have blanched. Excerpts from Chapter X, *Rum Millet*, appeared in *Mondo Greco*, published by Dino Siotis, to whom I owe a long-time debt of thanks for support both moral and literary.

The indefatigable and dedicated Fadi Dagher compiled the index. To the keen eye of my son, Anthony Reed, I owe the the maps that grace this volume. And, had it not been for the forbearance of my wife Ingeborg, who tolerated prolonged absence and often moody presence as I pursued shadows across real and imaginary landscapes, *Anatolia Junction* would never have been written.

While the hours of discussion, comments and criticism of many friends and colleagues informed and guided me in my work, its conclusions, judgements and, above all, its inevitable errors and oversights are mine alone.

Finally, this book is dedicated to Hassan Abdulrahman, *mujahid* with gun and pen who fears no mortal man, in whom I have long recognized the virtues I would find in Bediuzzaman Said Nursi.

# ISTANBUL

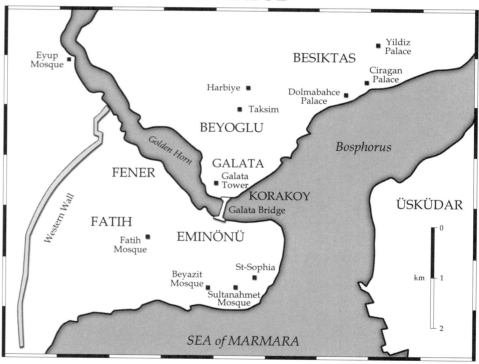

Map by Anthony Reed

Sacred pool at the Halilürrahman Dergah, Urfa.

*Photo by Anthony Reed*

# Introduction

MY VOYAGE TO HIGH ANATOLIA in the footsteps of the Muslim preacher, revivalist and ascetic Bediuzzaman Said Nursi began as a journey to Mecca: Mecca as metaphor for Islam's continuous quest to rediscover and remake itself. The paths that lead to it are many, often conflicting, complex and multi-faceted, as different as the societies that make up what we term the Islamic World, as diverse as the movements that sweep across it like wind sweeps across water, now ruffling the surface, now setting in motion mighty waves.

In my search for the wellsprings of the renewal movement—often called "fundamentalism" in the West—that has become an incontrovertible fact in that world, Mecca would be my ultimate destination. Not that I could have actually visited the holy city, of course. No Sir Richard Burton, I declined the subterfuge of concealing my cultural and religious identity. The tension that must underlie my enterprise of exploration and description would flow instead from the impossibility of reaching my goal.

If, in the Cavafian sense, we are to prize most those journeys which are their own purpose, then this journey, whose destination lay inaccessible, would be an exercise in application worthy of a Sisyphus, the mirage-chaser's Ultima Thule, its own rich reward.

When I began, I proposed to explore these paths, to compare the establishment of a modern Islamic theocracy in post-revolutionary

Iran with the struggle of Islamists, political and otherwise, in Turkey. But early on in the process of planning this book, I came to understand that the tale I wanted to tell lay not in the abstract generality of a world in flux, but in the gritty particulars of a cross-section of that world—that thin slice of living tissue excised from the body politic and placed beneath the microscope of the writer's and traveler's gaze.

Iran I knew well, as well as any frequent visitor can know the family from which he receives hospitality. I knew the cries, and had heard some of the whispers, though they remained indistinct. I had documented them in *Persian Postcards*, an exploration of that country in the aftermath of the Islamic Revolution of 1979. Not surprisingly, my overall understanding of the Islamic revival movement in Turkey was colored by my Iranian experience, in both its positive and negative aspects, perhaps more than I knew, or cared to admit.

My years of travel and journalistic investigation in Greece and the southern Balkans had long since driven home to me the powerful and lasting impact of the Ottoman centuries upon Europe's soft underbelly—although a more accurate definition might be that of an advance position of the Islamic Orient in the European heartland. For though the Ottomans have departed, their heritage has endured with startling tenacity. This was the subject of *Salonica Terminus*, in which I investigated the ravages of Western nationalism in the region. That book's subtitle, "Travels into the Balkan Nightmare," may have seemed, to some, lurid at the time. No longer.

The 1999 Kosova war, sold as a conflict between Evil in the form of a demonized and isolated Serbia and Good in the shape of Free Market crusaders dressed in humanitarian hair shirts—bearers of the rich man's burden, perhaps?—could better be described as another episode in the ongoing War of the Ottoman Succession, the raging imperative of replacing a multi-national dispensation with a plethora of tiny, discrete national entities forever separated by "ancestral hatreds" and "eternal truths," where one country's national hero is another's mass murderer.

Here I can declare parenthetically that no state system, no European-import regional security pact which will produce yet another restructuring on ethnic-national lines, no Drei Kaiser Bund, no US-dominated free-market protectorate, has been, is, or will be successful in eradicating this heritage. No need to skim over the failings of the Ottoman model, to conceal its cruelties, in order to acknowledge its success. A glance at the region today, from Bosnia to Kosova, is eloquent enough testimony.

The bravado of the Serbs, in their racialist crusade to rid their land of what they once termed the "Turkish-Albanian epidemic," seems to confirm the extent to which the old Empire still rules, deep in the national subconscious. The Albanians, yearning to join the West, would hide their own Ottoman connection, their own Islamic past, ill realizing that the more vociferously they abjure it, the more they point to it. Tiny, ephemeral Macedonia survives as a living relic, a lost land that seems to have emerged from a time warp, a throwback to the last days of Istanbul's last Balkan province, before the paroxysm of nationalism—that quintessential European import, let us remember—when peoples and religions contrived to live together as neighbors, and sometimes even as friends.

Then there is Greece, my first country of adoption. Clinging to Europe and claiming itself as the fountainhead of democracy, the Greeks cannot abide their own history; thus they luxuriate in the falsehood their own state founders devised to lend the new country its national and ethnic *bona fides*. But my years in modern Greece had convinced me that the country could not be fathomed without an understanding of the Empire from which it sprang, for better or for worse.

To understand why this is so, what better place to look than Turkey itself, where the original de-Ottomanization campaign has been underway from within for 75 years now? Thus I resolved to focus my attention on the land that lies between Iran to the east, and the Balkans to the west, the society that for nearly one thousand years was the standard bearer of Islam. Not the febrile, mercurial Islam of the Iranian Shi'ites,[1] torn between quietism and innovative volatility, but the established, disciplined orthodoxy of the mainstream Sunnis, those who wielded a cultural and spiritual tradition that gave unifying dignity to the lives of men and women from the Atlantic to the Philippine Archipelago.

Turkey not only occupies a geographical median space. It was—and remains—the great laboratory of Westernization in the world of Islam. And the epic battleground of resistance to it. In Istanbul, the capital of two empires, and on the steppes and in the mountains of Anatolia, a dynamic, aggressive European nationalism has encountered the intransigence of a concealed yet stubbornly powerful Islamic revival, often carried by Sufi mystics.[2]

My self-ascribed mission was to explore the spiritual heartland of this revival, to illuminate that part of Turkey that lies hidden, is shown on no map, described in no tourist guide. To carry out this mission, I travelled to the far reaches of high Anatolia, following in the footsteps of the enigmatic Said Nursi. I spent more than six months in Istanbul, exploring the distant and recent past in the great city's architecture and in its teeming sidewalks and market-places, its mosques and museums and libraries.

The structure of this book—the account of a voyage to far Anatolia interspersed with frequent returns to the hurly-burly and complexity of Istanbul—reflects the dual nature of my quest: to grasp the life of a man and his times, and to trace the social and historical forces that shaped the last years of one of the world's great empires, then brought it tumbling down, to be replaced by a modern, secular state.


ANYONE WRITING ABOUT Turkey must overcome an almost insurmountable obstacle. "The image of modern Turkey projected abroad is mainly a product of the prolific writings of Western authors," writes Muhammad Rashid Feroze. "This is, however, a partial and consequently mutilated image of a completely Europeanized Turkey where Islam is either dormant or dead in the public life of the people, and the few traces of Islam that remain confined to the four walls of the mosques and the minds of the 'reactionaries' may be wiped out soon by the torrents of Western culture. This picture of Turkey painted by Western writers betrays a studied attempt to convince the rest of the Muslim world that it can achieve progress only by following the example of Turkey in Westernization."[3]

Dozens, perhaps hundreds of such books exist. I had no desire to write yet another one.

If we, as Westerners, can look with comfort upon anything in our tormented cultural heritage—of which the now-expiring century of rationalist mass slaughter must mark the nadir[4]—surely it is to the dimension of self-doubt that now afflicts us. In writing about Turkey, and about Islam in Turkey, I would speak not from the point of view of the Islamists themselves, of whatever persuasion; that would have been presumptuous, and opened me to accusations of voice appropriation. I would write from the perspective of a Westerner who takes the simultaneous criticism of our own cultural and historical tunnel vision as his duty.

Seen from this vantage point, the work of generations of historians belonging to the school of Hegelian linear progress and Eurocentric inevitability is both overwhelming in its accumulation of fact and erudition, and stunning in the narrowness of its purview. These historians have fashioned a reverse prism, channeling the glorious spectrum of disparate events into a unidirectional, colorless shaft of light that blinds rather than illuminates. All is focus; nothing is field. The obligation of the anti-globalist is to reverse the prism, to restore the diversity of historical experience, to seek out the full range of the discreet, the singular, that which still presumes to define itself, that which insists in asserting itself as autonomous subject against the suffocating pall of commercial and cultural objectification.

To locate these voices in Turkey was no small task. It began in 1996 in Tehran where, during one of my frequent visits to the Iranian capital, I encountered a man called Ahmet Salahuddin, a Turkish citizen whose insistence on acting on his religious beliefs had landed him in exile, under threat of a death sentence, should he return. There, in a small, stuffy office not far from the money-changers' bazaar aptly called Istanbul crossroads, Mr. Salahuddin launched into an impassioned critique of Turkish historiography by pointing to Sultan Mahmut II, the early nineteenth-century Godfather of Westernization, as the man who would have delivered—culturally if not ideologically—the entire Empire over to Europe then and there. Had it not been for the intercession of the religious establishment, the *ulama*, the Sultan might have succeeded.

As my research deepened, the question of sources quickly reared its head. Historians whose work was accessible to me hewed to the prevailing canon, seeking only to elucidate aspects of it. The work of British authors I found vexatious in the extreme: in it, Istanbul appeared as some far and exotic suburb of London. Of the currents of religious mysticism that flowed through the Empire, both in time and in space, next to nothing had been written beyond obscure monographs on the dust-laden shelves of specialized libraries in the city on the Bosphorus. Fewer still suggested that Westernization in Turkey has failed in its unavowed but principle aim: to destroy Islam as a vital, unifying force, as a social cement of unmatched adhesive power, and as political potentiality.

Yet what I quickly ascertained when I arrived in Istanbul, with nothing more than a superficial grasp of elementary Turkish, was that very failure. Seen at close hand, my subject had become more compelling.

The "legitimist" Islamic movement—today incarnated as the Refah (Welfare) and its successor, the Fazilet (Virtue) parties—founded in the mid-seventies by Dr. Necmettin Erbakan had established itself as a political force. But the movement's strength was simultaneously its weakness. By pulling the faithful from the mosques and transforming them into voters, Refah/Fazilet had elected to play by the rules laid down by the ruling secular establishment. After being driven from the coalition government by the *coup d'état* of February, 1997, it found itself under increasing pressure to behave, not as an Islamist party, but as a secularist one. Its attempts to test the legitimacy of its politico-religious identity have been met, repeatedly, by unyielding repression.

When, in the aftermath of the April, 1999, election, newly-elected MP Merve Kavakçi was stripped of her citizenship for daring to wear a headscarf in the parliamentary chamber in Ankara, the absolute limits to political action informed by religion in Turkey became clear. In a meeting several months before, Dr. Recai Koutan, the party's leader, had taken pains to assure me that Fazilet, as it was now known, was first and foremost engaged in the defense of democracy. Without democracy, he insisted, there could be no freedom of expression in Turkey. Subsequent events, including the trials of several dozen young women arrested for protesting the banning of headscarves at the University of Malatya, have given the state's response to the implicit petition. The accused, some as young as seventeen, now face the death penalty. Journalists for the Islamist weekly *Selam*, outspoken in its advocacy of an Islamic polity, have been forced to flee abroad.

In the shadow of Refah/Fazilet's tightrope act over the thundering abyss of state repression, other powerful and influential Islamic movements thrive. One of them, led by a sybilline, charismatic preacher called Fetullah Gülen, is rumored to be recruiting a Golden Generation of devoted Muslim cadre, prepared to assume command of the state. And deeper still in the obscurity wrought by the Republic's banishment of its religious heritage, Turkey's controversial Alevis celebrate their fealty to the legacy of Mustafa Kemal Atatürk, the founder of the modern, secular state.

All, to invert the formula of the Communist Manifesto, seek to conceal their aims.

Hidden from sight, unassuming and self-effacing, lay another manifestation of the Islamic revival in Turkey. This one—call it a movement or a community, but not a political party—had no agenda, and had nothing to hide. It existed seemingly for the sake of religion, which alone, it claimed, could cure the ills that afflict modern society. It was powerfully traditionalist and disconcertingly contemporary. Against overwhelming armed force, it seemed to argue, what better weapon than absolute weakness?

IN OCTOBER, 1998, Turkey celebrated the seventy-fifth anniversary of the founding of the Republic, Atatürk's legacy to the descendants of the Ottoman Empire. There were military parades featuring heavily armed commandos dangling from helicopters as if in reply to the Islamist women's groups who, several weeks earlier, had staged a peaceful demonstration in the form of a human chain several million strong that stretched from Istanbul across the Bosphorus Bridge to Ankara and beyond.

Turkey's mainstream media, whose fealty to the military regime is exceeded—with a handful of honorable exceptions—only by its taste for vulgarity and sensationalism, had all but ignored the massive people's demonstration. Instead, it had hailed the devotion of the People to the founding principles of the Republic. But a mere handful turned up for memorial ceremonies at the pharaonic Atatürk mausoleum in Ankara.

Meanwhile, security forces carried out sweeping arrests of journalists and organizers of the earlier protest, including several of the individuals I spoke to in preparing this book. The meaning of these events was clear: nothing would be permitted to stand in the way of "progressivism," the Turkish political jargon term for what is termed Atatürk's legacy of secularization. As a corollary, "reactionism," shorthand for political Islam, was to be eradicated.

Three weeks later, yet another demonstration was held in silence to commemorate another anniversary: that of the establishment of the Supreme Board of Higher Education, known by the Turkish acronym YÖK. A creation of the September 12, 1980 military takeover, the Board has never missed an opportunity to demonstrate exactly where power lies. One day after the mass gatherings protesting its continued existence, the Board brought down sweeping new regulations, published in the official gazette, thus giving them force of law. The regulations, governing the

THIS BOOK BEGAN as an exploration of what we in the West call Islamic fundamentalism in Turkey. It did not take me long to realize that I had it backwards. We are the fundamentalists. Things must be done our way, the Western way, or not at all. The World Culture's time dishonored strategy of stigmatizing, marginalizing and destroying what it cannot assimilate is in full cry. Islamic fundamentalism, now cast as a synonym of terrorism and blind violence, was in fact the reflection of a civilization whose own accomplishments would cause the most outrageous caricature of putative Muslim rage to blush with shame and envy. Who was the pathetic yet shadowy Osama bin Laden, what could he hope to achieve against the cruise-missile arsenal of the Clintons, the Blairs and the Albrights of our fine, bright, inevitable world?

When I explained my views to my interlocutors in Turkey, they smiled with infinite courtesy. Why had I imagined I was telling them something they did not know?

So, though this book speaks to Westerners of a barely known (to them) religious and political personality, of a little-known past in an ill-known land, it does so in the certain knowledge that it holds up a mirror—cracked, imperfect, warped—to our own civilization.

It attempts something else.

In Herman Hesse's '60s cult novel *Steppenwolf*, Mozart proposes to Harry Haller, the incarnation of the wolf of the steppes, to listen to Handel's *Concerto Grosso in F Major* on a primitive wireless set: "… behind the slime and the croaking there was, sure enough, like the old master beneath a layer of dirt, the noble outline of that divine music. I could distinguish the majestic structure and the deep wide breadth and the full broad bowing of the strings."

Haller, the book's protagonist, protests the distortion as the last victorious weapon in the war of extermination against art. And Mozart replies: "Do you hear the basses? They stride like gods."[5]

Like Hesse's skewed metal loudspeaker trumpet with its crackling and hissing and static, this book attempts to suggest, however imperfectly, the long, loping strides of the gods, or whatever other convenient agency we designate as the force that structures and restructures the human condition.

Finally, whither Turkey?

Writing in the shifting ground between history and the present is an approximate art, akin to the reading of goat collar bones and chicken entrails or, at best, sifting through the shards at some archeological dig, for which the journalist's factual and statistical profiles provide a pale simulacrum. An author's efforts to intuit the future have much more in common with the uneasy grunting and lowing of barnyard animals who have sensed an incipient earthquake than with the dismal pseudo-discipline of aligning economic indicators.

Such was the method that led to this book.

In these pages, I also seek to explore an ill-known yet decisive moment in the history of a millennium-old culture: the slow collapse of the Ottoman Empire, its death agony in the form of the Young Turk revolution, and its replacement by the Turkish Republic—all in the shadow of that immense conflagration known as the First World War. In the life and times of Said Nursi, whose career spanned all three regimes, and whose views and teachings were inimical to each, I believe I have identified an emblematic figure, one who both expresses and evokes a civilization, a culture and a religion caught up in a process of impassioned reevaluation and reformulation.

That such a process can take place in an age that claims to have banished contingency, to have reduced all phenomena to micro-management, borders on the miraculous, and as such should compel our admiration in and of itself. But it is also the harbinger of something greater.

A shift is underway in Turkey. It proceeds not with the hair-trigger precision of military maneuvers, nor with the predatory dash of a corporate takeover, but with the glacial, rock-grinding singlemindedness of an entire society reasserting an identity that has been suppressed but never extinguished.

The sacred pool at the Halilürrahman Derga, Urfa.

*Photos by Fred A. Reed*

The empty grave, Urfa.

*Photo by Fred A. Reed*

I

# The Grave Robbers

IN URFA LIES an empty grave.

Why it lies empty today and whose remains it briefly held tell a tale of epic intransigence, and of the struggle for a country's soul.

In the conventional wisdom of the soldiers, politicians, businessmen, and intellectuals who make up its ruling elite, modern Turkey is the emanation of a singular, forceful intelligence, a dominating will: that of Mustafa Kemal Atatürk. At once creator and subject of a phoenix myth updated to fit the times, Atatürk is to be seen as both an architect and a master mason. Savior of a country reborn from the ashes of near-annihilation at the end of the First World War and hauled, half reluctantly, half enthusiastically into Western secular modernity. So claims the burnished but rusting boilerplate of what is still conventional wisdom, enforced, *in extremis*, at gun point.

Far from Istanbul and Ankara, in a distant, impoverished south-eastern corner of Anatolia, the empty grave in Urfa makes a silent claim that is every bit as bold. As absence reveals presence, its emptiness evokes a hidden Turkey, no less powerfully experienced for being unseen; a living negation of the myth of power inscribed in the republican Turkish state. Around it has grown a community that has willfully turned its back on the Atatürk cult. For lack of a centre, it is everywhere. For lack of an identifiable leader, it is multiform, protean. For lack of a political perspective, it is saturated with political potentiality. Though to the casual observer it seems vacant, it reverberates with the future of Islam in Turkey and throughout the Muslim world.

To this ancient city that overlooks the arid plains of upper Mesopotamia, in the spring of 1960, came an old man. The month of Ramadan fell in March of that year, and the weather across most of Asia Minor was bitter still. For much of his journey, which had begun two days before in the western Anatolian provincial town of Isparta, snow lay on the ground, and the primitive roads had been churned into muddy tracks.

The wispy old man's eyes were bright with the fever of pneumonia. Slumped in the back seat of a metallic gold Chevrolet sedan, sunken-cheeked, exhausted, his health destroyed by years of imprisonment and house arrest, he knew that this journey would be his last. Had he not prayed, then instructed that it be so? With him traveled three companions, younger men whose humble devotion to their elder's every wish marked them as followers. They had sustained themselves with cheese, bread and olives—the traditional Ramadan fast-breaking fare—as they drove south. Before they departed, a doctor had injected the elderly man with penicillin. But the miracle drug had no effect; he could eat nothing, drink little water and could barely speak.

On the way, they had stopped to smear the car's license plate with mud. To escape recognition by the police—how many metallic gold Chevrolets were to be found on the backroads of Turkey in 1960?— they drove by night. For all his advanced age and his infirmity, their passenger, whose head was wrapped in the traditional Islamic turban long forbidden by republican Turkey's draconian dress legislation, was considered by the authorities as a threat to the state. Now, his flight from the place where he had spent years of internal exile had touched off a country-wide alert and laid bare a bitter division at the heart of the regime.

The Republic itself was in turmoil, caught up in a political and economic crisis. The elected government of Democrat Party Prime Minister Adnan Menderes was faltering. With the ostentatious strut and hard eyes of men dangerously sure of themselves, high-ranking officers of the Turkish military had earlier that month visited the residence of former dictator Ismet Inönü, Atatürk's lieutenant and successor. Violent incidents instigated by operatives of the Republican People's Party, which for nearly three decades had ruled Turkey as a single-party semi-totalitarian state, were breaking out across the country. The nation's first faint experiment in parliamentary democracy was coming to an end. The mood in the country was ominous.

The Chevrolet and its four passengers arrived in Urfa late in the morning of March 21. The weather was milder in this city astride the historical caravan route to Syria where snow never falls. But the change of climate had come too late. Life was ebbing from the frail old man. Hurriedly his followers located a hotel and carried their charge up the stairs and to the end of the corridor, to a tiny, bare room that overlooked an enclosed courtyard.

No sooner had they learned the identity of this unlikely visitor than the people of Urfa flocked to the hotel to pay their respects. The paradox of Turkey's secular regime stood etched against the sharp edged glare of reality. He whose claim on the peoples' hearts exceeded that of the embattled Prime Minister was, judged against the official criteria of the Republic, a non-person, a reactionist relic, a cantankerous, disorderly throwback to an unlamented past. A dying man who exercised no power, who commanded no battalions, who owned nothing but the prayer rug and battered tea-pot that his companions now carried as they laid him down on the narrow bed that all but filled the room.

Soon a squad of plain-clothes police arrived. They had their orders from the Interior Ministry in Ankara, they said. The old man was to be bundled into his car and driven straight back whence he had come. His followers, encouraged by the swelling crowd that filled the streets outside the hotel, refused. After several hours of tense confrontation, while the telegraph wires between Urfa and the capital hummed with urgent messages, a doctor was summoned, examined the sick man and declared him unfit to travel.

Meanwhile the president of the Urfa section of the Democrat Party marched into police headquarters and slammed his pistol down on the police chief's desk. The warning was clear: any attempt to move the unexpected visitor would be met by widespread, violent resistance.

By evening the old man's condition had deteriorated further. He could no longer speak; fever had parched his lips. His followers, who had taken turns watching over him, kept his face moist with a damp cloth. In the small hours of the morning of the following day, he laid his hands across his chest and fell asleep.

The men attending him came and went softly. Gradually they noticed that the old man's labored breathing had stilled; his chest no longer rose and fell. But his emaciated body was still warm to their touch. Not wanting to believe the inevitable, they sent for a well-known religious scholar who happened to be visiting Urfa. On entering the room he uttered the words spoken by all Muslims to attest the advent of death,

"To God we belong, and to Him we shall return."[6]

In minutes the news raced through Urfa, where people stood waiting in the narrow street in front of the hotel. Rushing to the telegraph office, the companions sent the news to the clusters of faithful followers in virtually every city in Turkey. As the sobbing hotel owner hurried downstairs after certifying his visitor's death he encountered the Urfa police chief. Final orders had been issued, said the chief. A detachment of gendarmes was drawn up in the lobby. They were to return the old man to Isparta, in western Anatolia, by force if necessary. But it was now too late. Once more he had eluded their grasp.

As Wednesday dawned the town's tradesmen closed their shops. People flocked into the streets under a gentle rain. Doves circled in the air above the Halilürrahman Dergah, the shrine built around the cave devout Muslims claim as the birthplace of the Prophet Abraham. Here was to be the visitor's final resting place. After the body had been washed, the followers carried it to Urfa's main mosque, the Ulu Camii, where it was to lie until interment on Friday.

Again the authorities intervened. Such was the influx of mourners from across Turkey and beyond, they said, that the burial would have to be brought forward to Thursday. There would be no appeal.

As the shroud-wrapped body laid in the open bier was carried from the mosque, the crowd surged forward. Now it passed from one group of outstretched arms to another above the heads of the throng, until finally it came to rest in the Dergah were it was buried. The tomb, in a circular structure overlooking the courtyard and the clear blue-green waters of the sacred pool, had been built six years before by a local holy man. But in a dream this same man had been told that the tomb was not his. Changing his instructions, he ordered that upon his death he was to be buried in the general graveyard. [7]

The date was March 24, 1960.

Two months later, on May 27, a military coup overthrew Prime Minister Menderes. Ministers of his government, members of parliament, local officials and sympathizers were arrested and herded into camps and prisons. Martial law was proclaimed. A National Unity Committee became the new supreme organ of state power. The prime minister and his cabinet were hauled before a secret court martial on the island of Yassiada in the Sea of Marmara, where a guilty verdict was brought down. More than one year later, in September 1961, Menderes was hanged, along with his foreign and finance ministers.

Less than six weeks after the coup, in early July, the military authorities imposed an overnight curfew in Urfa. Tanks and armored cars took up positions at all downtown intersections; the Dergah itself was cordoned off by armed troops. Wielding sledge hammers, a grim-faced group of soldiers forced their way through the iron grill-work that enclosed the tomb and smashed the marble sarcophagus, exposing the shrouded corpse within. Waiting in the courtyard were two coffins, one of galvanized metal and another, larger one made of zinc. The body was deposited in the smaller coffin which was then placed within the larger one. It was then sealed, loaded onto an army truck and driven to the military airfield south of the city on the Harran road.

From Urfa, an army aircraft carried the coffin westward, to the city of Afyon. There it was once again loaded into a truck and driven south through the night with a military escort. Several hours later the motorcade stopped on a hillside outside a graveyard ringed by a low stone wall. A platoon of soldiers had dug a grave and were waiting, leaning on their shovels. Hurriedly they unloaded the coffin, placed it in the grave and covered it with the sweet, freshly turned earth.

Thus ended, in an unmarked grave, the last voyage of Bediuzzaman ("The Wonder of the Age") Said Nursi, the man whose turbulent career embodies the exemplary resistance of the Turks to a revolution whose aim was to wrench them from their faith and culture and haul them into a glittering European present.

Today, as the regime created by Mustafa Kemal Atatürk's unconditional acceptance of nationalism and secularist fundamentalism stumbles toward disintegration, its legitimacy in tatters, Said Nursi's legacy—the community grown up around his life's work, the *Risale-i Nur* (The Treatise of Light)—reasserts its implicit claim as the expression of Turkey's past and present, and as the force that bids to shape its future.

# II

# The Search For Said

IN THE SPRING OF 1998 I took the first fitful steps on a journey that was to follow Said Nursi's path—geographical and temporal; metaphorical and spiritual—toward the empty grave in Urfa.

For all my repeated visits to the Middle East as a journalist, I had somehow expected a bus trip across the steppes of Anatolia, interrupted by short visits to primitive villages and picturesque provincial towns. For all my precautions as an explorer of the spiritual world, my search for evidence of this elusive figure was to send me spiraling progressively deeper into the self-contained and self-defining microcosm of the universe that is the Islamic movement in modern Turkey. I had been naïve twice over, first assuming that my progress—if I could call it that—would be simple and linear, when, in fact, it became a constant process of departing, hesitating, and returning, only to begin again. I was naïve, too, in assuming such a thing as a single, identifiable, Islamic movement. It was not long before I came to realize that there were many, united only in their diversity, often bitterly at odds, locked in a struggle for legitimacy against the secular state, bitterly divided on the very definition of what might constitute a political, cultural or spiritual legitimacy.

\* \* \*

LATE ONE AFTERNOON I found myself standing in front of a pale green office building. The place was Yeni Bosna (New Bosnia), a western suburb of Istanbul that I recalled having visited several months before. Yeni Bosna, caught up in the great city's orgy of unplanned expansion, sprawls across hillsides cluttered with rudimentary *gecekondu* ("built in one night") dwellings, multi-story apartment blocks, narrow commercial thoroughfares, vacant lots in which sheep often graze, office buildings, small industries and workshops.

"Istanbul Ilim Kultur Vakfi" read the plaque on the door: The Istanbul Foundation for Science and Culture. The concierge directed me to an upstairs office, where a group of scrupulously groomed, mature men dressed in dark suits were waiting.

For a life-long practitioner of the intuitive method, the meeting into which I stepped with scant information, but with the tingle of awakening possibility, was like a gradual clearing of morning mists. Directed by the unseen hand of raw contingency and guided by solicitous acquaintances, I had stepped into the heart of the movement dedicated to propagating the thought of Bediuzzaman Said Nursi, the people known familiarly (and sometimes pejoratively) throughout Turkey as the "Nurcus," for followers of Nur, the Arabic and Turkish word for light.

It was a movement central to the Islamic dynamic of modern Turkey, but I knew nothing about it. For unlike its counterparts in Iran, where Muslim clerics now rule in the name of religion, in Turkey's strictly-policed secular system, the Nurcus had become masters of caution and of discretion. All but invisible, they are said by some to number more than six million, almost ten percent of the population. They collaborate with the military and the right-wing parties, say impatient students and left-wing radicals. They are quietists and mystics whose passive behavior only strengthens the state, say the anthropologists, political scientists and the proponents of political Islam. They are a *tariqat*, a Sufi religious order in new, modernist clothing, say the professional atheists who write for Istanbul's big circulation daily newspapers. They are dangerous fundamentalists, bent on submerging Turkey in a rising religious tide and taking over the government and the regime, warn the militant (and often military) secularists who view the community's dead namesake as the "very incarnation of backwardness."[8]

Nothing could have been clearer.

So, if this, and not the hoary cliché of a country torn between East and West, was the real mystery of the land hidden by the image of westernized, contemporary Turkey, then I would make it my mystery to explore and to elucidate.

* * *

ISTANBUL IS A BUSY Near Eastern megalopolis that works hard to appear Western and almost succeeds. It boasts the obligatory veneer of glass-fronted high-rise office buildings peopled with smooth-shaven puffy-faced yuppies brandishing cellular phones and briefcases, indistinguishable from their European or North American role models. Not lacking are the requisite international shopping streets, international luxury hotels and supranational monster malls with their omnipresent universal brands. The press, relocated now from the grimy teeming downtown precincts of Eminönü to mirror-clad corporate headquarters overlooking the freeways beyond Yeni Bosna has become, with a few brave exceptions, the ingratiating courtier of the mighty; has forsaken the third estate to enter the first.

For the visiting writer, these are far from reassuring signs. There is more daunting to come. Turkish media personalities are capricious, their egos almost as inflated as those of their western counterparts from whom they take example. Intellectuals can be diffident and remote, the pages in their date books filled with appointments, newspaper columns to write, talk-shows on which to appear. Other academics have withdrawn into the fastness of their faculties, venturing forth with jargon-clogged, turgid learned papers that resemble complex scale-model structures built from toothpicks.

To be fair, there may well be another factor involved in this syndrome. Since the strong, even astonishing, showing of Dr. Necmettin Erbakan's Welfare Party (Refah Partisi) in the municipal elections of 1994, and in the general elections of 1996, Turkey suddenly appeared vulnerable to the rising tide of that old reliable bugbear, political Islam. Never mind that Dr. Erbakan's showing astonished only the regime—all entrenched regimes are by definition blind. Foreign journalists, writers and academics, not to mention spies and secret agents and arms dealers, descended like a Biblical plague upon the country, seeking out the chinks in its secular armor, groping for the specter of the Islamic Menace, a new threat to the World Order and to the Market Forces that spawned it. Would Turkey become a second Iran, a replay of Egypt, another Sudan, a more refined version of the horror of Algeria? Would fierce-eyed, bearded Talebans suddenly roam the streets handing out stern punishments? Who would rise to the defense, once more, of the West and its Values at the close of the twentieth century— without contest *its* century.

Public figures, especially those few who speak foreign languages, could be forgiven for losing patience, for cranking out one-size-fits-all analyses, or for simply declining to talk at all. Turkey seemed to have been polled, probed, prodded, analyzed, investigated and explained to the point of saturation.

The men I met at the Istanbul Foundation for Science and Culture are of a different cut, in manner expansive and eloquent, their speech seasoned with expressions of traditional Islamic usage. Not for them the pseudo-savant babble of the social sciences. Despite appearing to be businessmen, they conveyed to me the impression that they possessed that most precious of all commodities, time, in apparent abundance.

After introductions, a first round of fragrant tea is served and the conversation may begin.

Professor R., a bespectacled lecturer at Istanbul University with a ready laugh and solid English, would perform the delicate and thankless task of interpreting. "Please do not use my name," he instructed me as I pulled out my notebook. "It is not because I fear problems with the authorities. They know us all in any case. But what I do, I do only for the sake of God."

Professor R., I was to ascertain, was much more than an interpreter. In his method—or perhaps his lack of an overt method—I was later able to grasp the subtle yet powerful difference between the Nurcus and their crypto-authoritarian emulators, the followers of the charismatic preacher Fetullah Gülen, whose movement I had encountered three months earlier in this same gritty semi-industrial suburb, and of whom we shall hear more later.

"It is very difficult to explain Said Nursi's views and ideas face to face." Breaking with a centuries' old Islamic tradition of the oral transmission of religious knowledge from master to disciple, he explains, Said Nursi had set out to institutionalize a new culture in the Muslim world. "To perform this work, there must be an organization, which is what we are. Our foundation includes a publishing and printing house, and a radio station."

But like their founder, the Nurcus eschew anything that suggests organizational discipline. Unlike the Sufi orders, where personal relations are paramount, contrary to the political parties like Refah and its successor, Fazilet, where structure and hierarchy are the rule, their aim is to establish direct, unmediated contact with the text of Said Nursi's voluminous *oeuvre*, which itself is an ongoing, open-ended meditation on and exegesis of the Qur'an. From that point on, believers are free to advance into the text as they will.

"Bediuzzaman was not a follower of any sect, scholar or *tariqat* [Sufi order]. He said our age is a time for reality, not *tariqat*. What he did was provide us with a shorter path to enlightenment, a direct line to the Qur'an, if we can call it that. The twentieth century is the century of science; he proves that all answers can be found there."

I was looking for a pretext to shift the discussion toward what I then thought was my subject, the latent (and now overt) combat between Islam, embodied in a political movement, and its arch enemy, the secular state. Time was to pass before I understood that my hosts, and the millions who feel as they do, see reality not in these terms, but instead as a primordial struggle between the forces of belief and disbelief, and themselves as combatants in that struggle. The arms they wield are forbearance, patience and stubbornness.

Yet on that cool March afternoon, politics hung heavy in the air. More than one year before, on February 28, 1997, the National Security Council, Turkey's shadow government—the one that wields real power—had pinpointed "political Islam" as the main threat to the integrity of the state, supplanting the bloody, decade-long Kurdish insurrection in the Southeast, which was now winding down, even before the capture and trial of Abdullah Öcalan. The Council, made up of the heads of the Armed Forces, the President of the Republic, the Prime Minister and key cabinet ministers, brought down a series of "recommendations" that were understood to be binding on the coalition government led by Dr. Erbakan.

The measures, as Draconian as they were sweeping, included closure of the Imam Hatip schools that dispensed religious education. Women wearing Islamic headscarves were to be banished from the universities and civil service. A few weeks before, tanks had rolled through the streets of the Ankara suburb of Sincan, following a public meeting to celebrate the last Friday of Ramadan, known throughout the Muslim world as "Qods Day," commemorating the occupation of Jerusalem, Islam's third holiest city, by the Zionist settler state. Within months, the Erbakan government was to resign, the Welfare Party was to be outlawed, and Dr. Erbakan himself barred from politics, but not before being humiliated by being constrained to authorize the generals' strategic alliance with Israel, at the behest of Washington. Daniel Pipes, one of the architects of the alliance, had publicly stated that the army's reaction was a function of the military cooperation treaty between the two countries.

In Turkey, where memories are long and sensitivity to the whims of the military establishment are almost as acute as the generals' obsequious regard for their American mentors, the events of February 28 were seen for what they were: a *coup d'état*. Wits promptly dubbed it a "post-modern coup," which differed from previous military interventions in that the generals now wielded influence from behind the scenes, through a minority government formed by a coalition of traditional rightist and leftist parties, united in their horror of the Welfare Party and in their dedication to stop the rise of its successor, the faintly Islamist Virtue Party (Fazilet Partisi), made up of former Welfare deputies.

What had been the most recent impact of the long-standing political, religious and ideological crackdown on the Nurcu community? I wanted to know. There followed a period of vigorous exchange in Turkish among my hosts, punctuated by gesticulations and clicking of tongues to signify the negative. Clearly there was no party line here, only shades of divergence on how to explain a delicate, and perhaps dangerous, question to a foreign visitor.

"Today, some people exploit Islam to get power, and we disagree with them," explains Professor R., in an allusion to the Welfare Party and its successor. "But others" (here he could mean only the military and their pliant acolytes) "use this to suppress sincere believers."

"Is there a test for sincerity?" I ask.

"See this picture?" says Professor R., walking over to the bookshelf, picking up a framed photograph and handing it to me. The sepia-toned print depicts a group of Turkish army officers of the last century seated on chairs in a coffee house amid squatting, dark-faced men in peasant garb. "Look how the soldiers are sitting with their legs crossed while everyone else sits on the floor. This has always been the attitude of the military towards the people."

I liked the answer.

"Today, some people are searching for anti-democratic means to suppress those who have not been approved by the official regime.

It's far from clear whether they can succeed or not. After all, Turkey has signed many international human rights documents. If we continue in this way, we'll be isolated from Europe. But, on the other hand, the United States seem to prefer the military option."

Since 1923, when Atatürk, with the proverbial stroke of the pen, disestablished the once-mighty Ottoman Sunni clerical establishment—and all of Turkey's thriving Sufi orders—secularism has been Turkey's orthodoxy. It has become, in the hands of his successors, an orthodoxy as narrow, scholastic, hidebound, punctilious and protective of its own virtue as the most disputatious of religious fundamentalisms—but without the divine dispensation that had given the former empire its legitimacy.

"Look, we accept true secularism," Professor R. translates for his colleagues. "As far as we're concerned, a person's belief system shouldn't affect his view of others. Our question is this: Why should our Islamic beliefs be any less worthy of respect than their secularist beliefs?"

One of my hosts is a slight, smiling man in his early forties named Safa Mürsel. Mr. Mürsel, Professor R. explains, is the author of a book on Said Nursi and the philosophy of the state. Its thesis is this: the state should be based on peace and freedom, understood as a prohibition of doing harm to oneself and others, and on cooperation. It should be a human-centered state, whose objective is to raise mankind up, and create prosperity. Such a state, he writes, must be based on consultation, the most advanced form of which is the parliamentary system. An opposition is needed for balance, and to make sure that justice is done.

"Every man has weaknesses," says Mr. Mürsel. "Even the Caliph. Today, the community can mitigate these weaknesses. The emphasis must be on righteousness, not power. This is the view of Said Nursi."

This sounded to me like the precise opposite of what we usually understand as "political Islam," which posits the creation of an Islamic state. The capsule formula is this: First political power, the means; then righteousness, the end. The twenty-year experience of Iran, if it had shown anything, seemed to indicate that there was no necessary link between the two, and that the end was often postponed, then forgotten while the means were further refined. Whether my hosts also had this in mind is a moot point. One thing was certain: the Said Nursi they were describing to me was unalterably hostile to the idea.

"Of course," he continued, "it is not forbidden in Islam to set up an Islamic state, neither is it compulsory. But here in Turkey, people are not ready for such a development. The truth of the matter is this: as Turkey has become gradually more democratic and grown closer to the West, people have become accustomed to the secular state."

On my journey eastward into Anatolia, I was to measure that claim and find it, increasingly, to be wanting.

The landscape near Erzurum, Anatolia.

Atatürk's office, Erzurum.

*Photos by Fred A. Reed*

# III

# The Journey to the East

A T FIRST GLANCE, the itinerary that Professor R. had sketched out for me seemed straightforward, perhaps even predictable. I began to wonder if my peregrinations in crisis-wracked places like Iran and Albania had inoculated me against the lesser but still powerful appeal of travel for its own sake.

"Fred Bey," he said, addressing me in the polite familiar form that simultaneously preserves the slightly archaic, ceremonial nature of address in spoken Turkish, and lubricates social interaction, "it is quite simple. You must see Nurs, Bediuzzaman Said Nursi's birthplace. From there you can go to Van, and on to Diyarbakir and Urfa, where he was buried. I hope you will accept the hospitality of our brothers in these places."

How could I refuse? At our first encounter several months before, Professor R. had won my confidence with his modesty, punctiliousness and finely honed sense of humor. Now, in the autumn, I had returned to Istanbul, intent on traveling to the East.

Professor R. set expertly to work. Flights to Van, the point furthest from Istanbul, were booked solid for a month, but through his good offices, I bought a ticket on the daily Turkish Airways flight to Erzurum the next day. From there, I could make my way by intercity bus—Turkey's preferred means of travel—to the city at the far extremity of the country's largest lake.

It was November. Already snow had fallen on the high ground in far Anatolia, and temperatures were dipping well below the freezing point at night. "You must leave as soon as you can," he said. "Soon winter will come, and you will be unable to travel to the mountain villages. There will be much snow."

On my much-folded map, I traced my itinerary with a finger tip. From Erzurum I would be traveling to the far eastern reaches of Anatolia, into the heart of insurrection-wracked territory, only a few dozen kilometers from the Iranian frontier and dangerously close to the border with Iraqi Kurdistan.

"Don't worry," Professor R. reassured me with his hearty laugh. "My information is that the security situation is under control." That it both was and was not under control I was only to attest later, in the wild, rock-strewn passes and barren hills of the southeast as my journey progressed in muffled counterpoint to the international hide-and-seek melodrama of Abdullah Öcalan, the fallen Kurdish leader—a messiah for some, a devil for others—careening toward its pathetic and hopeful denouement.

\* \* \*

THE MIDDAY FLIGHT from Istanbul touched down at Erzurum one and one-half hours after takeoff, breaking through low-hanging clouds, banking over the city, and then settling onto the runway of the military airport across the valley. As the THY jet-liner taxied up to the terminal, I noticed air force fighters crouched in their fortified camouflage bunkers. Against what invading force would they protect? I wondered. The USSR, whose putative threat had driven post-war Turkey into the arms of Uncle Sam, had collapsed into a welter of warring principalities and wounded grand duchies. Georgia, on the Black Sea frontier, engulfed in secessionist strife with a combative Abkhazian minority and rampant gangsterism, lay in impotent thrall to a consortium of US oil companies headed by Unocal. Armenia, Turkey's ancient bugbear, had now become a nominally independent state, but remained too enfeebled and mired in conflict with its Azerbaijani neighbors to the east to pose the slightest threat. Iran, twenty years after the Islamic Revolution, was still torn by the demons it had unleashed, while the Talebans lurked across its eastern border. Saddam Hussein's Iraq, bled white and bombed to a pulp by the Anglo-American bully coalition, will hardly be in a position to endanger the security of its neighbors for decades: now a morass of undiscovered horror weapons and casual death, the country's ultimate threat to its neighbors is that of its eventual collapse and dissolution. And Syria, which had lent shelter to the aforementioned Öcalan, supreme leader of the neo-Maoist Kurdistan Workers' Party (PKK), had been forced to bow to Ankara's threats of war and expel their honored guest. By any geopolitical measuring stick, Turkey's borders were secure and its eastern neighbors toothless.

"Peace at home; peace in the world," goes the Kemalist doctrine that encapsulates Turkish foreign policy. As ties between Israel and Turkey's ruling military establishment have shifted from cordial through warm to passionate, ending in the embrace of a US-brokered strategic alliance, the thought creeps into my mind that these aircraft might be used for more than merely the defense of Turkey.

Should hostilities arise between Syria and Israel over, say, the tinderbox issue of the Golan Heights, would Turkey's newfound friendship with the Zionists embroil it in a wider regional war? Should Iran push ahead with its plans to acquire what Washington and Tel Aviv label "weapons of mass destruction," might the World Policeman be seduced by the temptation of a pre-emptive strike to protect the Israeli WMD arsenal? Might its Turkish constable be chosen as regional enforcer? All legitimized by a suitably elastic United Nations resolution where possible, or a NATO ultimatum where desirable. Or, as a suitable dowry for this courtship ritual, did Ankara by any chance have secret designs on the oil-rich Mosul region of Iraq, currently languishing under the Allied no-fly zone that blankets Iraqi Kurdistan, a region that once belonged, let us not forget, to the Ottoman domains?

In a region that remains a morass of instability, torn by the latent, violent reordering of the status quo inherited from the division of the Ottoman Empire, jet fighters, far from offering a guarantee against instability, in fact generate that very instability.

These are dark thoughts indeed—*réalisme oblige*—but as I emerge into the biting wind, make my way down the steps from the jetliner and step around the puddles dotting the tarmac at Erzurum, they vanish. Just outside the gate, a man in horn-rimmed spectacles brandishes a piece of paper with my name on it. With an exchange of selams we bundle into a waiting car and speed off across the valley, through grain fields littered with frosty stubble, toward the city.

My guide's name is Harun, and he is a researcher at Atatürk University. He is also one of the academic members of the Erzurum Nur community, and eager to use his long-languishing English skills.

"I got my master's at college in the US," says the soft-spoken Harun. "Here I am forgetting my English," he says, speaking slowly. "In Erzurum there is not much opportunity to speak it."

Harun's American-learned English, though, is just fine compared to my Turkish, which consists of a short string of mumbled niceties.

\* \* \*

ASTRIDE THE MAIN overland route to Iran, Erzurum has a reputation as a dour town, a place where everything is quintessentially Turkish. Known as Theodosiopolis by the Byzantines, the city was named Arzan-ar-Rum, "land of the Romans," by the Arabs who first conquered it in 655. Like every city and town in eastern Anatolia, it has known many masters, and been home to a rich variety of religions and ethnicities, if we may project back onto the past a rather more recent construct. Some of them have left a lasting imprint, as witnessed by the startling turquoise-ribbed minaret I spot through the misty car window. Others have vanished without a trace. In fact, their traces have been effaced. Erzurum's Turkishness is, in historical terms, a recent development.

A fine, cold drizzle is falling as Harun parks his car near the centre of the old town. Across the main street stands the *medrese*, the fine old Qur'anic school that is but one of the pleiade of Seljuk architectural masterworks that dot the landscape of Anatolia. These buildings bear eloquent witnesses to the enlightened rule of the thirteenth-century Sultan Kaykubat II Alaaddin, prince of the dynasty of Rum and protector of the saintly Jelaladdin Rumi of Konya, revered by Turks and Iranians alike as Mevlana, the master.

The ancient *medrese* with the extraordinary minaret no longer fulfills its original function. The low-linteled chambers where theological students once bent in concentration over sacred texts, today house dusty exhibits of traditional clothing, weapons, writing instruments or illuminated Qur'ans. One of the chambers displays Sufi devotional artifacts. A curious artichoke-shaped pommel hung with short lengths of chain, and attached to a long, thick rusty needle catches my eye. Harun comes over and explains:

"These are used by the Rifa'i dervishes," he says, mimicking the action he describes. "They put it in one cheek and out the other." The Rifa'i had been one of the most influential *tariqats* of Anatolia and the Balkans. Born in what is today Iraq, Ahmad Rifa'i, the order's twelfth-century founder, had memorized the entire Qur'an by the age of eight and by adolescence had mastered Islamic law at the feet of several eminent jurisprudents of the Shafi'i school. According to legend—often superior to mere fact as a source of truth—Rifa'i, on hearing of the prodigies of another mystic whose name still looms large in Turkey, called Hajji Bektash Veli, traveled from his home in the marshes around Basra to faraway Khorassan to meet him astride a lion whose mane consisted of writhing snakes. It was then that Hajji Bektash famously mounted a stone wall and caused it to gallop away, leaving his guest speechless.

The Rifa'i, who survive even today in the Albanian-speaking regions of the southern Balkans beyond the borders of Albania proper, practiced not only cheek piercing. They devoured live coals, and handled scorpions and poisonous snakes. Because of their custom of shouting the *dhikr*, the invocation that subsumes three meanings—mentioning, invoking and remembering the name of God[9]—the Rifa'i have long been known as "howling dervishes."

In his autobiography, the late secularist author, provocateur and erstwhile translator of Salman Rushdie's *Satanic Verses*, Aziz Nesin, recounts his childhood memories of the order's ritual in the Istanbul *tekke* to which his father belonged:

"I too was among the chanters … As we chanted we were caught up in a wave of excitement. The atmosphere of contagion is difficult to explain. Some ten dervishes continuously whirled in the middle of the *sama'hana* and I was whirling among them. One felt that flight was so imminent that one's feet were about to leave the ground. While ten or so dervishes whirled, with billowing robes and skirts, a dozen others were burying skewers in their cheeks … driving them through their mouths until they protruded from the opposite cheek. With skewers protruding thus from their cheeks they began to whirl and chant."[10]

Drizzly, frigid Erzurum at oncoming dusk seemed a perfect place to conjure up, for a fleeting instant, the Rifa'i and their rites of ecstatic mortification. In an age that flees pain as it flees belief, the recombination of these two apparently antithetical qualities seem to pose a curious question: to whom—or what—dare we now to address our lives, to howl in ecstasy, to skewer, metaphorically, our cheeks?

From the Seljuk *medrese*, Harun leads me through the Erzurum bazaar, where tiny one-man workshops fashion a local soft black stone into *tasbis*, rings and necklaces, and then onto the cobble-stoned side streets of the old city. Here coal smoke hangs heavy in the air, and globules of water plunk from moss-grown tile roofs. Emerging as though from the dark, damp stone itself, a small religious complex suddenly looms before us.

"This is the Kursunlu *medrese*. Said Nursi lived here for one month, before he went off to fight the Russians," he says. "Would you like to look inside?" The ancient complex is still in use, though not for religious purposes. Each of its dark, domed cells with their low, arched doorways houses poor students from the surrounding villages, come to town to attend high school. With expressions fluctuating between curiosity and shyness, a group of adolescents wearing sweaters and fraying wool jackets shows us in. There is barely enough room in each cell for four bunk beds and a tiny kerosene stove to brew tea and provide warmth; there are no tables, no chairs, no bookcases. A single dim bulb hangs from the dripping stone ceiling. For their personal needs, the youngsters use the sanitary facilities built of rough-hewn stone more than nine centuries ago, and draw water from an antique fountain in the sloping, slick-stoned courtyard. If such is the academic life of the provincial town, I wonder, what must their home villages be like?

Here, in the bone-chilling dampness, on the cusp of night, I first crossed Said Nursi's path.

He had come to Erzurum at the head of a detachment of Ottoman irregulars in January of 1916. It was a curious job for a mollah, but utterly consistent with what I would after come to understand as the man's pugnacious character and commitment not only to a political view of Islam, but to a militantly combative one. It was a view that, like the empire he had sworn to defend, did not survive the war intact.

When hostilities broke out the Ottomans, encouraged by their German allies, had proclaimed *jihad*—the combat in defense of the faith that is incumbent on believers—against the Entente powers. Men of religion flocked to the imperial standard. With a rakish turban wrapped about his head, clad in a military greatcoat, sporting curved dagger and rifle, Said must have reminded the men under his command of the heroic Muslim fighters of old, the men who wielded sword and pen in the cause of Allah. [11]

But neither sword nor pen could stop the Russian Army as it marched southwestward out of the Caucasus and across Anatolia.

The irregular cavalrymen under Said's command, known as the "felt hats" for their distinctive headgear, numbered between four and five thousand. For all their brio and *esprit de corps*, for all their flaunting of death and their religious ardor, his militiamen could not infuse the ill-fed, ill-clothed and ill-paid Ottoman conscript troops with the desire to fight to the death.

On a bitter, snowy January 16, his militiamen and Ottoman regulars engaged the Russians at the strategic town of Pasinler, a few kilometers east of Erzurum. Outnumbered and outgunned, the Ottoman infantry broke and fled. Said's men were forced to withdraw southeastward, toward Van where they would make a last stand in that city's historic citadel. One month later, Russian troops marched into Erzurum.

They found a city emptied of all but a handful of its Christian Armenian population. They had numbered 20,000 in 1914; now only 80-100 remained. Several months before, the rest had been ordered deported by the Ottoman authorities, given a few days to sell their property and prepare their belongings, and then marched southwestward along the Sivas road and into the gorges of the Euphrates at Kemah, where most were killed. [12]

While beyond Turkey's borders, a majority of historians concur on the cruel facts of the mass extermination of the Armenians in 1915, the circumstances and events that emptied Erzurum and the other villages, towns and cities of eastern Anatolia of their vibrant Armenian population are written of obliquely—if at all—within the country.

Though they acknowledged that tens of thousands of deaths did indeed occur, the Young Turk nationalists who had seized control of the Empire and brought it into the war on the side of the Central Powers, argued, as do their Kemalist successors to this day, that they were acting in self-defense against an untrustworthy minority; that the Armenian leadership had treasonously thrown in its lot with the Russians and intended to carve out an independent Armenian state in the Ottoman eastern provinces.

There is more than idle truth to this version.

Erzurum had been the setting, in July 1914, before the outbreak of hostilities, of the general congress of Dashnaktsutiun, the Armenian nationalist organization. Members of the ruling Ottoman Committee of Union and Progress (CUP)—*Ittihad ve Terraki Cemiyeti*—attended the fateful gathering, where they pressed the Dashnaks to encourage Armenians living in Russia to take up arms against the Tsar in return for promises of a semi-autonomous Armenia. The congress voted down the proposal, but promised that "Armenian Ottoman citizens would enlist and fight as loyal nationals." [13]

But when the Empire entered the war on October 30, 1914, Armenian nationalists flocked to join the volunteer partisan units that were being set up across the border in Russian Armenia. The CUP rulers, whose hostile takeover of the moribund Ottoman state in 1908 might best be described as a high-level highjacking, could hardly have dreamed of a richer pretext. Two months later the Ottomans launched their great offensive against the Russian base at Sarikamish, deep in Ottoman territory. After capturing the fortress, the grand army planned to punch through to Baku, and liberate their Turkish-speaking brethren of what are today Turkmenistan and Uzbekistan from the Russian yoke. Perhaps it would even march through Afghanistan and into the Punjab, touching off a Muslim uprising against the British.

Led by the Minister of War Enver Pasha himself, the expeditionary force encountered calamitous defeat instead. Three quarters of the 100,000-strong Ottoman army perished, most from the extreme cold of the Caucasian winter, a casualty rate worse than that encountered by the Allied forces at the Battle of the Somme, the set-piece massacre of the Western Front.

Although he did not appreciate it, the disaster at Sarikamish marked the beginning of the end of Enver's military career, and sounded the death knell of the Empire itself. Never again, except at the end of his life, would he assume personal command. When he did, it was to be at the head of a band of Basmachi insurgents fighting against the Bolsheviks southeast of Bukhara in 1925. But the Armenians may have appreciated it all too well. They were to become the scapegoats for his monumental folly. Or were they already destined to be "cleansed," to use the contemporary expression, from the map of Anatolia, in which case Enver's calamitous expedition simply provided justification for pursuit of a strategic goal? Then, no less than today, representatives of the media were absent from the secret conclaves where decisions of war and peace, life and death, were taken.

Certainly, by 1915 and 1916, for Said Nursi and his men, the Armenians and the Russians were the enemy. Both had learned to fear the hard-riding, keen-eyed marksmen of his irregular forces, who gave no quarter and expected none. Bediuzzaman, who was known then as Mollah Said, led the charge on horseback, while at night, in the trenches, he would read from his books to the mystified but captivated militiamen.

As he waged war with his rifle, Mollah Said also took time to dictate in Arabic his Qur'anic commentary, *Signs of Miraculousness*. In it, he was to sketch out for the first time the "proper means" by which religion should be propagated in modern times. As the Qur'an's truths were being revealed by the advances of science, commentary must keep pace, he argued, laying the foundations of what would become his life's work: the combining and joint teaching of modern science and religious method which is even today the hallmark of the community that bears his name.

\* \* \*

NIGHT FALLS EARLY in eastern Anatolia. Though it is one thousand kilometers from Istanbul, and certainly no longer "Europe," Erzurum is captive of the same time zone. Already at 4 o'clock the faithful are streaming toward the mosques, and an acrid mist of coal smoke has settled over the town. The hour is propitious for a cup of Turkish coffee.

(Though coffee was adopted by the Ottomans in the seventeenth century after several years of theological disputation over whether, as a mild stimulant, it should be proscribed—declared *haram*—it is extremely difficult to find the bitter black beverage outside of Istanbul, Ankara, and the tourist resorts of the Aegean and Mediterranean littoral.)

There may be a place in Erzurum where we can find it, Harun ventures, as we exit the massive stone portals of the twelfth-century Ulu Camii—the Great Mosque—where he had paused to offer his pre-dusk prayers. A few blocks back toward the town centre, a left turn, and we slip through a glass door frosted with condensation, into a tiny coffee house lavishly decorated with kilims. Traditional musical instruments hang from the wall, alongside faded photographs of the city and bric-a-brac of unimaginable application.

Five minutes later a demitasse of foamy coffee appears in front of me, a glass tumbler of tea in front of my host. Contented, I sip the hot, bittersweet liquid as he tells me the tale of an American friend from his college days who converted to Islam, drawn by his own pious example and, ultimately, the teachings of the man they call *Ustad*, Master Said Nursi. It was a fair bargain, I thought. Harun travels to America to learn technique, and in return, gives one of them religion.

Among the Nurcus, as I was to learn in the course of my journey, idle conversation, or questions about my family, or life in the West, were concerns to be skimmed over, if not avoided altogether. Of more concern to the earnest and single-minded young men who would be my hosts and guides, were my views on religion, my own beliefs. As if malleable, these were constantly being probed and prodded, measured against the prescriptions of the community. And perhaps, though my hosts would never have uttered the words, found wanting. There were times when, under their searching though sidelong gaze, they seemed wanting too.

When we leave the coffee house and step out onto the street, night has fallen. The lights of Erzurum gleam on the rain-slick pavement; pedestrians hurry by, hunched beneath their dripping umbrellas. Though the hour is early, it is dinner time, Harun tells me. Besides, he adds, we are expected at a meeting later that evening.

Erzurum's specialty is kebab. Now sedentarized, but once a herding people of the steppes and grasslands of high Asia, the Turks long ago perfected the art of preparing meat fresh from the hoof. Here, the local dish is called *cagkebab*, tender morsels of lamb sliced from a large compact roll of meat rotating slowly over glowing coals. It arrives at the table on skewers, from which we slip the meat between folds of *lavash* bread whose texture evokes soft parchment, sprinkled with flakes of red pepper and washed down with frothy *ayran*, the yogurt-based beverage that best sets off the subtlety of Turkish food.

Restored and warmed, we drive to the home of a university professor where tonight's study meeting is already in progress. Twenty men, perhaps more, crowd the living room, most seated cross-legged on the floor. One of their number is reciting, in a slightly nasal, ceremonial voice, from the works of Said Nursi. This much I can recognize from the reverence of his tone, and by the red, gold-lettered binding of the book he holds. After each paragraph, the guests comment on the text, or raise questions.

Most of us are lecturers at the university, Harun whispers against the hum of amicable disputation. "Some teach in the high school." Impossible to distinguish. Even in the provinces Turks, Islamist or not, favor dark suits. And in these circles, shoes are an unreliable indicator of economic station. Practicing Muslims are always slipping shoes on and off, whether for ablutions and prayers at the mosque, or by custom and courtesy when entering a dwelling.

The subject of tonight's meeting, he explains, is the advisability of accepting Western technology and science, while refusing everything else. The question is a capital one throughout the Islamic world, where since the nineteenth century, Muslim intellectuals have been overwhelmed by the necessity of reaching an accommodation with Western science. "The psychological dissonance which caused Muslim thinkers to raise the issue in the first place … appears to have originated in a perception of a loss of power by Islamic societies," writes Serif Mardin in his provocative study of Said Nursi.[14]

Likewise, the touchstone of Said's career was more than a perception of a loss of power; it was the bitter certification of that loss, first with the collapse of the Ottoman state, then with the establishment of the secular republic. If I had understood my interlocutors correctly, the power involved was less that exercised in the political arena, and more the abstract, pervasive power of belief to inform individuals and the society they create. Arrayed against them, they saw the power of unbelief to subvert individuals and the society in which they live. This, they argued, was what Said Nursi tirelessly inveighed against, and against which they, his followers, hardened themselves through the spiritual exercises that I was witnessing tonight, and would encounter again and again, like a whispered leitmotif, like the rustle of the text.

NEXT MORNING, the clouds have dissipated. A bright winter sun beams down on granite gray Erzurum, and sparkles off the fresh-fallen snow on the surrounding hillsides. After a dormitory breakfast of cheese, olives, bread, honey and tea, which we take squatting cross-legged on the floor, Harun picks me up for a morning on the town. Puddles from last night's rain have iced over. The paving stones leading to the Cifte Minare Medresesi—the *Medrese* of the Two Minarets—are slick with hoarfrost; we must tread gingerly. Adjoining the *medrese* stands a tomb constructed by Kaykubat Alaaddin's daughter, square-hewn in its Seljuk sobriety. Even at this early hour, small groups of young men are strolling through the colonnaded inner court, open to the sky, as is the style in Iran, where the unseen heavenly vanishing point is the main architectural feature of mosque construction. Outside the main entrance, two older bearded gentlemen wearing knit skullcaps drag a park bench over into the sunlight, sit down and pull out their *tasbis*, the stringed beads on which Muslims enumerate the names and attributes of God.

Square in the historic centre of the city, just behind a tumble-down bathhouse, stands another monument, a monument to irreligion, as the Nurcus might put it. Here, in a two story house with a massive, ironclad door, Mustafa Kemal—not yet known as Atatürk ("father of the Turks")—had stayed in the summer of 1919.

The heroic defender of Gallipoli had sailed from Istanbul on May 16, on the day after a Greek expeditionary force, fired by greed, driven by nationalist delirium, and egged on by extravagant British promises of territory and imperial glory, had disembarked in Izmir to begin the dismemberment of Asia Minor.

Kemal's destination was the Black Sea port of Samsun. His ostensible mission: to end the disorder that was spreading through the eastern provinces. His true aim: reorganize the country's tattered armies and raise the flag of resistance. Reluctantly, the Allied forces that had occupied Istanbul as victors following the military collapse of the Ottoman Empire in October, 1918, issued Kemal, appointed Inspector-General of the Ninth Army by the Sultan, the necessary authorization. "Pasha, you can save the country," Sultan Vahideddin is said to have whispered to him in a farewell audience, little realizing that saving the country meant, for the steely-eyed Kemal, the fall of the house of Osman.

Three days later, on May 19, 1919, Kemal landed in Samsun. The date is considered to be the start of the national revolution that would bring down the Ottoman state. From Samsun he worked his way east, issuing at the town of Amasya a Declaration of Independence and calling on the Turks to send delegates to a conference to be held in Sivas; it would be preceded by a congress in Erzurum. The salvation of Turkey would come, not from foreign-occupied, corrupt Istanbul; not from the crumbling, compromised Ottoman establishment. It would come from deepest Anatolia, from the city that in the nineteenth century had been known as "the capital of Turkish Armenia," though by then it was all but empty of its Armenian population. On July 23, in the city's gymnasium, the delegates confirmed Kemal's preeminence in what was now being called the "War of Independence." Here too, they laid down, under his iron-handed guidance, the principles of what was to become the National Pact.

Adopting the language of French Jacobinism, Prussian nationalism and Wilsonian idealism, the Pact affirmed the right of the Turkish people to self-determination, and insisted that Anatolia and what remained of Turkey in Europe formed an indivisible entity in which there could be no Greek or Armenian state.[15]

For a building that embodies one of the defining moments of the Turkish Republic, the house in Erzurum is dank and ill-maintained. As the huge door creaks open, Harun and I step into the vestibule. No shoe removal necessary here. An ill-shaven, dour-looking caretaker shambles down the stairs, hovering around us as we visit the rooms containing the Great Man's furniture and assorted other micro-memorabilia. The house smells of dust and neglect. A wooden desk stands, surrounded by three chairs, at the centre of the room in a column of oblique sunlight, thick with brownian agitation. Behind it, moth-eaten red velvet drapes droop, funereal and tasteless.

On a far wall, half concealed behind a showcase, is a display of photographs showing the official visit of General Kenan Evren, the leader of the 1980 military coup that, paradoxically, gave new energy to the country's Islamic community. In the preceding decade, American Cold War policy had sought to establish a conservative Muslim "Green Belt" around the Soviet Union. The events leading up to the coup, including political killings and street warfare between extreme leftist and proto-fascist nationalists, had convinced the military, and more importantly their backers in Washington, that drastic action was necessary to preserve Turkey's integrity as NATO's southeastern rampart against Communism.

The defense of American interests proved to be an ill fit with the army's overarching objective, which was not the defense of Turkey, but the preservation of the Kemalist regime against the Turks themselves. In his effort to protect greater geostrategic interests, while remaining faithful to founding dogma, General Evren achieved neither. By bringing Islam from the periphery to the centre of Turkish politics as an antidote to communism, he contributed to the subversion of the very institution he was sworn by oath to preserve.

NOON HAD COME, and time for departure. Harun drives me to the Otogar, the bus station that in Erzurum, as in all Turkish towns and cities, is the intercity transportation hub. My host escorts me to the platform and, with a handshake, onto the bus for Van. It is with a certain trepidation that I board this brightly-painted, burnished chrome land-cruiser. Turkey's bus lines are private sector affairs, run by companies which compete on both price and service. Non-Turks tend to pay a premium fare, but all travelers are served hot tea, instant coffee or carbonated orange drink, and hands are regularly sprinkled with lemon cologne by the steward who makes his way up and down the aisle like a sailor on a heaving deck. The buses also have a reputation as rolling coffins, due perhaps to their drivers' propensity for passing slow-moving trucks on blind curves. As surely as day follows night, slow-moving trucks are always encountered on narrow uphill roads rounding blind curves. The bus driver's imperative is, of course, to pass, whatever the circumstances. In Turkish travel lore there exists an entire sub-narrative of bus disaster stories, tall but possibly true tales of head-on collisions with the inevitable on-coming oil tanker trucks, of plunges into ravines, of deadly skids and roll-overs, of hold-ups by Kurdish guerrillas or shoot-ups by trigger-happy gendarmes looking for "terrorists." "*Bismillah rahman-e rahim*" whisper the passengers as the steward swings aboard, the doors snap shut and the Mercedes-Benz bus roars through the gates of the Otogar and out onto the great Anatolian highroad. "In the name of God, the Compassionate, the Merciful," I whisper to myself. You can never be too careful.

As the bus speeds eastward through arid, snow-dusted hills and across broad plains where only wheat stubble remains in the fields, groaning upward through rocky passes, the towns and villages become poorer, dustier, muddier. Slowing only slightly, we skirt the citadel at Pasinler, then the farming town of Horasan, where we whoosh past a lone cyclist pedaling his way east. Between towns, the tiny roadside settlements, squat, random-seeming constructions of mud and straw bricks with a single, wood-framed window surrounded by conical haystacks, might just as well be Iranian. Only the water buffalo are missing.

Early dusk is falling as the bus stops in Agri, the junction. The main road continues east, toward Dogubeyazit, and the Iranian frontier. Instead of turning into the Otogar, our coach pulls up at a gas station on the outskirts of the town. Geese are foraging in puddles left over from the previous day's rain. On clotheslines strung between leafless poplars, veiled women are hanging laundry out to dry. Children wearing bright rubber boots are sloshing in the mud. From hundreds of chimneys, coal smoke drifts upward into the still, empty sky. As the sun dips below the horizon and the air grows chill, the call to prayer echoes across the flat rooftops.

The remaining three hours of the journey will be in darkness, through a landscape of roadside scrub-brush flattened by the glare of the headlights, dusty, dimly lit towns, and the occasional road sign.

To the right, an arrow points to Malazgirt. In Asia Minor, the relics of history lie, only faintly concealed by layers of dust, on the ragged edges of consciousness. On the plain known in European historiography as Manzikert, in August, 1071, a lesser force of Seljuk troops under Sultan Alp Arslan met a Byzantine host led by Romanus IV Diogenes, the *basileus*. For the Byzantines, the omens were grim: entire detachments of Turkcoman mercenaries, reluctant to fight their brethren, had promptly defected to the Seljuks. Despite the shift in fortune, the Sultan sued for a truce. Romanus, overconfident, refused. On Friday, the day of Muslim communal prayer, Alp Arslan attacked. After another mercenary detachment led by the Norman soldier of fortune Roussel de Bailleul, turned tail and marched off to safety, the panic-stricken Byzantines fled. Defeat had turned to rout as it so often did in this place, with its unforgiving climate and landscape.

Alp Arslan was magnanimous in victory. He and the captive emperor signed a treaty of eternal peace and friendship, and Romanus was released, only to be blinded by his political enemies when he returned, humiliated, to Constantinople. But the battle sealed the fate of Byzantine Asia Minor. "The cradle of civilization fell prey to Islamic barbarism and to complete brutalization," laments the nineteenth-century German scholar H. Gelzer. [16] This was the region where Alp Arlsan's successor, Suleiman-ibn-Qutalmish, later founded the Sultanate of Rum, and made Konya its capital. In that sink of barbarism and brutalization, German orientalism notwithstanding, would later be sheltered Mevlana, the poet of universal love.

Far-off lights glimmered from what could only be water, and before long the bus was winding along the shoreline of Lake Van. It was only 7 o'clock when we pulled up in the main square in a cloud of dust, but it seemed like the wee hours of the morning. Where in Erzurum the downtown lights were bright, those of Van glowed dimly, and the telltale acridity of coal smoke rasped in my nostrils.

# IV

## More Than Meets the Eye

THE UNLIKELY CHAIN of connections and coincidences that led me to Bediuzzaman Said Nursi, and later, to the amorphous, quiescent yet dynamic community of his followers, proceeded by the most convoluted of routes, along an often frayed, sometimes tenuous and often improbable narrative thread that stretched back to the fall of 1991.

That year, on a visit to northern Greece, I had encountered a brash young journalist named Abdülhalim Dede in the provincial town of Komotini, home to one of the most intractable minority dilemmas in the Balkans: the country's Muslim Turks. Protected under the terms of the Lausanne Treaty of 1923, Greece's single admitted though ill-loved minority is defined by Athens in strictly religious terms: as Muslims. Not without reason. The treaty gave international legal sanction to an accomplished fact: the expulsion of Orthodox Christians from Turkey and the reciprocal ejection of Muslims from Greece. Language, that modern marker of identity, had little to do with it. Many of the "Greeks" spoke only Turkish; many of the "Turks" spoke only Greek. In fact, Lausanne could be seen as the final act in the long-running drama of the Ottoman *millet* system, which classified minorities by religion, not nationality, or, to use current sociobabble, ethnicity.

(The other Lausanne-protected minority, the Greek Orthodox of Istanbul and two Aegean islands has suffered a similar, if not more tragic fate as I would later learn when I visited the Ecumenical Patriarchate.)

This minority contained within it, as an artichoke whose bristly, inedible choke conceals the prized morsel at its heart, yet a smaller minority, the Pomaks, a mountain people whose ancestral homeland straddles the Rodope Mountains along the Greek-Bulgarian border, and whom each country claims as its own. I visited the mist-shrouded upcountry Pomak villages, and there attested to the fervor of their Islamic beliefs; to the extent of their alienation from Greece; and to the ambiguity and intensity of their self-identification as Turks. That this self-identification frustrates, irritates and even enrages Greek officialdom is axiomatic. After all, it is an article of Greek nationalist belief, the archetype of the virulent Balkan variety later adopted by Turkey, that there was never and could not be such a thing as a "Turkish" minority, let alone a national minority of any kind, in the country.

Mr. Dede is a Pomak, an intense and mercurial man, who possesses the gift of outspokenness and displays a propensity for testing the limits of situations, was working then as a reporter for one of the city's minority newspapers. He was as diligent in introducing me to the leaders of the minority as he was in explaining their refusal to accept the Greek government's definition of them. What I did not know about at the time was his professional knowledge of the Turkish Islamic revival movement.

Six years later, in the closing days of 1997, I had once again encountered Mr. Dede, this time in Athens. Later, as we traveled together on the suburban electric railway toward Kifisia for a meeting with Panayote Dimitras, the intrepid and pugnacious founder of Greek Helsinki Watch, I spoke to him of my plans for a book about the Islamic movement in Turkey. Whipping out his notepad, he jotted down an address and a telephone number.

"Call these people. You may find them interesting," he said.

Several days later, I found myself in the Istanbul industrial suburb of Yeni Bosna, at the entrance to the five-story office building that houses the head offices of *Zaman*, daily newspaper and flagship of a media and educational conglomerate that spans Turkey and the Turkish-speaking world around it, from the Adriatic to the Chinese border, and is now branching out into the non-Muslim world. It is a conglomerate inspired by and dedicated to the personality and thought of a man named Mohammad Fetullah Gülen. It was a name I should have known, and would soon come to know well.

*Zaman*, however, rang a bell. I had met one of its reporters ten years previously on a reporting trip to Iran. There, the journalist had confided to me, with a touch of antipathy, that the Iranian Islamic revolutionaries parading past the Army Day reviewing stand in Tehran were "fascists." The journalist was no longer with the paper. But his name had given me an introduction. Today, as I listened to the paper's editor, Adbullah Aymaz, while sipping tea, I began to understand why there was no love lost between the followers of a worldly Turkish Muslim holy man and the Iranian mollahs.

Mr. Aymaz is short, bustling and energetic, with a well-trimmed mustache. He pads about his functionalist office, decorated with an arrangement of artificial flowers, in worn slippers. My explanation of the book project that has brought me to Istanbul draws scant attention. It is clear that I have come here less to talk than to listen. The message that I am expected to absorb is one of interfaith reconciliation, and of stern, unyielding opposition to the "clash of civilizations" thesis dear to the hearts of the Samuel Huntingtons of this world, and to their Muslim negative images, the shadowy fundamentalists we Westerners all love to dread and hate.

With a smile whose sincerity I later came to recognize as a hallmark of the movement, he presses into my hands, as if by way of illustrating his thesis, a photo album published by the Journalists and Writers Foundation, another manifestation of Fetullah Gülen's fertile organizational mind. In it, we see the spiritual leader dressed in his trademark turtleneck sweater, in the company of national and international dignitaries, ranging from the Refah Party mayor of Istanbul, now hounded from office by the military regime and his party disbanded, through former Prime Minister Tansu Ciller, to disgraced soccer star Diego Maradonna, who looks baffled, glassy-eyed and anything but overjoyed at the encounter.

Not one ill-dressed or downtrodden person is to be seen. The men are portly and plump of well-shaven cheek, the ladies sleek and impeccably groomed, their scarfless heads resplendent. How remote they were from the humble students, unassuming academics, calloused-handed workers and self-effacing merchants I would encounter in my travels through the Nurcu community.

Our aim, explains Mr. Aymaz, is not to erect barriers between the world's religions, but to build bridges. It was a mantra-like metaphor that was to recur again and again in my encounters with the movement's members. How could any reasonable man possibly oppose such an initiative? I kept on telling myself. What is it about this generous proposition that sets my teeth on edge?

The editor goes on to tell me the story of his encounter with the movement and its leader. As a young man, in the early sixties, he had gone to Izmir to pursue his training in the theological school there. Somewhere along the way, a book by the holy man Bediuzzaman Said Nursi had been thrust into his hands, a matter of chance. Suddenly, he says, a new, greater reality stood before him, luminous, beckoning. I made a mental note of the name.

This Said Nursi was a mystic, a Qur'anic preacher, a teacher and (say his followers) the bearer of a message as central to Islam as to Christianity: the rejection of the materialist ideology. Communism, explains Mr. Aymaz, was rampant in Turkey in those hard years. Said Nursi's deft deconstruction of the materialist world view and reaffirmation of the First Cause, and the ultimate unity of God, provided believers with the moral and ideological resolve to withstand its siren song of a worldly utopia. These ideas he encountered in this small book, and soon, from the mouth of a man perhaps ten years older than himself, who had just begun his career as a religious teacher in the Aegean coastal metropolis. That man was Fetullah Gülen, known to his growing numbers of followers, as Hoca Efendi, an honorific title granted to men of religious prestige and presence who have acquired reputations as preachers and spiritual counsellors.

"My plan was to go on to Istanbul and complete my studies," he says. "Instead, I stayed in Izmir to sit at the feet of Fetullah. Soon I became his follower, and decided to dedicate myself to his work."

As I would learn in the coming months, there are many such men in Turkey. Men of devotion and means who unstintingly plow back into the multifaceted organization that has grown up around Fetullah Gülen—and into a bewildering variety of cultural foundations and holding companies distantly connected to a spectrum of other factions of the Islamic movement—a large portion of their profits, and often their time.

\* \* \*

IN THE HILLS above Üsküdar, across the Bosphorus bridge in Asia, stands the headquarters of STV, the unblinking eye of the Fetullah Gülen community. With an audience it claims to be between 8 and 15% of all Turkish television viewers, and millions more throughout the Turkish-speaking world, STV expresses a curious non-Islamic public identity.

"Certainly, there is nothing Islamic about the content of our programs," program director Abdul Karim Gök assures me. "But we won't touch anything that shows sex or violence. Our programs are for the family, and they are designed to promote Turkish culture." As he tells me this, female employees in brightly colored print headscarves and modest ankle-length dresses flit by in the corridor. "This we do by supporting the state and working to educate the people. But, unlike other television stations in Turkey, we refuse to speak ill of Islam."

Neither at *Zaman*, however, nor at STV, will anyone speak ill of the Turkish state. Or, more precisely, of its stern, self-appointed and self-perpetuating watch-dog, the military establishment. Such a policy can be explained by the elemental need for self protection. A television reporter I met in the cafeteria confided to me in a whisper that journalism in Turkey can be a dangerous occupation. "You must be extremely careful what you say. And of course, you can say nothing critical of the military, or else you will end up in prison. Or worse."

If *Zaman* and STV are the visible manifestations of the movement that has coalesced around Fetullah Gülen, the Journalists' and Writers' Foundation is its intellectual arm. From its beginnings in 1994, the Foundation has rapidly become a factor in the country's complex, shifting political life. Its annual banquet, considered a hot ticket in Istanbul, presents awards to those citizens whose work has helped build bridges over the troubled waters of communal, social and political tension. The man telling me this is named Harun Tokak, the Foundation's chairman. Mr. Tokak is a journalist who worked, he explains with a wave of the hand, as if dismissing flies, in eastern Turkey before moving to Istanbul, there to be tapped by Fetullah Gülen to head up the Foundation.

"The Foundation gives awards to the best bridge builders," he says, reading from a list headed by President Suleiman Demirel, and including the Turkish army chief of staff, and prominent members of most political parties. A notable exception is Refah, the overtly Islamic Welfare Party that had been driven from nominal power ten months earlier.

"Well," I ask, "what about Mr. Erbakan?"

"Erbakan is not on our list," Mr. Tokak snaps back with a steely smile. "He is not interested in reconciliation; he is part of the conflict. In fact, he has publicly criticized the army, and that irritated people."

Could the Foundation be straying too close to the zone in which journalists slough off their critical responsibilities to become the handmaidens of power? I test the concept on Mr. Tokak, who replies that Mr. Erbakan, by virtue of the Welfare Party's strength at the polls, is the most powerful man in Turkey. That is why the Foundation will have nothing to do with him. What could be clearer?

"We are near who is near to us. We don't want to be close to power, but to truth," he says.

My next question concerns Turkey's international reputation as an unhealthy place for the practice of the journalist's trade. Mr. Tokak's response is as rapid as it is forthright. "I don't believe that journalists go to jail or are killed in Turkey."

Startled, I backtrack. Let me rephrase the question. "Do journalists in Turkey have to operate under political constraint?" I offer.

"If you're wrong, you're wrong, no matter who you are," says Mr. Tokak, not amused. "Yashar Kemal was wrong to demand an apology from the government of Turkey. (Mr. Kemal, perhaps the country's best-known writer abroad, had criticized the regime for its handling of what is euphemistically referred to as "the Kurdish problem," thus incurring the wrath of the authorities. He now lives abroad to avoid a prison sentence.) The whole world feels the impact of the lies spread by irresponsible writers and journalists."

Coming from the head of an organization dedicated to promoting and protecting all those who must live by their pens and their wits, these are curious words. Mr. Tokak may believe his claims that no journalists are singled out for mistreatment, arrested, let alone killed in Turkey. But as we spoke, at least twenty-five journalists were behind bars, and many more had been arrested and held incommunicado for periods of 48 hours or more without charges or trial, far more than in any other country. [17] In a court in a small town on the Aegean coast, the trial was getting underway of a group of eleven policemen alleged to have beaten to death Metin Göktepe, a young journalist, following a leftist demonstration in Istanbul.

(Five of the eleven officers accused in the beating were finally sentenced to seven and one-half years for involuntary homicide by a court in Afyon, a city in western Turkey, in March 1998.

However, another court in the same city in December, released the suspects because of the enquiry's "lack of depth" and the failure of certain witnesses to bring testimony. In a similar incident, uniformed and plainclothes police, in April, 1998, forcibly expelled journalists from a courtroom in the western market town of Aydin while the trial of police officers accused of torturing a student to death five years earlier was in progress. At least five of the journalists were beaten by police outside the courthouse.) [18]

The interview was not going well. Mr. Tokak's irritation and defensiveness were increasing with every question. This variant of Turkish Islamism was taking on a curious tint, a steely sheen that reminded me distantly of the glitter of brass buttons on the generals' dress tunics I'd seen in the photo album in the *Zaman* offices.

Before the meeting, I had applied for an interview with Fetullah Gülen himself. Now, I had little reason to believe that it would ever come about.


EDUCATION IS THE WATCHWORD of Fetullah Gülen's organization, its *raison d'être*. No less an authority than General Cevik Bir, the former second-in-command of the Turkish army, has publicly stated that the Gülen educational network's investment in colleges and universities abroad exceeds the budget of the Ministry of Education. Cut to the quick, Fetullah Gülen quickly responded that if the authorities had the slightest doubt about the educational integrity of his schools, he would immediately make them over to the State. Ever mindful of the struggle against the deficit, the authorities backed off.

As I stride through the hallways of the campus of Fatih University, an amorphous mass of raw concrete, brick and mortar, dominating a treeless hillside 30 kilometers from downtown Istanbul, I catch myself wondering if I've stumbled upon an Islamic version of the Jesuit order, which also swore by the virtues of education in its quest for pliant souls.

Like each of the movement's dozens of universities and hundreds of colleges and preparatory schools, there is nothing remotely Islamic about the new facility, except for the semi-concealed or unspoken religious identity of the men who founded and now administer it. The curriculum is focused on the Arts and Sciences, Engineering and Economics, and all instruction is in English. This, explains Professor Güçin, a mycologist by training, who is currently overseeing the start-up of the new campus, is because English is the world language, the language of the internet, of science and technology. "If we teach only in Turkish, we're speaking only to Turks. When we use English, we can communicate with everybody."

The unanswered question, that which my hosts contrive to avoid, is that of content. Do the schools operated by the movement offer a value free academic curriculum? That would be difficult to imagine, considering the number of posters promoting the business and management club that I see taped to the freshly-plastered walls. In that case, freedom from values could be interpreted as the expression of the liberal ideology. Perhaps I've misunderstood. Perhaps some faint resonance of their Islamic origin lurks deep in the syllabus, like a computer virus, to be activated at some future date, a kind of cultural millennium bug.

RAIN IS IN THE AIR on a cool spring afternoon as I make my way to the western Istanbul suburb of Avcilar, a voyage that takes almost as long as a flight to Ankara. At Sirkeci station, in the shadow of Seraglio Point, I hop onto the suburban railway that rumbles and roars along the shoreline of the Sea of Marmara, beneath the Byzantine walls and through the leafy waterfront settlements of Yesilköy, Florya and Kuçukçekmece where fish restaurants dot the waterfront and vine-grown villas, survivors of a time when these places were vacation haunts of rich Istanbuliots, slumber in the shadow of immense apartment blocks. The windows on the left-hand side of the carriages give a sweeping view to the ships riding at anchor in the roadstead, and the fishing boats putt-putting to and fro. But Istanbul connoisseurs know that the true spectacle of the suburban railway is to be seen inside the rattletrap rolling stock, with its missing window panes, grimy linoleum floors, cracked plastic seats and doors that refuse to close.

Whether at peak periods or during off-hours, the railway presents the elemental theatre of existence in constant, crazy, swaying motion. At each downtown station, situated at the edge of some of Istanbul's poorest, most crowded districts, crowds of raucous schoolboys practice their favorite extreme sport: jumping aboard at the last possible moment, timing their leap to coincide with the instant the accelerating train clears the far edge of the platform. One false step or missed handhold could mean a messy death beneath the wheels. Then, dangling casually from the open doors, hair swept back in the wind, scarves flapping, they disembark at the next station to hit the ground running with whoops of delight, and danger defied, as the conductors look on, impassive and powerless.

A succession of vendors work the cars, selling beach balls and balloons "for picnics," though the weather is cool and overcast, coloring books for children, wallets, pen-and-datebook sets, watches, socks, umbrellas, religious books for the holy festivals, posters depicting bucolic alpine scenes, wind-up toys. Some of them simply reel off their memorized sales pitch in a rapid-fire singsong, some speak with the fulsomeness of prevaricating politicians, others gesticulate, frown, smile, emoting like corporate motivational consultants or mutual fund touts. Some are blind, some handicapped, some apparently able-bodied.

In the maelstrom of the Kuçukçekmece station, amidst impatient taxis, shouting vendors and honking *dolmus*, I locate the Avcilar terminus and hop aboard. After a slow-motion slalom through suburban traffic as dense as downtown's, I step down from the minibus in front of City Hall where a man named Faïk Bulut is expecting me.

Mr. Bulut, to whom I'd been introduced by a mutual acquaintance, is guarded in manner. Born in the far eastern Anatolian city of Kars, of Kurdish parents, he defines himself as a leftist, pro-Kurdish independent intellectual. Any one of these qualities, the second in particular, are enough to land one in trouble in the tight ideological ship that is today's Turkey. Even the kind of group that he has recently helped found, called Kurdish Intellectuals for Peace, might well be seen, by the ultra-nationalists in and outside of the armed forces, as "separatist." The label, with which many Quebeckers are familiar, has here acquired a dire connotation, almost as dangerous to one's health as terrorism, which itself is shorthand for support for, or even acquiescence in the goals of, the outlawed Kurdistan Workers Party, the PKK.

"In fact, I've been charged more than ten times with undermining the unity of the state," he tells me as we sit down at the dinner table in his modest apartment, cup of tea in hand. Mr. Bulut's fascination with regional politics, of both the secular and religious variety, go back several decades to when, as a young man, he joined the Palestine Liberation Organization, was captured, and spent seven years in Israeli prisons. "Since then, I've written 18 books on Islamic issues and the Kurdish question. My book on the rise of Islamic capital was used to help bring down the Welfare Party government," he says in a flat voice that betrays no emotion, no sign of pride.

The low esteem in which Mr. Bulut holds the Islamic movement, and particularly the Fetullahcis, is reciprocated. Fetullah Gülen's supporters have described him as "wanting to use the Kurdish identity as a vehicle for Kurdish separation." [19] Worse, our author apparently has described the ninth Ottoman Sultan Selim I as a ruthless tyrant for ordering the pre-emptive massacre of 40,000 Alevis in his war against the militantly Shi'ite Safavids of Iran. As I was to learn later, the characterization of Yavuz "the Grim" Selim was accurate, though as controversial as the massacre of the Armenians four centuries later. What was most striking was that criticism of an early sixteenth-century sultan had become an argument against a current ideological adversary.

"Today, the followers of Said Nursi form at least 13 factions. The largest of these, Fetullah Gülen's sect, is attempting to make itself an umbrella type organization, something like a Masonic lodge.

But each of the sects pretends to be the true followers of Said Nursi," he tells me, using the kind of coded language that can be relied upon to infuriate Islamists, from radicals to conservatives, who abominate Free Masonry and all its works.

"When you first encounter Said Nursi," he tells me, warming to the subject, "he doesn't seem at all political. But he did not disdain writing to Menderes in support of American policy." In fact, according to Mr. Bulut, the Turkish state has used Said's theories to attempt to assimilate the Kurds and to overcome the Kurdish identity. "He made a point of religious brotherhood, and saw Islam as a bridge."

For this, I learned, Said Nursi had his reasons. They flowed from a historical document that seems as alive and relevant today—and as threatening to the territorial integrity of Turkey—as it was 80 years ago.

In August 1920, the internationally recognized government of Turkey, nominally still the Ottoman Empire, signed the Treaty of Sèvres. That document, which occupies a prominent place in the annals of Turkish infamy, legitimized the carving up and sharing out of what remained of the defeated empire among the victorious powers of the Entente. It was a worthy successor to the Sykes-Picot Agreements of 1916, which chopped up and distributed the territories that had once belonged to the multinational Ottoman state among the Great Powers, laying the groundwork for generations of conflict in the Middle East.

The Sèvres document had been signed at the political equivalent of gunpoint by an Istanbul government held hostage by foreign occupation forces. It had nudged the Ottoman regime even further along the path toward terminal discredit. France had already occupied parts of southeastern Anatolia; the Italians had landed at Antalya; the British held the strategically vital Dardanelles, returning victorious to Gallipoli where they had been defeated four years before; a Greek expeditionary force held Izmir. Plans had been made to set up a Kurdish state, and to carve out an independent Greater Armenia.

France's First World War hero Marshal Foch described the treaty as a threat to peace.[20] Not only did it touch off a campaign of violent resistance that was to catapult Mustafa Kemal into the role of national savior, it poisoned relations between Kurds and Turks in perpetuity and condemned the country's Armenians to life in a gray zone. Only Turkish nationalism, of the variety inherited by Atatürk from his Young Turk mentors, could hold the country together.

In a letter "written in order to avoid the disgust and insults that will be leveled at us in the future," Said Nursi lashed out at Turkism, the doctrine by which the Kemalist state denied even the existence of the Kurds. "Perhaps if you abolish the nationhood of the Kurds, of whom there are millions and who for thousands of years have not forgotten their nationhood and language, and are the true fellow-citizens and companions in *jihad* of the Turks, and make them forget their language, then perhaps your proposal [to utter the call to prayer in Turkish] to those like me who are reckoned to be of a different race would be in accordance with some sort of savage principle."[21]

This "savage principle" has ruled Turkey ever since, transforming Turks into oppressors, Kurds into non-persons in their own lands, and creating an atmosphere of suspicion and hatred. And now the argument at its core was being wielded by the followers of Fetullah Gülen to belittle critics like Faïk Bulut.

FETULLAH GÜLEN, charges Mr. Bulut, is cultivating a "Golden Generation." Trained in the movement's schools, sheltered in its dormitories and study centers where they are given religious guidance, this select cadre of top-flight scientists, technocrats, academics and entrepreneurs is expected, in the fullness of time, to assume the command positions in society, not only in Turkey but in the neighboring, fledgling republics that came into being with the collapse of the Soviet Union. Ostensibly they will owe their success to their superior intellectual and technical skills, honesty and competence. But lost on few is the fact that most of these high-achieving students are devout Muslims of both sexes, and that many of them look to Mr. Gülen as their source of inspiration.

"The difference between them and Erbakan's Refah Party is that Refah wants to take power as soon as it can. Gülen believes that you cannot succeed without the infrastructure of Islam. 'Suppose we gain power?' they say. 'Then what do we do with it?'"

The Fetullahcis believe that it will take at least 25 years to develop the fully Islamicized cadre they need, insists Mr. Bulut. "They cannot sacrifice the final goal for the short-term goal. The ideal of the 'Golden Generation' is to move into power when the season comes; their aim is not to set up an Islamic society, but a religious one, a Muslim one."

Mr. Bulut has finally become animated, his slightly protruding eyes growing darker as his pupils dilate. The subject has stirred in him some primordial, visceral reaction. It was not the first time I had seen a strong response to the name of Fetullah Gülen. Hoca Efendi's devotees are many and influential, as I was discovering; his detractors numerous and sometimes powerful. Neutrality, of the journalistic or the academic variety, did not seem the appropriate mode of appreciation.

Yet I struggled to maintain it. I'd seen no religious content at Fatih University, the movement's flagship educational institution, I remark. "You see," says Mr. Buluk, edging forward in his seat almost conspiratorially, "for Gülen, it is not the tool that matters, it is the use. His schools adopt the full, modernist curriculum."

Here's why, he adds: such a curriculum also creates a protective buffer. (I thought back to a conversation with a university student who told me it usually takes him and his classmates a week to identify the secret police informer assigned to every university course. This person's job is to monitor not only the students, but the professor teaching the course as well.) Then too, he reminds me, there are practical considerations. If the movement is to recruit among wider circles, it cannot rely on religious slogans alone. It must adopt liberal, democratic positions.

"There is religious indoctrination, no doubt about it, but it takes the form of discussion groups at the study houses after school hours."

Mr. Bulut is one of Turkey's fiercest public critics of the "Golden Generation" strategy, not an unreasonable position for a man stranded by a receding ideological tide. But in his criticism, in its virulence and categorical assurance, there may have been more than the whisper of that tide. Caught between the collapse of their socialist ideal and the rise of an Islamic movement that has made a serious claim on the principles of democracy, some old Lefties, like their counterparts in Algeria, have fallen, swooning, into the secular embrace of the State.

A FEW DAYS LATER, on one of March's frequent rainy, windswept afternoons, I made my way to the Gayreteppe district, on the hills that overlook the Yildiz Palace and, at the foot of Barbaros Boulevard, the ferry docks and bustling markets of Besiktas. In the lobby of the Dedaman Hotel I met Etyen Mahçupyan, a writer and free-lance analyst. A rangy man with a quizzical expression Mr. Mahçupyan, like many Istanbul intellectuals, wears several hats: weekly columnist with the left-centre daily *Radikal*, author of three books on Turkey, and entrepreneur.

A cup of Turkish coffee—welcome relief from the constant cups of tea—arrived. I sipped discretely as Mr. Mahçupyan explained that the Kemalist regime represents a break from the Ottoman past only on the cultural level. That split-off gave it the legitimacy it needed. But in the deeper terms of how the state defines itself, and how it behaves toward the people, there has been little change. "This is why Western writers will never really understand what's going on in Turkey," he said. "The state has remained as despotic as before. It may be in the hands of a minority with a new approach, but the underlying mentality is the same."

Mr. Mahçupyan is categorical about one thing: there is no such thing as civil society in Turkey. "In the minds of the people, the state is vital. The state and religion are intertwined, the idea being that the state should protect religion, which in turn should give legitimacy to the state."

Stated rather broadly, Mr. Mahçupyan's assessment is this: The policy of the westernizing ultra-secularists under Atatürk, who would relegate Islam to the individual sphere, was impossible from the start. The only way to sustain it was by repressive means, and those means were and are wielded by the state. At the same time, Islam is everywhere present in Turkey, invoked, acknowledged, even exploited by the self-styled Kemalists who operate the state machinery. The creation, in 1925, of the Directorate of Religious Affairs was an admission of the limits of secularist extremism. But at the same time, it placed the administration of religion and the elaboration of its "orthodox" content in the hands of government-appointed authorities, thereby subordinating Islam to the state—to politics. [22]

It was a roundabout, if transparent, way of perpetuating Ottoman practice, where an uneasy tension prevailed between the secular authorities, represented by the ruling dynasty, and the religious establishment led by the Caliph, which gave or withheld its benediction to state policy in the name of Islam. The sole difference was that for the Kemalists, the roles were reversed.

Today, he argues, the "high church" orthodoxy of a resurgent Sunni establishment is attempting to occupy the space created by the Directorate. "Their response is a communitarian one," Mr. Mahçupyan says. "They want to become the main interlocutor of the state, and the way to do this is to convince the state that they support it."

The preferred method is the recreation of a scale model of the old *millet* system, through which the Ottomans ruled and administered their religious minorities. This is precisely what Fetullah Gülen's strategy of building bridges, and organizing interfaith dialogue, hopes to accomplish, he explains. Several months later, I was to witness that strategy in action.

\* \* \*

RAMADAN, IN 1998, fell in late December. At this time of year, the days are short and the fasting is easy compared to the long, hot days of summer that never seem to end, a friend told me. A few days before the holy month was to begin, even as US and British aircraft were again bombing Iraq, I received an invitation to attend *iftar*, the traditional fast-breaking meal, at the Journalists' and Writers' Foundation. As I entered the Foundation's dining room, I recognized the stovepipe hat and white beard of the Ecumenical Patriarch, Bartholomeos I, whom I had encountered several weeks earlier. Soon the identities of the other guests stood revealed: the Papal Nunzio in Istanbul, the head of the Society of Jesus in Turkey, an embarrassingly sincere Turkish Protestant pastor, the Syrian Catholic bishop, the Armenian prelate, and two representatives of the city's small but influential Jewish community. Many men in black suits.

Hurrying through the meal (*iftar* is usually taken with the most deliberate haste: first the fast is broken with a handful of dates, a lump of cheese, a bite or two of *halvah* and a cup of tea, followed by an abundant and convivial meal) we repaired to a large meeting room. Here, each of the dignitaries delivered a short encomium to the virtues of dialogue, in which the name of Fetullah Gülen popped up frequently.

Under the *millet* system, each of the empire's religious minorities maintained full autonomy in the administration of the affairs of its community, of which the Patriarch, the Chief Rabbi and the Armenian Catholicos were the bellwethers. The only requirement was that they pay their taxes and create no disturbance. Instituted when Mehmet the Conqueror captured Constantinople in 1453, the *millet* system did not relegate the members of religious minorities to the status of sub-beings or chattels, as anti-Ottoman historians, especially in the Balkans, often claim. Nor did it suppress their beliefs or force them to convert. Orthodox believers, Armenians, and Jews were, in fact, people of the Book. As members of protected communities, they were free to practice their religion as they saw fit, with due regard for the primacy of Islam, and with a proper grasp of the realities of imperial power.

That night, at the Ramadan fast-breaking supper, Fetullah Gülen's organization was signifying to the country's all-but-insignificant and often uncomfortable religious minorities that it would henceforth be acting as their symbolic protector against the abuses of the secularist state. Whether it had either the power or capacity to do so was beside the point. What mattered most were its intentions. Among the guests, those intentions had been duly noted and certainly appreciated.

Nor had it escaped their notice that Mr. Gülen had been received by Pope John Paul II at the Vatican several months before, an arrangement that could not have been made without the active cooperation of the Turkish foreign service.


THE THOUGHT OF MEETING Fetullah Gülen had slipped so far from my mind that I all but overlooked the message from the Journalists' and Writers' Foundation that was awaiting me at my apartment in Galata when I returned to Istanbul from Tehran in the spring of 1998. Perfunctorily, I unfolded it. It read: "Interview with F. Gülen scheduled tomorrow at 10:00 a.m. Please confirm."

Early the next day, I was on my way to Üsküdar in a black Mercedes Benz sedan driven by one of the Foundation's officials. From the street, the complex that houses Fetullah Gülen's residence and headquarters reminds one of nothing so much as a bunker: a bleak, lowering building, windows glazed with a reflecting substance. The sharp-tipped steel fencing surrounding the concrete structure slides open, revealing a gate. Through it we turn into the compound, drive down a ramp to a below-ground entrance, slip from the car and walk through thick full glass sliding doors into the inner sanctum of the organization.

Moving expeditiously, we pass through a metal detector, then are shown to an elevator that whisks us to the third floor. It opens directly onto a spacious, high-ceilinged, carpeted room, decorated in a style less Turkish oriental than far-eastern. Against a windowed wall that overlooks a garden, an ensemble of chairs, tables and sofas form a reception area. Adjacent to it, like praying mantises, stand professional quality video cameras, floodlights and several microphones. To our right as we exit the elevator, a small fountain, nestled among potted plants, tinkles. (These fountains not only provide pleasure for the senses; the sound of falling water offers an ideal cover for confidential conversations. Paranoia or simple precaution: what could a religious, non-political movement possibly wish to conceal from the eyes and ears of the secret police? Was the building itself a fortified redoubt, complete with powerful computers and subterranean situation rooms, manned by armed guards prepared to fight to the death? To repulse an attack by helicopters and armored vehicles?)

Barely do I have time to sit down on the sofa and pull out the tools of my trade, a worn notebook and a pen, than a door swings silently open at the far end of the room and Fetullah Gülen enters, treading softly, accompanied by younger men with the unmistakable thick necks, sloped shoulders and square-jaws of weight-lifting security guards. Hoca Efendi himself wears a plain black suit over a white shirt buttoned to the neck. He is a strongly-built, stocky man, balding, with a small mustache and bushy black eyebrows that contrast strongly with his gray hair.

Tea and sweet cakes appear. A young man slips behind the video camera as another technician attaches tiny microphones to our lapels. Then he gives a signal: the interview may begin. The reconstruction which follows is a composite version of my own notes, and the transcript prepared from the video recording.

Through the interpreter, I address my question to Fetullah Gülen Hoca Efendi, using his full name and title. The response is immediate:

"Please call me Mr. Gülen," he interrupts.

Back to the question, then. What, I ask, is Mr. Gülen's relationship to the late Bediuzzaman Said Nursi?

His tone surprises me as much as the answer itself. "I prefer not to speak on my relations with Said Nursi. You can get information from our friends here later," he says curtly, pointing toward the listening men.

Well then, I offer, do you consider yourself to be a follower of Said Nursi?

"I am a simple and humble person," he says in a soft voice that suggests a mixture of lassitude and latent suspicion, his eyes obscured beneath half-closed eyelids. "A modest man. I am not attempting to follow anyone. To be his follower would be a great claim, which I am far from being able to make."

My next question, on his relations with other religious, and particularly Islamic groups, does little better.

"If society would benefit from a such a discussion, then I will talk about it openly. But with regard to the other groups in Turkey, I want to act cautiously. I know this policy may give rise to questions about what I've said, but this has been my policy for years, although it's likely to create problems. I am attempting to embrace all of humanity without discrimination. I am working to promote tolerance and reconciliation. My intention is the pleasure of Allah.

"I use caution when speaking on matters that I am not concerned with, and on anything to be published in a book or journal which would form the grounds for me to be questioned in the future."

That would mean me. Mr. Gülen would be erring on the side of caution today. But my next question, on the role of his movement in modern Turkey, did elicit an icy half-smile.

"First, I would like to make it clear that this is not a movement. I would never consider these things as being done as an organized movement, or myself as its leader. Ours is a gathering of people who share the same views and who come together around the common ground of the essentials of faith, and of the philosophy of service to humanity. If you define that as a movement, then I will not deny it. But if some people attempt to define it as such, I would like to emphatically note that this so-called movement makes no claim to bring about anything new or peculiar in Islam.

"Probably what began with Bediuzzaman [here Mr. Gülen refers to the man whose name he had earlier preferred not to mention] and impressed people most is an understanding of faith and religion whose main mission is to bring together the disunited and disintegrated sections of society and enable them to become a whole, integrated body again ..."

"We understand Islam no differently than the other Muslims," he continues. "However, in some respects, we may be further ahead of the rest in terms of accepting all people as they are, in their own status in society, and thus respect them too. I am a Muslim, and Hazrat Ali, Sheikh Gilani, Ahmad Yesevi, Mevlana Jelalladin Rumi, Yunus Emre and Bediuzzaman are all Muslims. And they all sought to embrace humanity."

Mr. Gülen's list of exemplary Muslims would also convey a sense of identification with Islam's mystical, anti-rationalist side, a marker of his approach to the question of faith and belief. In fact, the litany of names traces the lineage of the Sufi movement in Turkey. Ali, the son-in-law of the Prophet, and first Imam in the Shi'a tradition, is revered by the Turkish Sufis—as he is by all Sufis—as the greatest of all the Companions, for of all the Companions Ali was best able to discern hidden spiritual meanings. [23]

The founder of the Qadiri order, Sheikh Gilani, the eleventh-century spiritual master of Said Nursi, was renowned for his tolerance and charity, especially toward the other Peoples of the Book; Ahmad Yesevi, a Turk from Khorassan, that fertile seedbed of spiritual masters, ingratiated himself with the Turcoman earth shaker, Tamerlane, and left to posterity a compendium of poems of divine love, the *Diwan-i hikmat*, written in Turkish; Mevlana Jelalladin Rumi, the love-intoxicated master of Konya and inspirer of the Whirling Dervishes, needs no introduction; Yunus Emre, the Turkish Sufi poet who died in the late fourteenth century, gave voice to the teachings of Hajji Bektash Vali, one of the seminal figures in the propagation of mystical, syncretic "folk Islam." [24]

People today feel an enormous need for love, tolerance, dialogue and reconciliation, Mr. Gülen continues. It is useless to try to respond to those who are already tense, frustrated, angry, harsh or misinformed. But those who put aside their anger, hatred and malice and embrace mutual love, respect, recognition and acceptance see that the method works.

By now, the interview-*fleuve* with Fetullah Gülen was carrying me along on its frothing crest. My interventions were like those deceptively calm pools that open onto yet wilder stretches of white water. Was that the thundering of a waterfall that I heard ahead?

"But," I interject, "what is to be done about the kind of pressures that deny your belief itself?" a none-too-subtle allusion to the current situation in Turkey.

"The path to God is long, with no way stations," replies Mr. Gülen, quoting Yunus Emre. Muslims in Turkey in the past endured far greater difficulties than do their counterparts today. "They struggled and suffered much to learn their religion and its language, to open schools to teach the Qur'an and to train the hocas, the imams and the muezzins to read the *azan* ..."

Over the last fifty years, he continues, new movements began the task of establishing full democracy in Turkey. "This democracy has come close to providing people with the appropriate circumstances for living in and acting upon their religion." Up until two years ago, despite two military coups, people in Turkey have enjoyed "great freedom and comfort." And, in fact, when you compare Turkey with countries like Iran and Saudi Arabia, where "they do not tolerate the existence of different ways of thinking," Turkey provides "an agreeable atmosphere for Muslims who wish to practice their religion."

"Today, in the unfavorable conditions you refer to," he says, nodding in my direction, "I cannot help asking myself if some Muslims in Turkey have abused these circumstances. Extremists were unhappy, and demanded more. We, the Muslims, are the cause of the existing situation in Turkey. God Almighty has temporarily taken back what He bestowed as a blessing upon the Muslims."

It was as if Fetullah Gülen saw the National Security Council, whose "recommendations" of February 28, 1997, constituted, as he would put it, "the removal of a blessing," as an agent of the Almighty. Truly, God worked in strange ways. As I examine the official transcript (which I am assuming to be accurate), I note the wholehearted hope that, "the evil people plotting to make our country go backward will be detected and eliminated; that those who politicize the religion and exploit it for their own political ambitions will be separated from the pure and innocent believers."

I was struck by the resemblance between his formula and that of the censors of Turkish public life whose stated ambition—upon which any government must act if it is to be tolerated by the military—is to winnow out the advocates of "political Islam" from the great mass of "pure and innocent believers."

At the beginning of the audience (this was no interview, but a series of discreet sermons touched off by my questions), Mr. Gülen had been diffident, cool and remote. Now he was focused, concentrating on drawing the sharpest distinction between his beliefs and those of the political Islamists of the Refah Partisi, the main target of the February 28 coup. "If Islam is a system of belief, worship and morals, no one raises an objection to such a system in democratic countries. But conceiving Islam as only a way of ruling or governing people is nothing but a misrepresentation. This is why we must stay in Turkey and struggle against the politicization of Islam."

As a test of Mr. Gülen's views on society, I asked if he believed the dominant world order was a "just" one (the Refah Partisi had made "just order" its campaign slogan in the 1995 elections), and if not, what could be done to make it so.

There is disharmony and disorder in the world, he concedes. Capitalism's failed promises of equal distribution led to communism, which failed in turn. Today, the free market is supposed to bring peace and prosperity, but does so without taking the human heart and spirit, man's relation to the universe or the environment into account. If the superpowers wished to create new institutions, then our problems could be solved. Instead of investing in arms, we could invest in education, train teachers, open schools.

Then the world would be a more orderly and harmonious place. "But they only seem interested in applying their solutions to the world."

"What then is your solution?" I ask.

"All countries should build bridges between each other, and open themselves to mutual investments and commercial activities. Schools opening all around the world would be very fruitful. For example, Americans will open schools here, and we shall do so in the States."

Such measures would lessen the danger of conflict. "They would fight the ignorant and arrogant 'Bedouin' reaction that we see in society," he says through the interpreter (though the phrase has disappeared from the transcript, as have the words "tribal ignorance" from a description of the South as poor, desolate and uneducated as compared to the cultured, sophisticated North). What did Mr. Gülen mean by "Bedouin" reaction, by "tribal ignorance"? Had he even uttered the words? Perhaps the frail craft of meaning had run aground on the shoals of simultaneous translation.

The audience is ending. After a quick glance at his wristwatch, he sums up on a reflective note. Human beings must know themselves in order to resolve their problems as individuals, families and societies. This knowledge must be spiritual as well as scientific. For what is man, he asks, quoting Imam Ali, if not a tiny particle containing the whole cosmos. And this cosmos is knowable only through the names of God, those which the faithful click off on their *tasbis*.


BEYOND HIS WORDS, something about Mr. Gülen's manner left me feeling ill-at-ease. He seemed tired, detached, almost sad, though the core of his message to the faithful—and to the world at large— is a generous one of brotherhood and reconciliation. But in him I found an inner zone of opacity, an ambiguity that made it impossible for me either to warm to him, or to loathe him.

Neither the near-prophet claimed by his followers, nor the impostor alleged by his detractors, could he be a little of both?

The question was as simple-minded as the man himself was complex. Though he had responded at length to my questions, Fetullah Gülen had proven as impenetrable as the deepest mysteries of sufism, as indecipherable as an ancient kufic inscription whose sharp edges had been worn by time. Yet there could be no doubt about his charisma, his ability to sway the faithful by arguments that addressed both mind and heart. The young residents of his student dormitories were courteous, intelligent and selfless, all the more startling when measured against the stereotype of sullen adolescence prevalent in the West.

On the other hand, there could be little doubt about his worldly activities. Organizations like the Journalists' and Writers' Foundation sought out the favor of the powerful and cultivated a high public profile in an effort to surround the movement, or community, with a curtain of public legitimacy. A sophisticated media establishment propagated both Mr. Gülen's sermons or articles (available both in booklet form and on video cassette) and the image of the modern community of believers he claims to wish to create.

Etyen Mahçupyan views Fetullah Gülen's movement as an attempt to capture the religious franchise, to become the spiritual and temporal mediator between the powerful state and the pious believers, an up-dated version of the Ottoman model. For Faïk Bulut, the community was a modern-day *tariqat*, an offshoot of the Naqshbandis, a strictly Sunni Sufi order with a long history of support for the Ottoman state in its battle for survival against the West.

Where the "orthodox" followers of Said Nursi I was to encounter on my journey through Anatolia abjure the *tariqat* connection, Fetullah Gülen's behavior evokes that of the *murshid*, the exemplary leader in whom, the Sufis believe, the spirit of Mohammad lives on.[25] Where the followers of Said Nursi have supplanted the concept of leader with the primacy of the text, those of Mr. Gülen look to his person for guidance, not only in matters of the spirit, but in the affairs of the City.

"Fetullah Gülen Hoca Efendi is the richest man in Turkey, maybe even in the world," an acquaintance told me one evening over tea. "He has nothing. No house, no car, no money, no family. Only a few books. And yet, everything he asks for is his."

Whether he strives to replace with a "golden generation" the orthodox Sunni establishment of the imperial era, or to invest the state from within, Mr. Gülen's strategy remains one of extreme prudence, flattery of power and, suggest his critics, perhaps even the practice of dissimulation that is permitted to Shi'ites but not to Sunnis when the faith itself is in danger—though to suggest such a thing to a member of his organization elicits outcries of indignation. In such instances, the "Turkish paradox" kept popping into my mind.

Months later, on my second stay in Turkey, a friend asked me my opinion of Fetullah Gülen. I had found him tired, dispirited, remote, I replied, hinting that I had detected in him a certain empathy with the views of the regime.

"You are right, unfortunately. These are hard times for him," the friend sighed. "He is a good man but he is ill, and he is under pressure. The problem is that he does not want to displease anyone, and particularly the army. And they know it and take advantage of him."

If this is so, it becomes even more difficult to determine whether Mr. Gülen's opposition to "political Islam" flows from his religious convictions, or from his near-obsessive concern to remain in the good graces of the temporal masters of the Turkish state.

I cannot provide an answer. But the encounter with Fetullah Gülen Hoca Efendi's sect did arm me with the questions I needed to seek out the forebear he had been so reluctant to acknowledge, Bediuzzaman Said Nursi.

When I swung from the Erzurum bus in the early dusk at Van, the search for Said was to begin in earnest.

# V

# The Secret Garden

FAR ANATOLIA, in all its barrenness and thorny aridity, conceals a secret garden. Here, the harsher and more unforgiving the terrain, the rarer the trees, the more bitter the winters and searing the summers, the more verdant are the oases of mystical belief.

Perhaps the most extraordinary of the hidden spiritual gardens of Anatolia belongs to the Islamic scholar and holy warrior, rationalist and mystic, secret agent, political activist and quietist, the man affectionately known by many—but not all—Turks as Bediuzzaman Said Nursi.

At the urging of Professor R., I had come to Van intending to intersect not only the path of a man—his physical footsteps—but to seek insight into his spiritual progress as well. To trace the curious and compelling journey of a high and charismatic intelligence through an age of turmoil, the collapse of empire, the death and resurrection of the self, and finally the struggle against the unrelenting core of repression that lies at the heart of the Turkish state.

It would be, I suspected, a challenging task. Little did I realize how challenging. The object of my search travelled nothing so elegant as a straight line, his life trajectory resembled nothing like the cradle-to-grave progression that earnest biographers impose on subjects helpless to protest. Were one to plot his movements on a map, the pattern would be a dense cross-hatch, a series of loops and redoublings. Said's career spanned three regimes, each of which contained elements of the other. This meant, I soon realized, that I would not only be making my way across the Anatolia of geography, but into the Anatolia of history.

For the fast-moving tourist, lashed securely into the been-there-done-that straight jacket, skimming across the surface of societies, seeking to connect disparate stone relics to guidebook images, the region around Lake Van is as barren as its landscape. But for the traveler who burrows deep down into a society and into its history, the dry dust takes on the plasticity of primordial glaze, of mud enriched with blood and crushed bone, fallen empires and shattered but still vital dreams. In and around Van had long, long existed a finely wrought, though random and capricious, scattering of nationalities, tribes, religious doctrines and heresies, belief systems and remnants of ancient states and more ancient cultures, embedded deep in the compressed strata of time, forming a historical and social environment of immense fertility.

Van also lies atop one of the cultural fault lines that mark colliding worlds more surely than any frontier drawn on a map, in the middle of a border zone between warring empires, in the heart of contested territory whose inhabitants to this day bitterly deny attempts to define them, holding to the identity that clings to them like a shadow. Here—to speak merely of the last millennium—Byzantine *akrítes* skirmished with fast-riding platoons of Seljuk outriders on the eve of the great battle at Manzikert. Here the Black Sheep and White Sheep Turcoman hordes battled for tribal supremacy. Here the Sunni Ottomans under Yavuz Selim fought the red-hatted Qizilbash, the Shi'ite warriors led by Shah Ismaïl at Chaldiran for land, booty and the souls of the believers. Here the Kurds have for 70 years put up violent resistance to the efforts of the Turkish state to subsume, then erase them. Here languages, cultures, beliefs and dreams echo with greater resonance, greater intensity. Into this multi-layered, rich and complex society, Said Nursi was born, in 1293 AH, 1877 by the Gregorian calendar.

* * *

A FROSTY MIST hangs over the leafless poplars as Erhan, my guide for the day, and I hurry through the streets of Van toward the Otogar. Not until we climb aboard the Diyarbakir Express do the first rays of the sun begin to melt the ice on the puddles. Ten minutes out of the city, the bus sweeps onto the main highway that skirts the southern shore of Lake Van, trundling past reed beds, then along the coastline where the burnt straw of the early winter fields meets the deep blue of the alkaline waters. In the clear morning air, the snow-capped massif of Suphan Dagi floats above the distant shore, fifty kilometers away.

For the first third of the 150 kilometer run to Tatvan, the first leg of our trip, the road hugs the water. Then it veers inland and up through sheltered valleys where the shaded ground is still white with frost and wood smoke rises straight into the air. On the outskirts of villages, or guarding high passes, stand army outposts, protected by light tanks and armored personnel carriers beneath the red pennant emblazoned with the white crescent and star. They look lonely, isolated and vulnerable. The soldiers, most of them raw recruits, are far from home; the "enemy" omnipresent, yet unseen.

Two hours later the bus pulls into Tatvan, a sleepy town whose *raison d'être* is its situation at the western terminus of the rail ferry that crosses Lake Van, on the main line that runs eastward from Ankara and on to Iran. Here Erhan and I will wait for the minibus to Hizan, the jumping-off point for our day-long foray into the heart of the Taurus Mountains. Theoretically, as I am travelling into the war-torn region where Kurdish insurgents battle the Turkish army, I need authorization. I have no such authorization.

Unlike the clockwork precision of the interurban luxury coaches, Turkey's network of minibus lines, as dense and resilient as a spider's web, hews to an approximate schedule under which departure times are dictated by the filling of the last seat. Few people are leaving for Hizan at this early hour, so we stroll down the dusty sidewalks of Tatvan, under scrub pines and past tiny shops and the main mosque where workers are buffing newly cast concrete, throwing yet more dust into the atmosphere. Erhan, who claims acquaintances in every hamlet, thanks to the community's network of study houses, calls a friend, and the three of us step into a pastry shop for a glass of peach nectar where we continue to wait for the minibus to fill up.

My guide, a sharp-featured student at Van's Centennial University (in Turkey, "centennial" is understood to mean that of Atatürk's birth), has the kind of earnest intelligence that I was learning to associate with the residents of the country-wide system of dormitories the Nurcus call *dershane*, literally, houses of reading. In these houses, the reading, as I had observed the previous evening in Van, consisted of a recitation of the works of Said Nursi. In carefully-worded English of the bookish variety that flourishes in the absence of native-speaking instructors, Erhan plies me with questions, struggling to bring every thread of the conversation back to the writings of the master.

From the pastry shop we stroll back along the main street of Tatvan to the corner where our minibus is loading. By now, a small crowd of passengers is milling about, most of them Kurds sporting their traditional checkered headscarves and baggy pantaloons. Amid shouting and gesticulating the driver lashes cargo in the form of baskets to the roof of the vehicle, which sinks ever lower on its suspension. Erhan and I clamber aboard, and with a beeping of the horn in the faint hope of attracting one last passenger, the minibus creeps off.

Hizan, the second stage of our journey, lies at the end of a long, narrow valley sheltered from the north winds that sweep across Lake Van and distantly connected, by the stream that flows through the labyrinthine, intertwining network of canyons, passes and gulches, to the hot plains of upper Mesopotamia, and the far-away Persian Gulf. Here, the low-lying fields are still green, and the poplars that line the stream bed still cling to their yellowing, late-season leaves.

It is not the kind of town that appears on tourist itineraries, and the presence of a Westerner quickly sets tongues wagging and touches off intense curiosity. Around us cluster knots of wide-eyed boys with close-cropped heads. From tea-houses and barbershops, eyes follow our progress across the public square. Meanwhile, Erhan has encountered a friend of his called Burhan, the prefect of the Hizan study house, who has agreed to guide us the final 40 kilometers. After some inquiry, they locate a plumpish, ill-shaven man with a prominent gold tooth. His name is Adil, and he is the owner of a Turkish-built Renault "Toros" taxi. It is aptly named, for Hizan lies in the heart of the famous and forbidding Taurus mountain range. Adil is also a follower of Bediuzzaman and therefore overcomes his doubts about the condition of the road: God will provide, he assures us. Quickly agreeing upon a price, we set off. Time is short; nightfall comes rapidly among these rugged peaks and deep valleys. And at night, the roads are closed. "The area is not safe," people warn us. In this part of the country, that can only mean the PKK, the dreaded—or venerated—Kurdistan Workers' Party.

My journey into Anatolia had coincided with the expulsion from Syria, under threat of Turkish military intervention, of PKK chief and founder Abdullah Öcalan and his spectacular flight to Italy. As "Apo" lounged in a suburban Rome safe house to plot a political offensive that he hoped would transform him, with the ill-disguised complicity of left-wing members of the Italian parliament, from desperado (or liberation fighter) into a non-violent media-amenable personality, Turkish ultra-nationalists howled, wolf-like, for his blood, or at minimum, for his extradition. Bizarre events occurred. The Turkish Grand National Assembly quickly advanced legislation to strike down the death penalty, for Italian law forbade extradition to countries where capital punishment was in force. Turkish politicians boasted that though the death penalty was still on the books, it had not been enforced for years. (Extra-judicial capital punishment is frequent, disguised as traffic accidents, suicide or unexplained murders by unknown assailants.) Turkish businesses "spontaneously" ceased to import Italian goods. The government suspended purchase orders for Italian military hardware. Black wreaths were laid, and brawny, mustachioed men marched at the head of delegations of martyrs' families, as the people whose sons have died in anti-PKK operations are known. People accused of being "soft on terrorism" were beaten on the streets. Human rights activists were threatened.

Öcalan's decision to found the PKK in November, 1978, had fallen like a seed on fertile ground. Five decades of republican "progress" had meant little more than exclusion of the entire region, where Kurds form a majority of the population, from the country's social and economic development. From its inception, Atatürk's Republic had postulated itself as an ethnic monolith and imposed a single Turkish supra-identity. Unlike the Turks, however, who had migrated in waves into Anatolia from Central Asia one thousand years earlier, the Kurds were an indigenous people related by language and custom to the Iranians, distant heirs to the ancient civilizations of the region.

Kemalism, for all its totalitarian national claims, was an urban phenomenon. When modern Turkish nationalism—it must never be forgotten that nationalism, as surely as the Atatürk variant of republicanism, which is an extreme variant (or perhaps mutation), was a Western graft—finally arrived in the poor, backward southeast, it encountered a formidable rival:[26] a diffuse but intense, historically-rooted sense of Kurdishness, of which Öcalan's PKK was to be only the latest, but certainly not the last, expression.

For, as Hugh Poulton writes, despite the relative liberalization that accompanied the advent of a multi-party system in Turkey in the 1950s, "the modern Turkish state has remained antithetical to a Kurdish national consciousness separate from the Turkish one." In fact, the Turkish state makes not the slightest concession to the multi-national and multi-ethnic character of the republic's citizens. The Turkish nation—in Kemalist doctrine—is a "monolith without ethnic minorities and comprises the entire population of the republic."[27]

Article 26 of the Constitution of 1982, written by General Kenan Evren's military junta, declared Turkish to be the mother tongue of Turkish citizens. [28] In Kurdistan, application of the law meant the criminalization of Kurdish for over a decade, until President Turgut Özal's decision not to enforce restrictions on its private use. (To this day, many in Turkey are convinced that Özal's readiness to acknowledge the existence of the Kurds, not to mention his tolerance for the overt practice of religion, may have contributed to his untimely death.)

In Turkey, the PKK must be publicly referred to as bandits, and "terrorism" must be identified as the main obstacle to development of the dirt-poor Southeast, which for many years has been ruled as an Emergency Law area. Since the early 1990s, government policy—dictated by the military, like every other key aspect of national life—has been to uproot the logistical base of Öcalan's party. This is has done by destroying crops, burning villages, and forcing their inhabitants to flee, either to the large cities of the region, or to Ankara and Istanbul.

Simultaneously, the same forces concentrated deep within the hard core of the Turkish state have crushed any attempt to set up a legal Kurdish political party. The few courageous individuals that dared to speak as Kurds in the Ankara parliament found themselves stripped of their parliamentary immunity and imprisoned on charges of promoting separatism. The effect (could it have been desired?) was to lend legitimacy to the claims of the PKK to speak on behalf of the Kurds, and to create, in the manner of all self-fulfilling prophesies, a violent, brutal, desperate and ruthless opponent. Abdullah Öcalan, whose name means "avenger," may have been all of these things, but it remained for Turkish policy to create and consolidate his constituency.

FOR THE FIRST DOZEN KILOMETERS the surface is smooth asphalt and Adil makes excellent time, slowing only to dodge errant cows, to defer to flocks of sheep crossing the road, or to avoid darting goats and their tiny, underage herders. Now and again fierce-eyed, burly shepherd dogs dash after us, howling with protective fury. This is no countryside for casual strolling, and not only because of the presence of Kurdish "terrorists."

As we branch southeastward into a narrow canyon with soaring walls the road surface has become dusty gravel, forcing us to travel with closed windows. Our speed drops to a crawl as Adil negotiates miniature crevasses and puddles of indeterminate depth. From the canyon walls waterfalls gush down to join the river.

As we round a sharp bend, Adil points upward, to what appears to be a tiny hut perched on a crag overlooking the river far below. Erhan translates: "It is Tag. This is where Said Nursi first went to school." At first I can barely make out the rocky excrescence against the cliff, a sub-locality of the town of Isparit, itself so small that it appears on none but the most detailed maps.[29] The young Said, so legend goes, was a proud, pugnacious and headstrong lad. Constantly involved in fights, he did not last long at the Qur'anic school in this place.

Around us the canyon has broadened out to form a narrow valley. Houses built from split stone begin to appear. A few minutes later we encounter donkeys laden with huge piles of twigs to be used as firewood, then little girls with bright-hued headscarves tending a few goats. The road has now deteriorated to a muddy track. Adil's Toros churns, whines and bucks in the mire. Suddenly we are surrounded by a grove of trees, still in late-season leaf.

"We are in Nurs," exclaims Erhan. "There is Bediuzzaman's birth house. Look, that house there!"

Through a translucent veil of amber-green foliage, I can make out a complex of stone dwellings built atop one another, clinging to the canyon wall. Adil brings the car to a stop in a wide spot in the road. We climb out and cross a worn plank bridge across the stream. Seen close-up, the village is not a relic but a living organism that may well have existed in this forbidding yet beautiful and fertile valley for millennia. Puffing from the altitude—we are well above 2,000

Bediuzzamon Said Nursi at the tomb of Sultan Mehmet the Conqueror, Istanbul, 1952.
*Courtesy of Istanbul Ilim Kultur Vakfi*

Said Nursi's distant relatives in front of his birth house, Nurs, Hizan.

*Photo by Fred A. Reed*

meters now—I follow my guides up a rock-strewn path that winds along the flank of the mountainside.

Abruptly we round an outcropping. Before us stands Said Nursi's birth house, a split stone construction with a mud and straw roof. In fact, to call this dwelling unassuming is to commit a grievous overstatement. It is little more than a rocky hovel nestled against the steep slope, almost indistinguishable from it. The place is still inhabited by a family of distant relatives. The man of the house shows us into the kitchen, a corridor with a stone step atop which a small bottled gas burner balances precariously. This kitchen, Erhan explains, was added to the house at a later date. From the open window—more precisely, a hole in the wall—we look across a narrow cleft toward another stack of houses, where women are going about their Saturday afternoon chores. On catching sight of us—male interlopers—they adjust their headscarves and turn their backs.

When we visit places connected with men of unique qualities—the usual shorthand term is "great," but it is ill-adapted to the singular career and character of Said Nursi—the first reaction is often one of disappointment, and anti-climax. What possible connection can exist between this tiny, rock-poor village in a remote canyon of the Taurus and a man whose action and dogged insistence on inaction are still shaping, in unforeseen and mysterious ways, a country and a religion?

Had I been expecting a commemorative plaque, perhaps? Suitable "improvements," perhaps a religious theme-park, through which would tramp legions of the curious, shopping for souvenirs and gaping at the remaining inhabitants who, in turn, would silently curse the visitor-tormentors, who might be parted with a few loose coins? None of the above. Nurs, with the exception of the roadway and a lone electric line, stands today as it would have when the young Said would scramble up the hillside and spend the night searching the stars for the meaning of the universe.

Genius, that simultaneously inflated and debased term, is often the unexpected product of the most humble of circumstances. As a journeyman provincial violin teacher and court composer fathered Mozart, the wonder of his age, here a small landholder whose family hailed from Cizre, on the banks of the Tigris, called Sufi Mirza, and his devout wife Nuriye, bore their son Said, the fourth of seven children.

"From my mother I learned compassion, " he later wrote, "and from my father, orderliness and regularity." [30]

But early on, Said Nursi's character reflected more than compassion, orderliness and regularity. He was a youngster of extreme pugnaciousness, intense pride and a disputatious temperament who could not endure, writes his biographer Sükran Vahide, even the smallest word spoken to him in a commanding tone. Later he was to describe himself in these terms:

"When I was ten years old, I had great pride in myself, which sometimes even took the form of boasting and self praise, although I myself did not want to, I used to assume the air of one undertaking some great work and mighty act of heroism." [31]

Said was displaying a preternatural modesty. The great work, the mighty act of heroism would be nothing less than the attempt to establish a reformed, democratically responsive Ottoman Empire as a bulwark of Islam and, when that failed, to preserve Islam against the depredations of republican secular fundamentalism.

Who could have predicted that such a man would emerge from such a place? To ask the question is to misread the "primitive" nature of Nurs, and of southeastern Anatolia. For Said Nursi, as his intellectual and spiritual faculties expanded, found around him the conceptual tools he needed to grapple with what we now describe, with some embarrassment, as "the great questions": whence, why, whither? He found them, reworked and adapted them, in a family environment of piety, closely connected to the rhythms of the soil and the seasons, in the rich and multiform natural surroundings of Nurs, its trees, animals and rushing water, never straying from the tradition of Muslim devotional erudition that owes as much to these uneducated but spiritually rich Kurdish villagers as it does to the high theological postulates of the Sunni mainstream.

And yet, at the core of the conundrum of genius lies the insoluble, the unapproachable, the inexplicable. No more can a Said Nursi (or a Mozart) be explained simply by his family, social, natural and intellectual environment, than by the currently fashionable binary and genetic reductionism, or by DNA analysis. They must be defined in their own terms. But not only in those terms. Wonders of the age are children of the age as well, and they speak its language.

\* \* \*

DURING THE LAST HALF of the nineteenth century, the region into which Said Nursi was born may have been, compared with Istanbul, a remote and primitive place, but it was far from isolated from the rapid changes sweeping the Empire. At the centre of the district, the town of Bitlis had become a thriving centre of trade and agriculture, a rich and humming caravansary of goods, people and ideas. Since the time of the Ottoman conquest in the sixteenth century, Bitlis and its surrounding region had been ruled by a Kurdish Bey, and enjoyed substantial autonomy—typical of the fiercely independent spirit of the Kurds themselves, whose allergy to remote and foreign rule is legendary. The whole area, observes Serif Mardin, "was still a crazy-quilt pattern of tribes, loose tribal federations, ethnic units and religious groups."[32]

So the region was to remain until the great cleansing that accompanied the collapse of the Empire. But the gradual penetration of the Ottoman reform movement into the hinterland, the liberal trade politics and legal, administrative and educational policies copied from the West, touched off massive shifts in the conservative, traditional, tribally oriented Kurdish society. These shifts—or rather, upheavals—were to create a climate of tension and national tragedy, and to provide the backdrop for a young man's expanding awareness of the natural world, and of Islam's threatened place in it.

Between 1871 and 1894, the imperial authorities imported and adopted a system of provincial administration modeled on the French Second Empire. In the Bitlis region, reflecting its complex ethnic, religious and cultural composition, the semi-representative local council consisted of the governor, the mufti, the presidents of the civil and religious tribunals, a secretary general, two Muslim and two Christian notables and the Armenian Gregorian bishop.[33]

A census carried out in the region in 1889 gives figures of 254,000 Muslims, more than 130,000 Armenians and 6,000 Syrian Jacobites, 2,600 Chaldean Catholics, 3,862 Yezidi, a heretical Muslim group known as "Devil worshippers," 210 Greek Orthodox and 372 Copts. The Turks were primarily townspeople; they formed part of the notable class and accounted for the near totality of the bureaucracy. The Armenian population encompassed both wealthy and influential town notables and poor though industrious villagers. Kurdish-speakers made up the tribal and village population.[34]

The Ottoman reform movement of the early nineteenth century, known as the *Tanzimat*, brought with it increased solicitude on the part of the Empire's creditors. Having obtained a precious foothold, they acted rapidly to consolidate and expand what they saw as a beach head. It was an odd invasion that elicited an equally curious defense.

For two centuries the Ottomans had been the world's dominant military power. Their armies had once threatened Vienna. But by the late seventeenth century, this once invincible force had begun to taste military defeat at the hands of a resurgent, and better-armed Europe. Emboldened, Hapsburg Austria and imperial Russia launched successful campaigns against the Empire. In their dismay at military defeat and the shrinking of their dominions, the sultans concluded that they must learn from, mimic, and eventually surrender to, the West.

Encouraged by the spirit of the *Tanzimat* as early as 1820, Western Protestant missionaries, Americans for the most part, began to flow into the Empire. Their initial intention was to convert its Muslim and Jewish subjects. Misjudging their quarry, they fastened on the Christian Armenians of Anatolia. Here their prospects were brighter by far. By the end of the century, there existed 127 Protestant congregations with 13,000 members, and 400 schools with an enrollment of 23,000 pupils, the vast majority of whom were Armenians. [35] These schools acted as a conduit for a new way of thinking; they also provided Armenians with an attitude of pragmatic, down-to-earth realism to replace the fatalism of a subject minority.

Such ideas, combined with an influx of radical Russian populism from across the Caucasus border, and the influence, through Constantinople, of the European-educated sons and daughters of wealthy Armenian merchants and bankers, fueled an intellectual and social ferment that was not long in seeking political expression, first in the shape of secret societies, then, of revolutionary parties committed to the creation of an Armenian national state on the Balkan model. European statesmen were drawn to the Armenians. They found them ideal proxies in their on-again, off-again battle to the death against the Islamic Ottoman state, from which such a new country would be carved. What the Armenians did not fully appreciate (as the Bosnians and the Albanian Kosovars of todays' Balkans do not fully appreciate) was that a new country would only be created if it served European interests, not their own.

By century's end the climate had turned sour, the atmosphere growled with distant thunder. Newly-roused demons prowled the land. And in far capitals, the decisions of frock-coated, top-hatted statesmen to accelerate the reform process in the Empire—their motivation being, of course, purely altruistic—had a devastating impact. The finely wrought Ottoman needlepoint of multi-ethnic, multi-religious coexistence was about to ripped from the hands of its artisans and torn to bloody shreds.

At the same time as the Empire was being infiltrated from the West—often at its own express desire—by European culture and the European economy, in a process commonly described as cultural fertilization, another kind of infiltration was taking place from the East. In the early nineteenth century, coinciding with the arrival of the American Protestant missionaries, the wandering dervishes of the Naqshbandi Sufi order established themselves in Anatolia, an event entirely overlooked by popular Western histories of the rise and fall of the Ottoman state. Already in the 1830s, Naqshbandis had led the resistance to Russian expansionism in the Caucasus, where their legacy persists to this day among the fierce and rebellious Chechens. Now, settling in places like Hizan and Bitlis, they insinuated themselves into the fibre of society and politics. It was not long before their program of resistance to imitative westernism and European imperialism won them a strong and devoted following. Their following proved as vigorous among the Kurds as had been that of the Protestants among the Armenians.

For the Naqshbandi sheikhs, the upsurge in the activity of the Empire's Christian communities was nothing less than a threat to Islamic civilization. The existence of proselytizing missionaries among heretofore docile subject populations was a scandal, and a mortal danger to the integrity of a social system, and a way of life.

Little wonder, then, that by the middle of the final decade of the century, overt activity by Armenian reformers and revolutionaries had given rise to the creation of Muslim secret societies determined to stop them. These groups may have been set up by Naqshbandi dervishes or not; the spirit of resistance that the Naqshbandis preached dovetailed with widespread popular resentment against the Westernizing upstarts.

That was not all: Sultan Abdülhamid had created special irregular detachments officered by Kurdish tribal chieftains known as the *Hamidiye*, "Sultan Hamid's men." One of their tasks was to "combat Armenian terrorism" in Anatolia.[36] When, in October, 1895, the central government announced a reform program dictated by the British that was seen as favoritism toward the Empire's Christian (read Armenian) population, violence flared.[37]

A bloody incident occurred in Bitlis, where at least 200, and perhaps 600 Armenians were killed, depending on the sources. It had been preceded several weeks before by a massive protest march through the streets of Istanbul by the Armenians of the capital to deliver a Protest-Demand to the government calling for an end to "systematic persecution." The demonstration rapidly turned ugly; the cry of "Liberty or Death" was raised and the crowd surged forward, was met and violently dispersed by police. Rioting and an anti-Armenian pogrom followed.[38]

\* \* \*

NURS SHELTERS in a grove of poplar, walnut and oak on the northern side of the valley, situated for maximum exposure to the sun. A well-trodden path connects clusters of stone houses built in stepping-stone form, up and down the slope. In single file I follow Erhan, Burhan and Mehmet Bey, Bediuzzaman's distant relative, along this path, our feet crunching in dry leaves, upward across the gentle pitch of the hillside. Atop a knoll stands a tiny graveyard: the burial site of Said Nursi's parents and elder brother Abdullah, whose religious piety helped the headstrong youngster find his vocation. The gravestones are inscribed with crudely drawn Arabic letters, as a reminder to the wayfarer that this place hews still to the old-time religion.

On the way back to the village we encounter a young girl spinning wool. She looks us straight in the eye and greets us with a cheery "selam." Further on, where a chattering rivulet flows into a small pool, we stop to admire the village goldfish, plump, lustrous, reddish carp that have somehow contrived to flourish in this micro environment.

Noon. My guides beg my indulgence while they pause to pray at the village *mescit*. While they perform their ablutions I wait in the minuscule prayer-room, squatting on the carpet strewn, packed-earth floor. Through a small unglazed window next to the *qible*—the point designating the direction of Mecca—I enjoy the view southeastward up the canyon, through half-bare poplars, to the cliffs and beyond, a patch of sky.

How many people live here? I ask Mehmet Bey as we leave the *mescit*. Perhaps one hundred souls, he explains. The inhabitants till tiny terraced patches of flat land, harvest fruits and vegetables, and raise sheep, goats and chickens. Some migrate to regional centers like Hizan, Tatvan or Bitlis. Some have even gone to Diyarbakir. But this is not a village populated only by the elderly: I see able-bodied men, women minding their children, adolescent shepherds scrambling up and down the steep hillsides, whistling and slinging rocks sidearm to keep their four-legged charges in line.

Prayers completed, and with the spring of anticipation in their stride, my guides strike off toward a house overlooking the stream. I have picked up the Turkish equivalent of "let's eat," and increase my pace to keep up with them. Within minutes we are seated cross-legged, amidst expansive gestures of welcome, on the carpeted floor in front of the *sofra*, a large round brass platter that does duty as dining table. Then, as though by magic (I saw no kitchen and no cook), plates and bowls begin to appear through the doorway. The meal begins with a bowl of fresh, warm sheep's milk, followed by a spicy stew of tomato, onion and potato, a pilaf of bulgur, plates of cheese, olives, chunks of oozing comb honey that gleam like raw cut gemstones, and rounds of village bread, chewy, fragrant, substantial—as far from the extruded semi-styrofoam that passes for bread in Istanbul as Nurs is from Taksim Square.

The meal is a time of few words. Short bursts of conversation give way to the sounds of bleating sheep, wind rustling in the dry leaves, and, in the middle-distance, the rushing stream. Soon the table is bare, save small piles of bread crumbs and olive pits. For my hosts, getting up after sitting cross-legged through a meal is a lifelong reflex unencumbered by the logistical considerations that I, a long-legged, no-longer-young non-Turk must grapple with. By the time I have massaged circulation back into my thighs, straightened my knees and ducked through the low-hanging doorway, good-byes are already in progress.

As we were finishing our meal, distant gunshots had rung out. Impossible to know whether they had come from hunters' shotguns or the automatic rifles of insurgents.

"Security problems?" I asked.

"No," they laugh.

Moving now with a certain purposefulness, we make our way downhill, where Adil is waiting. The sun is edging toward the canyon wall; perhaps two hours of daylight remain. Erhan and I consult briefly; we have a problem. If we return to Hizan, we may be trapped there overnight for the usual, euphemistically described security reasons. If I offer Adil a few million more lira, will he drive us directly to Tatvan? Indeed he will.

Waving to our hosts we roar off, churning up a cloud of dust and rousing sheep dogs from their midday lethargy long enough to pursue us with bared fangs and blood-curdling snarls. "Can you believe," says Erhan, "that from this poor place Said Nursi went to Istanbul."

The vibrancy with which he says the word Istanbul gives me the measure of its meaning. Ankara may be the administrative and political capital of Turkey, but Istanbul is the city of empire, the centre of culture, the economic powerhouse, the magnet. Yes, I nod, I understand. From the village, its most illustrious son went up to the metropolis, daring to engage the mighty of the day in debate about the future, presuming to propagate faith among the profligate, and to offer living testimony of a rigorous righteousness whose only possible equivalent would be (though Bediuzzaman's followers would recoil in horror at the comparison) the late Imam Khomeini.

If in the mind of a devout follower like Erhan the path from Nurs to Istanbul seemed, in the diffuse light of history as it blends into legend, straight and narrow, for Said Nursi it would have been tortuous and roundabout, and illuminated only by a young man's overpowering self-assurance and sense of mission. Not only had he to acquire the language of religion; he needed to acquire the kind of reputation that would precede him, the qualities of physical and moral steadfastness that functioned as markers of personal influence in the unforgiving, turbulent, male-dominated society of the Kurdish provinces of Anatolia. [39]

Throughout the forced modernization of the Ottoman Empire, the Islamic idiom in which Said Nursi's first mentors cast their arguments, their instruction and their lives, had lost nothing of its richness and flexibility. Mastery of it gave people firmly rooted in the rural world, yet alert to the forces changing society around them, the ability to step confidently into an increasingly Western-influenced urban culture. [40] By the time he departed Nurs for Bitlis, the first stop on his long pursuit of religious legitimacy, a singular combination of stubbornness and extreme mental agility had already given him a reputation that spread to the neighboring villages. In a dream he had encountered the Prophet Mohammad, who confided to him: "Knowledge of the Qur'an will be given you on condition you ask no questions of any of my community." Thenceforth, the young Said refused on principle to ask questions of other religious scholars, and answered only questions put to him.

The *medrese* of Sheikh Emin Efendi, in Bitlis, was one of the most prestigious in the region, its master one of the leading theological personalities of the day. Several years later, the Sheikh himself was offered, and refused, the post of Sheikholeslam, the supreme religious position in the Empire, by Sultan Abdülhamid. It was unthinkable that a stripling from a back-country village, no matter how bright, would be taught by such a lofty figure, instead of by a junior seminarian. Wounded by the slight to his ever sensitive *amour-propre*, Said one day leaped to his feet in the mosque and challenged the master: "Sir! You are wrong, it is not like that." [41] Shortly thereafter he departed Bitlis, moving from town to town through eastern Anatolia in search of the circumstances that would provide his uneasy spirit with the stimulus it sought.

As Adil's Toros churns and yaws back down the dusty canyon road toward Hizan, the cliffs close in around us; dramatic earlier in the day, now they seem threatening. The sun has vanished beyond the canyon rim, and darkness is rising from the riverbed. Suddenly, ahead of us, we encounter a military vehicle drawn up diagonally across the road. What if I am challenged for an authorization? We surrender our documents to dour-faced young soldiers who trot over to the armored car, show them to the commanding officer, then come trotting back. No further questions. Soon night will fall, and any vehicle traffic daring to travel this road must have excellent reasons for doing so, or else be dealt with as an enemy. Here, in the canyons of Kurdistan, the soldiers will no longer be the rulers. Shadowy forces may emerge from the darkness; worst of all, these shadows, all but indistinguishable from the rocks, may be the very villagers who earlier that day had served them tea. I thought back to the photograph I had been shown in far away Istanbul.

A few kilometers further along we overtake a group of three uniformed men strolling along the roadside. Less well attired than the soldiers who had stopped us earlier, they are dressed in camouflage outfits and carry rucksacks emblazoned with the national flag. In addition to the automatic weapons slung over their shoulders, the men also carry shepherd's staves; their sun-wrinkled faces are covered with stubble. They are members of the "village patrols," recruited by the armed forces to keep the terrorists and separatists at bay, and may well be courting mortal danger by sporting the Turkish insignia in these parts. Part of the PKK's reputation for ruthlessness arises from its policy of attacking and killing these patrol members who, like school teachers, they claim to be instruments in the army's pacification strategy.

The sun is dropping beneath the jagged western horizon, bathing the folds of the eastern slope of the Taurus in golden light, as we reach the Hizan turnoff on the Tatvan road. Providentially for Adil and Burhan, whose concern is mounting with every kilometer traveled into the deepening gloom, a taxi is waiting at the cutoff. We transfer into the other vehicle, say quick good-byes, then the Toros roars back down the valley to Hizan and safety. Our new driver, unlike the pious Adil, is a chain-smoking loud-mouth who guffaws and imitates the sound of machine gun fire. But the imperative is the same: reach the town before nightfall. Within twenty minutes we crest the final hill. Below us Tatvan emerges, ghost-like and faintly lit, from the ground-hugging mist. The taxi speeds down the now-deserted main street through the coal fog, to deposit us at the station where we board the return bus to Van with minutes to spare. Instead of taking the direct route, the vehicle will be skirting the lake along the north shore. The south road—the main highway—is already closed.

Three hours later Erhan and I disembark on the outskirts of Van city and hike rapidly through the chilly, dark streets to the dormitory. The weekly Saturday night reading session is in progress; we slip off our shoes and wind our way upstairs through knots of young men listening in the staircase and hallway to the proceedings being broadcast over a loudspeaker system. Elsewhere in Van, trendy youngsters may be carousing in some smoky club (though I doubted very much that such a place exists in this dour town), but for the devoted young followers of the Nur movement, this is as wild as life is likely to get.

We step into the main meeting room, where more than 150 men of all ages are kneeling or squatting on the carpeted floor as one of the community leaders reads the lesson. The reader, Erhan whispers, has done several years in prison for what, in today's Turkey, is called "reactionism," shorthand for illegal religious activity. Throughout, the attention of the listeners is total, imperturbable. The only sounds in the room, aside from the incantatory voice of the reader, are an occasional cough, and people shifting position.

After the meeting, over a light meal, I remark on the absence of state symbols in the *dershane*, and particularly of the obligatory portrait of Atatürk. "Well, you see," explains one of my hosts, "this is really a private house, so we are not obliged. Besides, if we were to hang up the flag, it might offend some of the people here, who are Kurdish."

The personality cult, the constant invocation of the state founder's name and principles, the lowering, glaring presence of his photograph, steely-eyed, purposeful, heroic and threatening, may have the opposite of the intended effect, he explains. "Young people go through the education system, from elementary school to university, and as soon as they get out, they become Marxists or Nurcus!"

What he dared not say, and what a student whispered to me on the street in Istanbul one day, is that the cult has created not love or admiration for Atatürk, but hatred of the man in whose name freedom is denied.

* * *

WHEN SAID NURSI, now an adolescent, departed the *medrese* in Bitlis he turned northeastward. Passing through Van, he headed for the town of Dogubayezit, today the last stop on the road to Iran. His stay in the *medrese*, run by Sheikh Mehmet Jelali, was to last a mere three months, but it grounded him in the religious sciences upon which he would draw in the works of his maturity. The fourteen-year-old displayed a phenomenal memory. During his stay he absorbed the entire curriculum, including annotated works, commentaries on them, and commentaries on the commentaries, a course that normal students usually completed in fifteen to twenty years before graduating as certified preachers and *ulama*. [42]

In Dogubayezit, too, Said encountered the strain of mystical Islamic thought that was to become a "constant theme in his religious imagery and a central fulcrum of his theories, the theory of light or illumination." [43] The followers of the Illuminist school—known as *ishraqi*—held that asceticism expands the mind and leads to knowledge of God. Bypassing the formal structures of academic learning, this knowledge would only be vouchsafed in a flash of illumination—a metaphor that was to become the hallmark of Bediuzzaman's mature thought. Not only would illuminism lead him onto the highroad to religious knowledge—through it he could challenge, then surmount the charisma of his Naqshbandi teachers.

Finally, it would become the method that would inform his life's work.

Clad in the robes of a dervish, Said set out for Baghdad, where he intended to visit the tomb of his revered spiritual patron, Abd al-Qadir Gilani, the eleventh-century founder of the Qadiri *tariqat*. Born in the Iranian province of Gilan, on the south coast of the Caspian, Gilani died in Baghdad having attained the perfection of love—*kamal-i ashq*—respected by all, even such rigorously anti-Sufi Sunni theologians as Ibn Taymiyah, the man considered to be the father of "fundamentalism." [44] Sidetracked by his own insatiable curiosity and lust for religious knowledge, Said wandered instead through southeastern Anatolia, visiting theological schools and disputing the finer points of doctrine with astonished men of religion.

In the town of Tillo he withdrew, hermit-like, to a small stone building. There his younger brother Mehmet, who was accompanying him, brought him soup and bread, the crumbs of which Said fed to the ants. This he would later describe as a "reward for their republicanism." [45] He may have been drawn to mysticism, but he was alert to the great social and political sea changes taking place around him.

In Tillo, as well, the young man was visited in a dream by Sheikh Gilani, who ordered him to summon a certain Mustafa Pasha, one of the area's most notorious Kurdish warlords, to the way of guidance. If the Pasha did not desist from his evil ways, Gilani commanded, Said was to kill him. Coming from a man of perfect love, it was a curious request, but it well fitted the young man's charged emotional state.

Only a fool—or a man of blind self-confidence—would have done what Said did next. He packed his meagre belongings and headed south to Cizre, overlooking the Tigris. Mustafa Pasha had a reputation of his own, as a caravan robber, and as a bloodthirsty and tyrannical despot of the sort that for centuries had flourished in these wild and desolate parts. The young man in the dervish's robes had no sooner encountered the fearsome Mustafa than he threw down a challenge:

"I have come to guide you to the right path. Either you give up your tyranny and start performing the obligatory prayers, or else I shall kill you."[46]

A man of little patience, who preferred the language of knives and rifles to religious injunctions, Mustafa Pasha was taken aback by the cheek of his visitor. Killing a member of the *ulama*, he must have reflected, would not stand him in good stead among the devout tribesman who rode under his command. He withdrew from his tent to consider possible solutions. The answer was not long in coming. A competition would be organized, in which the leading religious scholars from the region would match wits and erudition against the brash upstart. Were Said to emerge victorious (an unlikely prospect in Mustafa Pasha's eyes), the tyrant would relent and repent. Were he to be bested, Mustafa would order him thrown into the Tigris.

Against all odds—except in the light of latter-day hagiography where fact meshes with faith—Said easily prevailed over the baffled experts, answering their questions, asking none, and astonishing them with his knowledge. True to his warrior's word, Mustafa presented him with a Mauser rifle and began to perform his prayers.

The incident in Cizre (Mustafa Pasha later reverted to form and threatened to kill him) illustrated Said Nursi's conviction that by using the lever of religious injunction he would be able to raise the mighty to the path of righteousness, halt the disintegration of the Empire, and restore Islam to its ancient glories. Provincial governors, high-ranking officers, the leading religious authorities of the Empire, and finally the Sultan himself—none could avoid or ignore the passionate pleas of a man seemingly invested by God Himself with a mission.

* * *

FOR THE NEXT FOUR YEARS, he criss-crossed the southeast, preaching, disputing, encountering the leading scholars of the day, and displaying his extraordinary memory. While established again in Bitlis, he received an invitation from the governor of Van, a certain Hasan Pasha, to establish himself in that city. In the first decade of the twentieth century, Van was a showcase of Ottoman administrative reform. The Armenian community was influential, enlightened, and only partially attracted to the burgeoning revolutionary and separatist movements that were later to bring about its downfall. [47]

Several months later, Hasan Pasha was replaced by an official close to the Sultan himself, a man called Tahir Pasha. The new governor enjoyed a reputation as a patron of learning, kept abreast of developments in western science, and boasted a substantial library. More important, Tahir was, writes Sükran Vahide, the first state official to grasp Said Nursi's talent and potential, and gave him unstinting support until his death in 1913. [48]

Two things happened during Said's four-year residence with the governor. He committed to memory some ninety books of Qur'anic exegesis, a feat of learning that reinforced his title as "Wonder of the Age." At the same time, he became convinced that the classical formulas that he had used to refute the arguments of the unbelievers—the skeptical, westernized *Tanzimat* intellectuals—were useless. The only possible course of action was to study and master their idiom, the secular sciences. [49]

For all the political turmoil that wracked the Empire, the first years of Abdülhamid's reign witnessed an outpouring of scientific literature, as the Ottoman elite, having turned its back on all but the ceremonial aspects of Islam, ate and drank itself into a stupor at the table of the West. Pocket libraries on the sciences were published. Bediuzzaman's direct experience of the new knowledge and his encounters with its advocates combined to convince him that the true path of enlightenment lay in demonstrating the truths of religion in a manner appropriate to the dominant understanding of the century. [50]

This he set out to do, by opening his own *medrese*, which he onomatopoeically named Horhor, at the foot of the Van citadel where a gurgling spring flowed from the ancient rock. Here, the limitations of the traditional curriculum became apparent. Here, the power of secular science to inform religion, and to corroborate its truths, shone with a new intensity. Said Nursi, ever the innovator, would combine the two. The next decade of his life would be dedicated to the aim of setting up a university in far Anatolia, where his method would be applied. This institution would remedy the backwardness of the region; it would also open the door to the solution of its multifarious social ills; it would reconcile the fractious Kurds with their Turkish brothers-in-religion.

But he could not hope to raise support for his daring venture in Van alone, for all the solicitude of Tahir Pasha. The city was small; it soon became narrow, constricting. Only in Istanbul, seat of ultimate power, could he act upon his visionary idea. At the age of twenty-three, dressed now in his Kurdish turban, with daggers thrust through his sash, he traveled to the capital, seeking audience with the man whose command alone could satisfy him. That man was Sultan Abdülhamid.

Said Nursi ("The Old Said") in 1918.

# VI

## Galata Diary

Spring was threatening when I returned to Istanbul in March, 1998. In a southerly breeze, flags snapped and sunlight ricocheted off the Bosphorus and the gilded crescents atop the minarets of St. Sophia and Sultanahmet mosques. Gulls wheeled and darted on the updraft.

In the two months I spent in the apartment hotel in Galata, from the top-floor window of which I had taken in the first, throat gripping panorama of the Istanbul skyline, I had also heard a whisper, a faint rustling. Its source was impossible to trace. At first I thought it might have been the call to prayer echoing through the dark, claustrophobia-inducing alleys like the plaintive chanting of some demonstration drawing ever closer but never finally arriving. Or it might have been the soft footfalls of the neighborhood cats on night patrol. But it was neither of these. The sound I heard—more like a hum or a subterranean rumble—seemed to emerge from the creaking floorboards, to creep from the mortar between the stone blocks, to rise from the basements of abandoned synagogues, to be carried on the hiss of the wind or the patter of the raindrops as they impacted on the gray dust of fine-ground rock and bone that seemed to coat the entire city, rising from its depths like the uncontainable past.

As Istanbul buildings go, this thick-walled structure was a recent one. It had originally been constructed at the end of the nineteenth century as a revenue property for the Comte Moïse de Kamondo, one of Istanbul's wealthiest stock brokers. From the narrow lane that fronts Felek Han, as the building used to be called, a flight of stairs named for Kamondo plunges into the traffic-clogged maelstrom of Karaköy, the steamer pier and open-air fish-market where the gulls gather, and the northern end of Galata Bridge.

When the Kamondo family departed Istanbul for Paris to seek and make its further fortune in international banking, it rented out the building to the Alliance Israélite Universelle, the international Jewish organization founded in France to propagate the French language and French republican ideals among the Jews of the Orient. Such was its influence in the fading years of the Ottoman Empire that to this day, most Istanbul Jews speak French, while Ladino, the Iberian dialect they had brought with them from Spain at the time of the Great Expulsion in 1492, is used by an ever diminishing handful. Such, too, was the westernizing zeal of the Alliance that at the height of its influence and prestige, few of the Empire's Jewish subjects bothered to learn Turkish.

The Alliance was born of an ideology that would see the Jews assimilated into an emerging transnational society in which national boundaries would disappear, the kind of world so brilliantly evoked by the Austrian novelist Stefan Zweig in his memoirs. But it was soon to be overwhelmed by the onrush of Theodor Herzl's Zionist movement, which brilliantly tapped into the subterranean currents of a resurgent Jewish identity that rejected assimilation in favor of a radical racial-religious nationalism. With the Alliance's decline, Felek Han was rented out to small shops and offices. Moïse de Kamondo's heirs perished in 1943 when the Jews of Paris were deported, via the roundup at the Velodrome d'hiver, to the Nazi extermination camps.

As many of the city's Jews emigrated to Israel in the 1950s, Felek Han, as did the synagogues and charitable institutions that surrounded it, fell into disrepair. Only in 1995 was it returned to its former glory, as the flagship of lower Galata, when it was rescued, then revitalized, by a consortium led by Cemal Ekingen, an interior decorator of Kurdish descent who is today the hotel's owner, and architect Mete Göktug, a native Istanbuliot who had moved into the neighborhood, determined to make it his own.

Galata, at the southernmost tip of Pera, the "European" quarter known today as Beyoglu, was for centuries the city's most brashly cosmopolitan district. It was the entry point not only for the technology of the West, but for the ideology which that technology nourished. City within a city, semi-colonial enclave within an empire, Galata became a haven for banks and warehouses, trading houses and spy dens, and home to a distinctly non-Islamic mercantile elite. Not that Galata was a late-comer, though. Like much of the infrastructure of the empire, the conquering Ottomans had inherited it from the Byzantines, the former landlords in this place. In their wisdom—or realism—they changed little but the tenants. Only with the ultimate collapse of the Ottoman state, and its replacement by the unitary Turkish Republic was the hillside precinct facing Seraglio Point reduced to the status of just another district of a city that had lost its status as capital.

Of the Genoese, Venetians, Jews, Greeks, Armenians and Levantines who once inhabited this place, of the French and English whose embassies it once housed, little remains but their buildings and street plan, Mr. Göktug tells me as we wander down Galata Kulesi Sokak toward the Golden Horn. Synagogues, churches, charitable institutions, administrative buildings and schools lurk in the lanes that branch off from this narrow, cobbled thoroughfare, linking the waterfront, now hidden behind the rubble of ancient fortifications to which cling, like so many mussels, the habitations of subsequent centuries, with the Genoese Tower, the neighborhood landmark.

"I moved here in 1990," the architect continues, his tone modulating to wistfulness. "As a native of Istanbul, the area always fascinated me. When I was a kid I used to come here all the time to explore. The sea front was a pleasant place then, before the municipality decided to rip down all the old buildings. Playing with the city is a wonderful experience for children. I remember I used to swim at Karaköy, right at the foot of the bridge. Today the water is so polluted not even the fish can survive."

"This street we're walking on, it used to be the main street of Galata," he adds with a proprietary grin, coming to a stop at the foot of a wall coated with ancient grime. "Look at this building, look at the size of the stone blocks! This was the residence of the podesta, the Genoese governor."

With only a slight effort of imagination, I conjure up a street transplanted from the Ligurian republic, strewn with refuse, teeming with fishmongers and greengrocers, along which strut expatriate pseudo-aristocrats in thigh-revealing tights and bulging codpieces, plumed hats perched jauntily atop their heads, as ready for mortal combat with knives as to stand and declaim in the newly emerging Latinate demotic.

One of the paradoxes of Istanbul is that the imprint of the lesser power, the Republic of Genoa, today overshadows that of its predatory maritime adversary, the Republic of Venice. La Serenissima had long held the monopoly of seaborne trade with the Byzantine Empire. Why content ourselves with a mere monopoly? Let us instead seize the Empire, reasoned the brilliant and ruthless Doge of Venice, Enrico del Dandolo, as the Christian thirteenth century opened with yet another call for a Crusade to liberate Jerusalem. The Holy Land, we must remember, had been recaptured in 1187 for Islam by the victorious Kurdish dynasty founded by Saladin al-Ayubbi, not to be relinquished until delivered to European colonialism and thence to its Zionist junior partner by the crusading triad of Balfour, Lawrence and Allenby.

Agreeing to transport the Frankish Crusaders for a princely sum, Venice schemed to return the dethroned *basileus*, Isaac Angelus, to the throne in Constantinople. His son had made the Western coalition a proposition it could ill refuse: if they would restore his father to the throne of Constantine, he in gratitude would subordinate Byzantium to Rome and participate in the Crusade.

Transported by a Venetian fleet, the crusaders appeared before Byzantium in late June, 1203. Having rapidly captured Galata, the knights of the consortium prepared for an all-out assault on the City itself. Nine months later, in April, 1204, the Crusaders—like IMF experts sizing up some feckless and corrupt southeast Asian economy—reached agreement on a plan to parcel out the Empire amongst themselves and launched the attack. Despite their spirited resistance, the defending forces were quickly overcome, and the ruling Emperor Alexius V Ducas fled leaving the citizens at the tender mercies of their fellow Christians from the West. For three days "the Latins treated the city with appalling cruelty ... Neither churches, nor relics, nor monuments of art, nor private possessions were spared or respected. The western knights and their soldiers, as well as the Latin monks and abbots, took part in the pillaging."[51]

As for the solemn promise to reinstate the deposed Isaac Angelus, it was promptly forgotten.

Eastern Orthodoxy never forgave, nor fully recovered from, the Fourth Crusade. To this day the destroyers of the City are roundly cursed, not only for their terrible depredations, but for the greater crime of undoing the Empire. The rape of Constantinople was the penultimate act in the fall of the Second Rome, and, of the two, perhaps the worse, for it was an act of betrayal, a stab in the back by putative co-religionists. May God, in the form of the stern-eyed Pantocrator who glares from high in church domes, preserve us from such friends, have since chanted legions of popes in the nasal intonations of archaizing Greek which renders anathema with such sweet vituperation.

The Latin Kingdom set up by Dandolo and the mercenary knights was an ephemeral creation. From the hinterland, the Byzantines fought back, often recruiting bands of their erstwhile mortal foes, the Turks. By the seventh decade of the thirteenth century,

Constantinople had been restored to the imperial purple. Soon thereafter, trade privileges were granted to Venice's arch-enemy Genoa, not within the City walls, but across the Golden Horn in Galata, where Mr. Göktug and I are strolling as a gentle rain begins to fall.

By the end of the century, the Genoese had supplanted Venice as the leading maritime power in the Byzantine East and as the banker to the Empire. So it would remain until that fateful day in 1453 when Mehmet the Conqueror breached the western walls, and Constantinople, in one of those historical turnarounds where all things change and nothing is any longer the same, ceased to exist, and became Istanbul.

* * *

EVEN BEFORE THEY acquired their new capital, the Ottomans, as the dominant military power in near Asia and southeastern Europe, had occasionally entered into contact with the Christian West, but only if and when they deemed it appropriate to their interests. As their empire reached its zenith, from western traders and merchants they acquired the luxury goods and necessities lacking in their far-flung territories. But only when Ottoman power began to wane, after the death of Suleiman the Magnificent in 1566, when the fearsome army no longer swept its terror-stricken adversaries before it, did the sultans gradually open their doors to European diplomatic missions. Embassies were soon established at their doorstep, in Galata, which was of the City but not in it.

Powerful but not omnipotent, the Ottomans were constrained to recognize their limits. Ever since it had established itself in the tiny principality of Bursa, in 1326, the house of Osman had quickly mastered the politics of alliance and treachery crucial to the building of a powerful state. As staunch Muslims, the Ottomans believed they could distinguish in the Protestants newly challenging Rome's vise grip on Europe, spirits kindred to their own. Like the Muslims, so the argument went, the followers of Martin Luther abhorred the doctrine of the Trinity and excoriated the cult of images. The sultans may have been advised by the most astute of the court *ulama* that these dour thesis-posters were throwbacks to the Iconoclasts, the early Byzantine heretics who abolished images in order to combat the inroads of advancing Islam, thereby accrediting and legitimizing it.

All the while the rising national states of Western Europe, searching for allies in their bitter conflicts with one another, learned that the "Terrible Turk" could prove useful, even precious. England, caught up in its struggle against Spain for mastery of the seas and unimpeded access to the plunder of the New World, sought to gain Ottoman favor. Queen Elizabeth herself described Sultan Murat III as "the unconquered and most puissant defender of the true faith against the idolaters,"[52] and soon after dispatched an English ambassador to Istanbul to lay down the foundations of what was to prove a long and often acrimonious relationship.

Galata, where the embassies clustered, enjoyed extraterritoriality under the lavish concessions—known as Capitulations—granted by the sultans. The French had been handed the right to protect the Christians of the Empire; the English, wide-ranging mercantile privileges that quickly transformed the Levant Company into an adjunct (if not architect) of imperial policy.

Of the British, only the jail house that operated during the Allied occupation of Istanbul, from 1918 to 1921, remains. This I have from a privileged source, Mete Göktug himself. The architect has transformed the dreary building with its massive walls and tiny cells into a studio and gallery, where he holds forth over tea in seminars for architecture students from nearby Mimar Sinan University.

From their listening posts at Galata, the European powers monitored the Ottoman Empire's vital signs. When it became, in the nineteenth century, the "Sick Man of Europe," they dispatched medical diplomats, whose cure was worse than the disease. Like their latter-day imitators of the International Monetary Fund, they were one-cure doctors. Stiff doses of westernization and debt would surely achieve the desired results, they droned, nodding their heads with the appropriate *gravitas*. Dazzled, trusting the hand-wringing mountebanks, charlatans and leeches in frock coats, the patient agreed.

By the last decades of the nineteenth century, supranational finance capital had achieved direct control over Ottoman affairs. This was accomplished through the ministrations of the *Tanzimat* bureaucrats, who were convinced that the empire's rightful place lay with the "International Community" of the day. They willingly adopted measures of economic liberalization—structural reform in today's parlance—that they believed would improve their chances of receiving protection, and money in the form of loans, from the European powers. The strategy was successful beyond the promoters' wildest dreams. Established in 1881, the Ottoman Public Debt Administration (PDA), consisting of a seven-man council representing the creditors of the state, administering a huge permanent bureaucracy, controlled between one quarter and one third of all government revenues.[53] Only after it was too late did the Ottomans begin to realize that *their* disappearance had been the ultimate remedy all along.

\* \* \*

THE GREAT CAPITAL on the Bosphorus was, in the first decade of the twentieth century, a city in turmoil. As state sovereignty shrunk, foreign capitulations expanded; Galata had become a semi-independent enclave within a regime whipsawed between its own multinational heritage and the new doctrine of national exclusivity in the name of which it was being disassembled. As the Great Powers of Europe, favoring radical amputation, schemed to dismember and portion out the remains of the Empire, within what remained of the Ottoman power structure, conspirators plotted its overthrow. In order to save it, some insisted, it would have to be destroyed and replaced by a modern, secular state on the European model. In order to save it, others contended, it would have to be revitalized through Islamic rebirth.

Enter Bediuzzaman Said Nursi.

In 1899, when he first came up to Istanbul from Nurs by way of Bitlis and Van, Said stepped into a debate whose distant echoes, as they had reverberated to the far Anatolian provinces, had already shaped his sensibilities and his outlook. Now, those sensibilities and that outlook were to be tested not against provincial *ulama* or Kurdish warlords, but against the imperial establishment itself.

He carried with him a letter of introduction to Mustafa Bey, the Sultan's Head Falconer, in whose residence near Yildiz Palace he lived for eighteen months. He had also brought a petition addressed to Abdülhamid himself, calling on the Sultan to establish a university in Anatolia. The time was not ripe. Preoccupied by more weighty matters, the Sultan never noticed the Head Falconer's recommendation. But during his sojourn in the capital, Said became fast friends with the Falconer's son. In the turbulent years that followed the re-proclamation of the Constitution, both men would join the *Teshkilat-i Mahsusa*, the State Security Service set up by the Young Turk revolutionaries. [54]

His stay in the capital being without result, Said returned to Van, where, in the house of Tahir Pasha, the governor, he experienced a radical awakening. A British Colonial Secretary had been quoted in a newspaper as declaring that, "so long as Muslims have the Qur'an we shall be unable to dominate them." [55] The statement galvanized Said, who vowed to marshal the knowledge he had gained, and defend the Holy Book against all attempts to discredit it. The Qur'an would be the ultimate shield and weapon against the designs of the colonialists.

While I have been unable to trace the putative Colonial Office statement, it jibes both with historical truth and British colonial policy. Several years earlier, following the anti-Armenian pogroms of 1895 and 1896, William Gladstone, the humanitarian moralizer who had built a career of lashing out at "the unspeakable Turk," called, in the same tones that Anthony Blair would employ more than 100 years later with regard to Serbia, for the Ottoman Empire to be "'rubbed off the map" as a "disgrace to civilization." [56] The European Powers agreed on the need to liquidate and divide the

Empire; they diverged only on how this was to be done, and on the division of the spoils. Said Nursi was responding not to a rumor, but to an unusually clear articulation of policy long understood in Europe, but only faintly grasped among the Ottomans, and then only by the keenest minds among them.

\* \* \*

BY 1907, WHEN SAID traveled to the capital for a second time, the disintegration of the imperial regime was clear for all to see. For decades, intellectuals and military men had been searching for ways to halt the decline. Westernizers and reformers, dazzled by European brilliance and power, anticipated remaking Ottoman society on the Western model. Their counterparts in the military, stunned by defeat against superior arms wielded by better-trained forces, clamored and plotted for access to those arms and that training, which were inevitably European. One question lay on everyone's lips: how could the state be saved?

Not all agreed that, to survive, the Empire must deliver itself over, body and soul, to its self-proclaimed saviors, the European statesmen and bankers who lavished advice and credits on its gullible administrators. The *Tanzimat* reforms sat badly with dissidents like Namik Kemal, who believed that the reformers had been too quick to jettison the religious component of the state. The problem, Namik and his associates—who were known as the Young Ottomans—asserted, was Ottoman absolutism, for which there was no precedent in the Qur'anic tradition. Constitutional, representative government, they argued, did not conflict with the *Shari'a*, the Islamic legal code, itself derived from the practice of the Prophet Mohammad and his immediate successors.[57]

A confluence of intellectual agitation, dynastic upheaval, military reversals in the European province of Bosnia and Herzegovina, and Western diplomatic and financial pressure had, in 1876, combined to force the adoption of a constitution, followed by parliamentary elections. Held in the spring of 1877, the vote yielded a representative assembly whose deputies included members of 10 nationalities who spoke 14 languages. But this first experience of democracy soon foundered. Russia, eight days after the newly-invested Sultan Abdülhamid had proclaimed the constitution, declared war on the Ottoman Empire, in the name of "Orthodoxy and Slavdom."[58]

A Russian winter offensive soon amputated the Empire of its Bulgarian provinces and set the stage for the loss of all its Balkan possessions. In Istanbul, the newly-elected deputies sought answers for the collapse of the imperial army. Instead of providing them, Abdülhamid suspended the parliament he had inaugurated. It was not to reopen until thirty years later.

The debate opened by the Young Ottomans could not be easily closed. Soon overcome by circumstances, however, they lost the ideological initiative to a second generation of reformers schooled in the very belly of the Western beast. Shaped from the merger of a group of Paris-based intellectual dissidents with discontented junior officers of the Ottoman army, the Committee of Union and Progress—*Ittihad ve Terakki Cemiyeti*—was founded in 1907. Its organizational locus was Macedonia, along with Kosova, the jewel of the empire's remaining Balkan possessions. Heavily influenced by European republicanism and Free Masonry, of which Salonica was then a hotbed, the Young Turks declared themselves constitutionalists respectful of Ottoman diversity. But beneath their multicultural exterior lurked, like a slow-acting contagion or a deep penetration spy, a virulent nationalism that, in the able hands of Mustafa Kemal, was to become the founding ideology of the Turkish state.

* * *

ACROSS FROM GALATA and up the Golden Horn, the Fatih district, named for the Conqueror who delivered the City over to the armies of Islam, is Istanbul's spiritual Anatolia, an assertive precinct of the Islamic East, in the heart of the would-be secular West. Lying astride the teeming west-east boulevards that converge from the ancient ramparts to the mercantile centre at Aksaray, the district is a densely populated warren of streets and alleyways clustered around Fatih Camii, the Mosque of the Conqueror, built atop the ruins of the Church of the Holy Apostles in 1470, to shelter the remains of Sultan Mehmet II. During my months in Istanbul I came to know the mosque's huge courtyard well. It was here, beneath the great plane trees that I would meet my student guide and interpreter, Nazim, before following him deep into the labyrinths of the Islamist movement.

Fatih's reputation for religious rectitude of the Sunni variant is well-deserved, Nazim told me on one of our strolls through the district. Here people had poured into the streets to demonstrate against the government's decision to close the Imam Hatip schools that not only gave their children religious instruction, but taught them Arabic, the language of the Qur'an.

Around the corner from the sprawling mosque and *medrese* complex is a cobbled street filled with small shops and restaurants, some of them located in the ground floor of an ancient building. As we walked down the middle of the street one afternoon, Nazim stopped and pointed to a padlocked doorway: "This was where Said Nursi stayed when he came to Istanbul."

Like many of his contemporaries, Nazim is a militant political Islamist, critical of the cautious calculations of the Refah Partisi and its even milder-mannered successor, Fazilet, the Virtue Party. His disrespect for the regime and loathing of the generals was exceeded only by his lack of reverence for Fetullah Gülen. "Gülen, he is like this with the military," he would tell me, rubbing the first fingers of both hands together in the typical middle-eastern gesture of complicity. But when it came to Said Nursi, Nazim's attitude was different. "I do not agree with everything he said and wrote," he told me as we sat down to a bowl of hot soup in a cubbyhole of a restaurant at the foot of the lane, "but he was a courageous man who fought for Islam."

At the beginning of the century, the building where Said took up residence, known as Sekerci (Sweetmakers') Han, operated as a hostelry. Its tenants included several of Istanbul's leading religious intellectuals who gravitated to the Fatih *medrese*, the most prestigious in the city. To the door of his room, the newcomer tacked a sign which read: "Here all questions are answered, all problems solved, but no questions are asked."[59]

This curious mollah who strode around Fatih dressed in the garb of a Kurdish mountaineer quickly made his mark, not only for his encyclopedic knowledge of matters theological and philosophical, his mastery of Arabic and Persian scripture, but for the singular fact that he would accept neither gifts nor alms, highly uncharacteristic of a man of religion. On this visit to Istanbul, his second, as constitutional ferment worked its way through the Empire, Said's mission met with success. His petition for the establishment of an educational institution to be located in Van and which would combine the teaching of religion with the scientific disciplines imported from the West, had finally reached the Sultan. (It is not known whether the Head Falconer or his son had a hand in the matter.) Shortly thereafter, Abdülhamid granted him an audience.

The 28th Ottoman ruler since the conquest of Constantinople would not have been, in common parlance, an easy man to get along with. A British historian catalogues his dark and darting eyes, hooked nose, pallid skin, chiseled cheekbones and luxuriant beard as features that "emphasized the mistrust and suspicion inherent in his character."[60] Yet this son of Sultan Abdulmecid and a Circassian (or, say some, an Armenian) dancing girl had become a strong-willed and determined head of state who, in his spare time, produced finished furniture at the wood-working shop in Yildiz Palace. Now, he was intent on taking an active hand in the day-to-day administration of an empire that had already begun to crumble when he girded the sword of the Prophet in Eyup Mosque in September, 1876.

Another author, writing from a pro-Armenian bias, speaks of the man whose "paranoia and cowardice were to be the main distinguishing features of Near Eastern politics for the next thirty years."[61] Accused of fomenting the Bulgarian Massacres of 1877, Abdülhamid early on had won himself the title of "the Red Sultan" in Europe, a title he was to confirm during the violent suppression of the Armenians in 1895. And in her biography of Said Nursi,

Sükran Vahide notes that the ruler's "successful foreign policies were paid for by internal repression of considerable severity," while insisting that his was not a bloody despotism.[62] In fact, Abdülhamid's complex personality and career concentrates within it all of the contradictions of Ottoman and Turkish historiography. Western scholars, writing with the lofty serenity of the historical victor, lay down merciless strictures against their once fearsome but now vanquished foe. In Turkey, though his despotic character cannot be concealed, Abdülhamid is seen within the context of a foundering empire and, from the Kemalist perspective, that of the new Turkish state-in-the-making. Beset on all sides by foes whose rapacity certainly exceeded that of the Ottomans, faced with the upsurge of nationalism in the Balkans, in Armenia and in the Arab provinces, the Sultan appears as a ruthless, clever, yet farsighted statesman, adept at playing rivals off against one another, and at defending the empire's interests. To have expected any less of him would have been naïve.

True, the 1876 Constitution and parliament amounted to little more than eyewash, conjured up to first please, then neutralize the European Powers who had demanded and ghost-written it in the first place. But, at the same time, Abdülhamid returned Islam to the vital centre of state policy, rehabilitating the place of the Caliphate in an effort to strengthen the bonds that held the empire together. This royal pan-Islamism, argues Hugh Poulton, was a device "propagated to combat outside (Western) influence both in the heartlands of the empire and on the fringes ..."[63] However, his reaffirmation of the primacy of Islam and the language of the Qur'an paid political dividends in the empire's Arab provinces though it was of little utility in the Balkans or amongst the Armenians. Did Abdülhamid believe what he proposed as imperial policy? Though it is impossible for us, as we play the bright spotlight of hindsight across events, to draw such a conclusion, his over-bold visitor apparently took the Sultan at his word.

Bediuzzaman Said Nursi's reputation as a man of forthrightness and religious acumen was gaining him a following in the capital. Where eight years before doors remained closed to him, now, in

1907, those same doors swung open. At the peak of his powers, Said cut a dashing figure, with dark skin and penetrating eyes, wearing on his head a turban wrapped around a conical hat and clad in the flowing robes of an Anatolian mollah, sporting a dagger and pistol thrust through his sash and a bandoleer slung across his chest. His sense of mission and self-confidence, combined with a mastery of Qur'anic exegesis unmatched in his day, made him a formidable—and fearless—debater in matters temporal and spiritual. There was a religious state to be saved in its hour of need, and the creation of a faculty of higher education in far Anatolia was the only way to address the burning issue.

The two men met at the Sultan's audience chambers at Yildiz Saray, high atop a forested hill overlooking the Bosphorus. Pushing aside the niceties—failure to observe them would have cost a lesser man his head—Said cut quickly to the point. The ruler's duty, argued the petitioner, was to attend to education and the religious institution, the *ulama*, key to the revitalization of Islam. And Islam alone could provide the cement that would hold the crumbling empire together. Abdülhamid's main failure (did Bediuzzaman actually use such words in the Sultan's presence?) was to have performed his duties as Caliph, God's regent on earth, in an unsatisfactory manner. Despotism, he argued to the despot's face, was not only contrary to God's will; it was the greatest obstacle to progress in the empire. "Despotism has no place in Islam," he declared, lashing out at the system of spies and secret agents run from the Sultan's antechambers, of which he had recently come afoul. "To give a ruling on a person is the right only of courts acting openly and within the justice of the *Shari'a*." [64]

Those present testified, dumbfounded, to Said Nursi's courage in presenting his proposals, and in criticizing the Sultan's passivity as Caliph. "It is this unheard-of behavior which led the Sultan's officials to wonder whether Said was mentally deranged," writes the normally impassive Serif Mardin. [65]

The encounter at Yildiz, which was to land the reckless Bediuzzaman in a mental hospital, had all the stuff of high drama.

Prescient in his diagnosis of the ills of Kurdistan, farsighted in his identification of education as the salvation of the empire, accurate in pinpointing despotism as un-Islamic, Said's was the voice crying out in the wilderness, that of the prophet unheard in his own land. What the Sultan said has never been recorded. Did he slump in his throne, peering at the wiry Kurdish mollah as he stroked his luxuriant beard? Did he finally dismiss the petitioner he himself had invited with an irritated wave of the hand, as one would swat at a bothersome fly? Did he fly into a frenzy?

How long the patient-captive was held at the Toptasi mental hospital in Üsküdar remains unknown. What is certain is that Said engaged his captor-examiners in a vigorous debate that led ultimately to his release. In his report, the doctor who ordered him discharged, wrote: "If there is the tiniest trace of madness in Bediuzzaman, there is not a sane person in the world."[66]

The doctor's diagnosis dispelled the illusion of mental illness, but still Said remained in custody, while the palace drafted plans for a new tactic to silence him. This time they would, in the time honored Ottoman custom, buy him off. Nothing could have been more inept. Not only was this outspoken mollah fearless, he had no desire for wealth, status or position. In fact, his refusal to accept gifts or emoluments of any kind was the bedrock of his intractable devotion to his ideals. So when Abdülhamid's Minister of Public Security visited him in custody with a generous salary offer, were he to return to the East, Said indignantly waved the proposal aside. "Are you rejecting an imperial decree?" asked the stunned official. "An imperial decree cannot be rejected. The result will be disastrous."

Said replied: "I have been free. I grew up in the mountains of Kurdistan which is the place of absolute freedom. There is no point in getting angry ... Send me into exile ... I do not mind."[67]

In tragedy, the denouement is known, and only the inexorable mechanisms of fate need be exposed by the dramatist's pen. In true tragic manner, Said Nursi's audience with the Sultan prefigured a second encounter fourteen years later with another absolute ruler,

Mustafa Kemal, on the eve of the founding of the Republic. Then, instead of being sent to a mental institution, Bediuzzaman was consigned to an ordeal of internal exile, house arrest and prison that was to last 30 years. Which man was the greater despot?

* * *

WITHIN THE YEAR Abdülhamid had fallen to the enlightened cutthroats of the Committee of Union and Progress, who shipped him off into exile at the Villa Alatini in revolutionary Salonica. Meanwhile, Said Nursi was spirited away from his place of custody—by whom remains unclear—and taken clandestinely to that same city.

In the first decade of the twentieth century, Salonica was the second city of the empire, a commercial and industrial dynamo, and home to a diverse and vibrant Sephardic Jewish population. These were the descendants of the Jews who had come to the Ottoman lands where they prospered after their expulsion from Spain, on the invitation of Sultan Bayezit II. In Salonica, more than anywhere else in the Empire, they left their mark, forming an entire social pyramid, and imprinting on the city their language, culture and religion, all of which has been erased. [68]

Intense political, social, industrial and religious ferment was the hallmark of that decade in Salonica. The insurrectionists of the Internal Macedonian Revolutionary Organization plotted their desperate campaign of uprising and terror bombings against the Ottomans in the heart of the city. In the Macedonian garrisons of the imperial army—in places like Monastir, Resen and Skopje—discontented officers chafed under the constraints of poor pay, low social esteem, and dissatisfaction with the political and economic backwardness of the empire. Through the writings of the Young Turk ideologues in Paris, they had been exposed to a radical patriotism that blended the ideal of a modern, multi-cultural state with the dream of a Turkish national awakening. Through their contacts with Free Masonry, which flourished in free-thinking Salonica, far from the eyes of the Sultan's spies, they encountered radical republicanism, secularism and a certain view of the European Enlightenment.

Into this explosive atmosphere strode Said Nursi, who possessed a knack for finding himself in the most critical situations at the times of highest tension. The CUP's stated program of replacing Ottoman despotism with a parliamentary system based on equality before the law attracted him, as he saw in it confirmation of his own conviction that justice, freedom and brotherhood were the fundamental characteristics of Islam. His boldness and originality likewise impressed the seditionists of the CUP, who praised him as the personification of freedom and justice in religion. The two soon made common cause.

On July 24, 1908, from the balcony overlooking Liberty Square in Salonica, Enver Bey, who had emerged as the de facto leader of the Young Turk movement, acclaimed the re-establishment of the constitution. Crowds milling in the streets below chanted "Liberté, egalité, fraternité, justice," as brass bands blared out *La Marseillaise*. Turks, Greeks, Jews, Bulgarians, Armenians and Macedonians embraced in an outburst of brother-feeling that was as intense as it was short-lived.

Following Enver's appearance, Said Nursi stepped out onto the balcony, where he delivered his Address to Freedom. From his first words, it was clear that his audience was not simply the delirious multitude looking on in Liberty Square, but the entire population of the Empire, and particularly the people of his native Kurdistan. Adhere to Islam and its morality in the new era, he enjoined them, describing the crippling legacy of despotism and the bright new prospect of freedom. As sovereignty now lay with the nation, through the restored constitution, so Islam must be the "fountainhead and spirit" of nationhood. Beware of uncritical acceptance of all that is Western, he warned. "We must imitate the Japanese in acquiring civilization, for in taking only the virtues of civilization from Europe they preserved their national customs, which are the leaven of every nation's continuance. Since our national customs grew up within Islam, they should be clung to ..."[69]

The Committee of Union and Progress, being a conspiratorial coalition, rather than what one would term a "vanguard party," encapsulated all the contradictions of a rapidly evolving Ottoman society. Some of its members were dedicated westernizers, intent on carrying the *Tanzimat* reforms through to their logical conclusion and delivering the empire, body and soul, to Europe. Others were fervent Islamists who supported Abdülhamid's invocation of Islamic unity, while condemning only his despotic behavior. The followers of a third trend, irritated by the increasingly vocal demands of the minority nationalities, favored a unitary Turkish nationalism. Under the guise of unity and progress, a bitter battle was about to begin.

As many a revolutionary has learned to his dismay, overthrowing the tyrant is the easy part. A few days after the tumultuous events of Salonica, the Sultan proclaimed a general amnesty for political prisoners. On August 1, a *hatt-i hümayun* (imperial prescript) ordered the disbanding of the secret police, freedom from arbitrary arrest, equality of race and religion, and announced that a new parliament would be elected within three months.[70] The military mutiny in Salonica had brought the bearded carpenter of Yildiz to his knees.

"You want power?" Abdülhamid seemed to ask the insurgents, apparently acquiescing. "Well, take it then and wield it."

* * *

ON A BLUSTERY DAY in mid-December, I walked rapidly beneath the plane-trees, now bare of their leaves, that line Çiragan Caddesi, the thoroughfare that winds its way along the Bosphorus shore beneath the hills of Yildiz park, still dark green under its canopy of conifers. The high walls that conceal aristocratic buildings and enclosed gardens block off the view to the water, but the slant of the rain driven by a north wind down the narrow maritime corridor from the Black Sea told me that open water was near. Several hundred meters north from the Besiktas ferry landing and bus terminus, a breach in the wall opens onto the entrance to the Kempinski Çiragan Hotel, the most luxurious in a city where monumental luxury is never far from view. I had been invited to attend a breakfast press conference staged by the municipal authorities, from the Islamist Welfare (now Virtue) Party, to introduce the city's new mayor, the former administrative deputy who would now fill the considerable shoes of Tayyip Erdogan. The charismatic Erdogan had run afoul of Turkey's real rulers, the secular fundamentalist generals and would soon be entering prison, stripped of his political rights. Erdogan's "crime" had been to recite, in the Kurdish city of Siirt, a poem by Ziya Gökalp, the nationalist ideologue of the late nineteenth century who laid the foundations of the Young Turk movement, the man considered by many to have had a decisive influence in the shaping of militant Kemalism, that peculiar hybrid of Jacobinism, nativism and collectivism.

"One must be careful whom one quotes," I remarked to the attaché who handed me my press kit.

"Especially if he does it in Siirt," the man answered wryly, without missing a beat.

For all its Islamic modesty, the Istanbul municipal administration, which runs a jurisdiction richer and more powerful than most members of the United Nations, has a taste for the expansive gesture. In their choice of the Çiragan Palace, I wondered if they were making an oblique reference to certain events that had occurred here in the heady days of 1909, long before the Kempinski chain acquired and refurbished the building. In vain I search the lobby, with its towering windows giving onto a formal garden and then the churning waters of the Bosphorus, for a commemorative plaque. There is none. But perhaps somewhere in the deepest recesses of the huge structure there lurk imprisoned echoes of the voices of the men who thronged its halls, the members of the first and only freely-elected Ottoman parliament.

Çiragan was the creation, better, the embodiment in stone and mortar, of Sultan Abdülassiz, the "Giant Sultan," who intended it as a counterweight to the extravagance of Dolmabahçe Palace, built by his baroque-minded predecessor, Abdülmecid. For all his physical size, Abdülassiz had no surfeit of courage and less of mental balance. When, in early 1876, he was challenged by an angry crowd of students demanding the dismissal of his foreign minister for appeasement of the Great Powers after two foreign consuls had been assassinated in Salonica, he retreated to his throne room to enjoy a cock-fight. It was there that he was confronted the next morning by the Commander in Chief. In his hand the *Serasker* held a *fetva* of deposition issued by the religious authorities, always sensitive to the needs of the army. Bowing to the inevitable, Abdülassiz was transported by royal barge to Çiragan, along with the members of his harem. Four days later the deposed sultan's dead body was discovered; his wrists had been slashed with scissors. The wounds had been self-inflicted, concluded the royal physicians. The agency, people whispered, may not have been the Sultan's own hand.

The new ruler, Murat V, a westoxicated sot, survived a mere three months in office before being likewise deposed on grounds of insanity, illustrating that even at the heart of Oriental despotism, a certain system of checks and balances prevailed. In the background, constitutional agitation was becoming a clamor. Abdülhamid, Murat's younger brother, had let it be known that he supported reform. On the last day of August, 1876, he was declared sultan. The hapless Murat was transferred to Çiragan, where he lived in luxurious confinement until his death from diabetes, in 1904.[71]

Perhaps there was something about the palace. Perhaps the deputies, flushed with the enthusiasm of the people's mandate, would have been wiser never to have relocated there after the events of March and April, 1909. Was it a building cursed by its past? If this was so, then the Istanbul municipal administration should have given some consideration to the omens. At Çiragan, as befits its somber history, the omens are invariably grim.

They were grim not only for the infant Ottoman parliamentary experiment, but for the new constitutional order itself. For if the centre would not hold, it was because things had begun to fall apart in the Balkans. Ostensibly, the Empire's neighbors wished to test the limits of its authority in the European tinderbox. This wish was particularly strong in Vienna. In October, 1908, the Dual Empire decided to annex Bosnia-Herzegovina outright. In short order Bulgaria declared its independence, and Crete proclaimed *enosis* with Greece.

In Istanbul too, as the tumult and the shouting of the constitutional revolution quieted, murmurs of discontent began to be heard. The changeover was too rapid, they whispered; the traditional values of the state, in which lip service was paid to Islam, were being slighted, or worse, ignored. Opposition to the Young Turks swiftly concentrated in an organization called the Society for Islamic Unity—*Ittihad-i Muhammedi*—which was set up in February, 1909. Among its founders were the Sultan's fourth son, and Bediuzzaman Said Nursi. The palace may have channeled funds into the Society's coffers, says one historian.[72] But opposition to the constitutional regime was widespread and growing as the Great Powers greeted Ottoman reform with a shameless grab for Ottoman lands.

On March 31, the anniversary of the birth of the Prophet, the *Ittihad-i Mohammedi* organized a *Mevlid*, a commemorative ceremony, in the great mosque at St. Sophia. The main sermon was given by Said Nursi, who ascended the pulpit clad in his customary Kurdish warrior's dress. Outside, a peaceful crowd estimated at more than 100,000 people had gathered. "The truth has risen naked from the grave of the heart," he thundered. "Let those for whom it is prohibited not gaze upon it." The sermon had not been a call to arms against the Empire's new rulers, but a warning against failure by Muslims to observe their religion. "We are more in need of moral improvement than government reform," he wrote several weeks later.[73]

The Committee of Union and Progress, the organizational core of the Young Turk movement, labeled all opposition to itself as "backward" and "reactionist." These two words are still part and parcel of the Kemalist aesopian vocabulary, in which they designate anyone connected with "political Islam." Like the generals who run Turkey today, the CUP brain-trust wielded power but accepted no political responsibility. As the euphoria of constitutionalism yielded to sober reassessment, critical murmuring became widespread. The empire was losing territory, its minorities were mistaking freedom for license, new appointees to key posts in the armed forces, replacing officers loyal to the Sultan, mocked Islam, Western ways and behavior were gaining a foothold, moving from Galata and Pera into the wider Muslim society of Istanbul. A showdown had become unavoidable: from Salonica, the CUP branded the March 31 Incident as "reactionary," and affirmed the responsibility of Sultan Abdülhamid. The war of words, waged in newspapers controlled by the constitutionalists on the one hand, and in *Volkan*, the organ of the Society, on the other. Within two weeks, quantity had been transformed into quality, to use the dialectical materialist formulation: words became deeds.

The soldiers of a light infantry battalion that had been transferred to Istanbul from Salonica mutinied in the wee hours of April 13, locked their officers in their quarters, and swarmed out onto the streets of the capital. As they made their way toward St. Sophia and the old Ottoman parliament building (the parliament had not yet been transferred to Çiragan Palace), theological students and passers-by joined their ranks, calling for dismissal of high officials closely associated with the Young Turks, and the application of the *Shari'a*. Breaking into the legislative chamber, the insurrectionists murdered two deputies, both cases of mistaken identity. The government resigned, but the unrest spread. Unruly soldiers attacked and destroyed CUP headquarters.

When the news reached Young Turk headquarters in Salonica, where the insurrectionist tail wagged the imperial dog, the CUP assembled a volunteer force from bands of Serbs, Bulgars, Greeks, Macedonians and Albanians, strengthened by several contingents of the regular army. Its chief of staff was the Salonica native Mustafa Kemal, a Young Turk co-plotter with a distinct political agenda of his own. Despite stiff resistance from the mutineers, the "Army of Action" made short work of the rebellion, and within two weeks martial law had been declared in Istanbul. Three days later Abdülhamid was deposed, to be succeeded by his half-brother, 65-year-old Mehmet Reshad. Meanwhile, military courts martial had been set up to try the instigators of the anti-constitutional rebellion. As a leading member of the Society for Islamic Unity, one of the prime suspects was Said Nursi.

* * *

BEYAZIT CAMII, Istanbul's most visible, most venerable great mosque, stands at the edge of a broad, cobblestone square, an urban no-man's land inhabited mostly by pigeons, and frequented by ambulant vendors, students hurrying to classes at Istanbul University, and tourists catching their breath after the ordeal of prodding, sleeve-plucking and pleading at the nearby leather shops, and incessant glasses of tea with the carpet merchants of the great Covered Bazaar. A tea garden nestles beneath the east wing of the mosque, and from it a passageway leads into the Sahaflar Çarsisi, a tiny open-air courtyard ringed by booksellers specializing in foreign-language works about Turkey.

At noon on a raw Friday in late fall, beneath a fine drizzle that had turned the paving stones slippery and glistening, I found myself hastening across the square. Instead of the customary hum and bustle, the area was silent, empty. Ominous. The clothes-sellers' stalls on the periphery had been closed, their Eastern European customers had dispersed. From further away I heard the creak of metal shutters being lowered across store fronts. Turning a corner I saw why: hundreds of riot police were drawn up in battle order behind their plastic shields, helmet visors pushed back. Down the slope that separates the cross-town trolley tracks from the square, reinforcements waited in buses equipped with steel-mesh screened windows. I slipped between two armored cars and hurried across the open space in the direction of the mosque. My destination was the bookseller's bazaar; to reach it, I had to pass in front of the main entrance to the mosque.

Friday prayer was in full swing. In the courtyard, stragglers were performing their ablutions before being frisked by beefy cops guarding the entrances. Most of the worshippers were humbly clothed; many of them wore a three- or four-day beard that would not have been at all out of place in revolutionary Tehran. These men were not the kind of people who would attend one of Fetullah Gülen Hoca Efendi's black-tie bridge-building galas. In fact, they might at that moment have had the feeling that those bridges were being built on their backs. From inside throbbed the intensity of communal devotion, the piercing voice of the *hoca*. The tension surged in a muffled roar, aching to burst out across the square and tumble downhill like a flood tide, driven on by repressed anger.

The protesting Muslims had a grievance. The Imam Hatip high school system, created under the military regime of 1980 when Islam was promoted as a counterweight to communism, and expanded under the late president Turgut Özal, had been abolished by one stroke of the pen by the same generals who first forced Welfare Party Prime Minister Necmettin Erbakan to sign on the dotted line of the odious act. Playing for time, Erbakan had gained nothing but humiliation. The generals had then cashiered and replaced him with would-be Eurocrat Mesut Yilmaz, who was later to lose his job to the "leftist" Bulent Ecevit, judged the best political rampart against creeping fundamentalism. After a suitable time, suitable arrangements and excellent good fortune, Ecevit would return to power at the head of a new coalition government after the election of April, 1999.

On this day the party's supporters, and they are many, had closed their shops, and made their way uptown from Fatih to register their discontent, first with God, then with Turkey's secular authorities. The latter were unlikely to listen, for they owed their sinecures, if not their heads, to the benevolence of the bemedalled commanders, with the paunches and dark glasses, who regard the country as their private preserve.

Beyazit Square is the kind of place where the collective public emotion of the ruled often encounters the imperatives of the rulers. In the years before the 1980 coup, it had been the scene of violent confrontations between Left- and Right-wing students, between shadowy fascist groups recruited among the city's sub-proletariat, operating on the far edges of deniability, and bright-eyed young believers in the Working Class paradise wielding clubs, knives, and often guns.

Seventy years earlier, in the aftermath of the March 31 Incident, in 1909, the broad cobblestoned surface had been transformed into a macabre theater that proved premonitory. Here were erected the gallows from which the guilty were summarily hanged. The courts, staffed by officers loyal to the Salonica plotters, prefigured little good for Turkish justice. Formalities were few, and sentences were carried out immediately and without appeal. Hundreds were to die, including the founder of the Society for Muslim Unity and publisher of *Volkan*, the hot-headed Dervis Vahdeti. On the day of Said Nursi's appearance, the bodies of 15 men dangled from ropes outside the courtroom. Fists clenched, lips tight in anger, a crowd milled silently in front of the ancient mosque.

"I opposed this branch of despotism here, which has destroyed everyone's enthusiasm and extinguished their joy, awakened feelings of hatred and partisanship, and given rise to the formation of racialist societies, whose name is constitutionalism and meaning is despotism ... Since I am pledged to true constitutionalism based on the *Shari'a*, whatever form that despotism takes, even if it clothes itself in constitutionalism and calls itself that, I shall strike it wherever I encounter it," he told the uniformed judges. "If constitutionalism consists of one party's despotism and it acts contrary to the *Shari'a*, let all the world, men and jinn, bear witness that I am a reactionary." [74]

Said Nursi had entered the court martial with the full expectation of being hanged, and spoke accordingly. Instead, he was unanimously acquitted. When the verdict was announced, he spoke not a word of gratitude to the military judges, turned his back, strode from the hall and out onto the square. There his followers were waiting for him, chanting, "Long live hell for all tyrants."

HAD IT BEEN A PROVOCATION orchestrated by the CUP, whose aim was to bring about the final fall of Abdülhamid, the March 31

Incident achieved its aims. Though in appearance acquiescing in the advent of constitutionalism, the Sultan had attempted to undermine the new order. In this, his foes in Salonica and in the capital provided him with every opportunity. The saviors of the empire, once their veneer of multiethnic Ottomanism had been peeled away, stood revealed as Turkish nationalists. For all his grotesque imperfections, the Sultan still represented a historical continuity which, while claiming to preserve, the Young Turks sought to undermine and destroy. But the failed uprising may not have been a conspiracy at all. It may have been the last gasp of a mortally wounded ruling establishment, and at the same time, the faint harbinger of a force both old and strikingly new: Islamic revivalism.

From their clandestine headquarters in Salonica, the Empire's new rulers saw March 31 as their triumph, a triumph they intended to press to the full. In this new, vindictive spirit, the Chamber of Deputies, now relocated to Çiragan Palace, once again set to work. In August, 1909, the 1876 constitution was amended to give parliament the right to depose the Sultan, now the nominal ruler, should he violate his oath of loyalty to the Fatherland (an ominous new concept in a multinational state) and the Nation. New laws forbade political groups identified by race or nationality, with the exception of those claiming a Turkish identity. Conscription was, however, extended to non-Muslims, as if to illustrate the new rulers' professed rejection of racial or religious distinctions.

But even as it strove to enact the Young Turk legislative program, the parliament was enacting its own marginalization. The deputies would be called upon to rubber-stamp decisions ostensibly taken by the government in Istanbul, but ultimately made by the CUP central committee, meeting in closed chambers, in Salonica. As if to underline the impotency of parliament, the newly-appointed legislature burned to the ground in January, 1910, leaving Çiragan Palace a smoldering hulk, and the deputies without a deliberative venue.

That same year, as though by coincidence, a shift had taken place in the membership of the CUP central committee. Where Ottomanism, Islam and Turkish nationalism had been the three original pillars of the Young Turk movement, Turkism now moved rapidly to the fore. The shift may have been the product of the exceptional circumstances of the day: the implosion of the empire, Great Power rapacity and the narrow nationalist motivations of the leaders of the great historical millets, the Armenians and the Greeks. It may also have been hidden all along beneath the official rhetoric of racial and religious equality, itself inherited from the *Tanzimat* reforms. Were this the case, the "separatist" movements that shook, then destroyed the empire, first in the Balkans, then in the Arab world, were the result, and not the cause.

Spearhead of the new, assertive Turkish nationalism, was Ziya Gökalp, whose poem had brought Tayyip Erdogan to grief with the military junta. Ziya, a native of the Kurdish city of Diyarbakir, early on had become an advocate of reuniting the dispersed Turks, from Central Asia to the Adriatic. In his eyes, Islam should be a purely ethical construct, freed of any social and political dimension. Separated thus from society, religion would be no impediment to that most desirable of all outcomes, the adoption of European civilization. Turks, he wrote, could accept "the three ideas [Turkism, Islam and modernization] at the same time by determining the respective fields of operation of each."[75] Islam and Turkish nationalism could coexist, he argued. All Turks were, after all, Muslims, and Turkey was the fortress of Islam. But in his Turkey of the future, there would be little room for the peoples who had for centuries been part of the complex Ottoman mosaic.

Foremost, but not alone among them, were the Armenians, who for centuries had been known as the *Loyal Millet*. The hidden policy of the CUP amounted to nothing less than their dispossession and ultimate assimilation. As they had been in the last decades of the nineteenth century, the Kurds were to act as the instruments of a policy designed by master cynics. They would do the regime's dirty work; in payment, over the decades that followed, they would receive the banishment of their language, the rifle-butt, the machine gun and the burnt-out village. Out of deference to the CUP ideologues, we must also add that they were willing pupils of the even greater cynics who ruled from the chanceries of London, Paris, Moscow, Vienna and Berlin. They had the interests of their shareholders to attend to, and this necessity overrode, as it does today, all other considerations.

After his acquittal, Said Nursi rapidly departed Istanbul to return to his beloved Anatolia, to make a "*medrese* of mountain and plain," dispensing lessons on the compatibility of constitutionalism and religion. With the curse of despotism removed, constitutionalism and the idea of freedom could now spread throughout the Islamic world, he argued, bringing progress and great changes. To his Kurdish brethren who could accept his definition of freedom as a good thing, but to whom that of the Greeks and Armenians seemed distasteful, he said: "… your freedom consists of leaving them in peace and not oppressing them. And this is what the *Shari'a* enjoins. (…) Our enemy and what is destroying us is Aga Ignorance, and his son Poverty Efendi, and grandson Enmity Bey. Even if the Armenians have opposed us in hatred, they have done so under the commandership of these three corrupters."[76]

* * *

"I PREFER THE WILD nomad tents of the high mountains of Kurdistan, the place of absolute freedom,"[77] he had written shortly before he left Istanbul, shaken by his brush with death at the hands of the usurpers of the constitutionalist dream. In the spring of 1910, he again traveled eastward, where he spent several months among the mountain tribes of high Anatolia, preaching his vision of hope in an Islamic rebirth. In early 1911, he arrived in Damascus where, at the invitation of that city's religious authorities, he delivered a sermon in the historic Umayyad mosque before an audience, claim his biographers, of ten thousand believers.

In the sermon, which has today become an exemplary component of the Said Nursi textual corpus, he addressed the sicknesses that had arrested Muslim material development. They were six in number: despair and hopelessness in social life; the death of truthfulness in social and political life; the love of enmity; ignorance of the luminous bonds that bind the believers to one another; despotism; restricting endeavor to the personally beneficial. Having set out his terms, he went on to elucidate "the lesson I have learned from the pharmacy of the Qur'an, which is like a faculty of medicine."[78]

Though Said Nursi belongs, like the bulk of Islamic theological tradition, to the historical era, it has become difficult today to determine what words of his famous sermon were actually uttered from the pulpit of the Umayyad mosque. As, two generations after his death, he has been overtaken by the accretive power of legend, so too the surviving text has been added to, modified and revised, growing organically like a coral reef. This was done both by Said himself, who sought to bring it into line with the great shift in his life, his forced withdrawal from active involvement in politics and social issues into a world of writing and contemplation focused on defense of belief, and by his followers, in an endeavor to explain its inconsistencies.

"Europe and America are pregnant with Islam," he proclaimed. "One day they will give birth to an Islamic state. Just as the Ottomans were pregnant with Europe and gave birth to a European state ... it is Islam that will be the true, and spiritual ruler over the future, and only Islam that will lead mankind to happiness in this world and the next; and that true Christianity, stripping off its superstition and corrupted belief, will be transformed into Islam; following the Qur'an, it will unite with Islam."[79]

While no rational (or intuitive) person can rule out the possibility of this happening, most would probably agree that a fusion of these two monotheistic religions still belongs, ninety years later, to the realm of the improbable. Likewise, Said Nursi's rousing appeals to material progress as essential to proclaiming the Word of God, may cause eyebrows to arch with skepticism. Yet, in the sermon, he established the theme that was later to become central to the success of the Nur movement in Turkey, the source of its subversive strength and of its weakness as well: the primacy of religion over politics. All politics may serve Islam, he concluded, but no politics can make Islam a tool for itself.[80]

The voyage to Damascus had another objective: that of reconciling the empire's Arab subjects with the new doctrine of consultation. For although Said had not yet joined the Ottoman secret service, and despite his burning critique of Young Turk despotism, he still viewed the new regime as the least of available evils and continued to cooperate with it. The preservation of the Empire, he reasoned, was the best way to protect the interests of Muslims everywhere. Shortly after the sermon, he traveled from Damascus to Beirut, and thence by sea to Izmir and on to Istanbul, where he would pursue his dream of setting up a university in far Anatolia. This time the omens were favorable.

Far from being an anonymous provincial mollah, Bediuzzaman had by now acquired a considerable reputation. When, in June of 1911, the new Sultan set out on his journey to Rumelia—the last visit by an Ottoman ruler to the Empire's soon-to-vanish European provinces—the fiery-eyed preacher was invited along.

Several months earlier, Albania had erupted in rebellion and civil strife, as the southerners, bent on westernizing themselves, confronted the conservative landowners of Kosova, loyal to the Porte. The Sultan's task was to reconcile the warring factions and awaken renewed feelings of patriotism. The stakes were high: Great Power vultures were circling. Around polished tables, men with pork-chop whiskers were issuing preliminary mobilization orders. Soon, where the elderly sultan trod, troops would march, fight and die, just as they were to fight and die 80 years later as Yugoslavia's unwilling province imploded for the same reasons.

From Salonica, where he was given a triumphal welcome, the Sultan's retinue made its way north by rail to Üsküb, today's Skopje, the Albanian-Macedonian city on the Vardar, and then proceeded to its northernmost destination, Pristina, where Friday prayers were performed before a congregation of 200,000 near the tomb of Sultan Murat, victor and martyr of the battle of the "Field of the Blackbirds" where, in June 1389, an Ottoman army had defeated the Serbian knights of Prince Lazar, opening a wound on the body of the Balkans that has yet to heal. At a festive gathering held later that day, local notables pressed upon the Sultan the necessity of establishing a university. Such an institution would anchor the refractory province to the Empire, they argued. This same university, after the establishment of socialist Yugoslavia, would become a hotbed of a virulent Albanian nationalism that was to deny not only Kosova's deep historical ties with the Ottoman state, but with Islam itself. [81]

Said seized the opportunity and submitted his own proposal for a similar faculty in Anatolia. While his biographer suggests that the proposal was accepted on its merits, Serif Mardin has another, more seductive hypothesis. Sultan Mehmet Reshad was known to be in sympathy with the Mevlevi order, the "Whirling Dervishes" of Konya. "Perhaps this is what made him take sympathetic notice of the petition which Said Nursi presented him." [82]

The project, like the Empire itself, was doomed. First the Balkan Wars stripped the Ottoman state of its European provinces; then the First World War brought Istanbul to its knees. Said Nursi, who had returned to Van, was swept up in the turmoil that was to end a dynasty that had endured for six centuries.

# VII

## In the Shadow of the Citadel

S UNDAY MORNING IN VAN dawned bright and crisp. One of the
particularities of Turkey, a country whose population is 98%
Muslim, is that Friday, the day of communal prayer, is not the
communal day of rest. Why it is not forms part of the country's
denial of itself. Having seized the state after the War of
Independence in 1922 and eliminated the Sunni religious
establishment from which the Ottomans had drawn their spiritual
legitimacy, the victorious secularists replaced the Islamic calendar
with the pagan/ Christian/modern one. By leaving behind them the
embarrassing encumbrances of the faith they associated with
ignorance and backwardness, they aspired to step into a radiant new
era of prosperity. It cannot have occurred to them that imitation
would not bring them that which they imitated. Nor would it have
crossed their minds how tenacious that faith and its encumbrances
would prove to be, how fluid-like in its ability to seek out and flow
through the tiniest pin-holes in the dike of secularism, enlarging
them as it went, how resistant to the new dogma would be the old
belief.

This secular Sunday would be a day of exploring the ruins of Van
in the company of two academics from Centennial University.

These ruins possess none of the vivid though ersatz three-dimensionality of computer-generated images, little of the stony palpability of ancient sites. They must be evoked by imagination, by the projection of knowledge onto and into a past that can speak to us no longer in its own voice. But in their powerful virtuality they have left an indelible trace on society, in the human heart and spirit.

The languid look and feel of the far provinces envelops Van, a small city of drab concrete buildings and perhaps 300,000 souls, most of them Kurds and most of them poor, like a fine layer of dust. A nether zone of mud-brick huts surrounds the downtown core. Here scrawny chickens graze the roadside pecking for specks of grain, and barefoot infants gambol in the mud puddles. Bushes still in yellow leaf and bare-branched poplars and willows overhang the narrow road.

The Nur movement is a patient one, explains Hasan K., the man behind the wheel, as we swerve off the paved road and onto a dirt track, winding up the hillside. Professor K. is a member of the philosophy department, who took his graduate training in England. The author of several books, he is also the most outspoken and articulate member of the community I was to encounter on my journey, a man with quick eyes, a keenly cultivated sense of that quintessential post-modern virtue, irony, and an appetite for wide-ranging give-and-take that never once veered off into Qur'an thumping or the sanctimoniousness that comes from a too certain possession of the Truth.

The movement has no political aims, he explains as his colleague Bulent G., an instructor in the science department, nods approvingly from the back seat. Only the modest and potentially explosive intention of becoming, peacefully, quietly and with determination, a majority. "Said Nursi tells us, 'Never attempt anything unless you have sixty or seventy percent,'" he adds, glancing at me. "Our movement, when you get right down to it, is one of peaceful disobedience. Our approach is to demonstrate in our daily lives, among our friends and our families, what Islam really is, and how it can make people happy."

Bediuzzaman's world of ethical commands flows, writes Serif Mardin, "from the family and the community—the basic components of society according to Said Nursi—to the state." In the view of his followers, the state exists for the benefit of the family and the community, rather than vice versa.

"Kemalist ideology was long on views concerning the virtues of Turks, the benefits of secular republicanism for personality expansion, and the contribution of universal education to progress," Mardin continues, adding, "it was short on methods that would enable individuals to tackle issues arising in the family circle."[83] The Nur movement, by refusing to engage the regime in the political arena, had located its weakness. Where the regime could not, it provided individuals with the methods Mardin describes. What were the *dershane*, the discussion groups, the informal networks of friends and colleagues, but an extended, sophisticated and ramified family circle whose unspoken credo was to ignore the state, to create a peacefully disobedient extra-parliamentary non-political opposition that is both everywhere and nowhere.

Fine in theory, but politics still loom over the lives of individuals and of the Nur community. The movement may discourage political discussion in its dormitories, it can hardly forbid individuals from supporting parties. In fact, Mr. K. tells me as we climb higher up the barren late fall hillside, it can endorse certain candidates it feels meet the minimum religious requirements of probity and piety. Most such candidates gravitate to the traditionalist, conservative parties. Endorsement of the political Islamists of Refah-Fazilet would be unlikely, support for the radicals who openly favor an Islamic state, unthinkable. Though the group finds its internal cohesion in discipline and good example, a central policy-making body meets regularly to discuss problems, debate issues and make decisions. But as befits a movement which draws its dynamism from voluntary adhesion, no ruling can do anything more than offer moral guidance. "If you wish to go your own way, to run for political office," he adds, "you must leave our community."

As he talks and steers, I crane my neck, straining for a glimpse of the cadmium blue, alkaline expanse of Van Gölü. Suddenly we crest a rise and the car shudders to a stop. A few meters from our stopping place stands a pile of rubble that a trained archeologist would have certainly recognized and classified. I turn to Hasan K. "This was an Armenian church," he says. "Here is where Said Nursi came to, what do you say in English—to meditate? Ah yes, to meditate. They were bringing him some bread from the town so he would not be hungry."

Those were the days, in the first decade of the century, when Bediuzzaman had come up to Van at the invitation of the governor, Tahir Pasha. During the summer months, while acting on the governor's behalf as a conciliator in tribal disputes and pursuing his avid readings in Islamic theology and Western science, he would range these arid hills, studying the "book of the universe" and seeking to unlock the secrets of the Qur'an. [84] Across the valley, cold water from a mountain spring flows down a ravine through clumps of poplars. "This is the water he drank," says Mr. K.

The sun has risen higher in the sky , and a southeasterly breeze has swept the horizon clean. In the distance we can pick out the roofs of the barracks that house the villagers driven from their homes in the fight against the Kurdish insurrection. Having applied the "strategic hamlet" approach perfected by its American patrons in Vietnam and Guatemala, to no avail, the concentration camp model was now favored by Ankara's counter-insurgency experts. For more than a decade, the Turkish government has pursued a scorched-earth policy as unforgiving in its thoroughness as in its violence, torching villages whose inhabitants are suspected of sympathy with the PKK. Hundreds of thousands of Kurds have been dispersed throughout the region. For many of them, Van has become the first stop.

Official insensitivity to that euphemism, the "Kurdish problem," is endemic in Western capitals, despite the pleading of human rights advocates in Turkey and the troubling revelations of a generation of non-mainstream journalists and authors. At the heart of this curious deference (discounting for a moment the Turkish state's fealty to Washington and its status as a NATO member) must surely lie the circumstances surrounding the rise of the modern Turkish state from the rubble of the Ottoman Empire, and to a lesser extent, the way in which this story is told.

Although the Ottoman heartland was never directly seized by European colonialism, it was subverted from within by its own European desires, by the West it had internalized. On the periphery, the empire's former provinces were shared out among the proxy states created by the Great Powers, and predicated on an uninterrupted flow of oil westward to Europe, and later, to the United States. The price for Turkish independence may well have been an implicit undertaking to abandon Islam. Certainly, its *quid pro quo* was the abandonment by the Powers of the idea of a Kurdish state which had been mooted (along with the creation of an Armenian equivalent) in the stillborn Sèvres Treaty of 1920.

Turkey's image abroad has been shaped over time not only by such geostrategic considerations, not only by the West-worshipping policies of the secularist elite, but by the work of a cohort of Western scholars attuned to the overriding ideological imperatives of the regime: the unicity and indivisibility of the country, coupled with the inevitable, irreversible nature of the "Atatürk reforms," the eurocentric notion that "progress"—defined strictly as modernity— is somehow possessed of nothing but positive attributes, and the tacit acceptance of Great Power domination of the Islamic heartland. These professional Turcophile scholars, as exemplified by Bernard Lewis, "are surely paid by the government," says Mr. K., who is intimately familiar with their writings.

(Several months earlier Mr. Lewis had been the guest of the Turkish government which wined and dined him in Ankara, then awarded him the Atatürk Prize, in recognition of his meritorious services to the State.)

But, continues Mr. K., "we Turks are always blaming foreigners for our troubles. The truth is that if outsiders do not find people they can purchase or collaborate with, they cannot carry out their plans. In fact, this is the situation in our country: there are two Turkeys, the 'official' state, the institutions, and the army, that make up 10 percent of the population; then you have the rest of the people, the other 90 percent. How can 10 percent rule 90 percent? Only by force, fear and intimidation."

* * *

IN AUGUST, 1913, the Balkan Wars ended in defeat for the Ottoman Empire. The Balkan League, a short-lived alliance of pathological micro-nationalisms, had driven Turkey from all but a corner of the peninsula.

Earlier that summer, Said Nursi had returned to Van hoping to begin construction of his Islamic university. In a letter to the Grand Vizier's office in Istanbul, his old friend and protector Tahir Pasha underlined the importance of such an institution for continued Ottoman predominance in an area where Shi'ite propaganda was present and where the Kurdish tribes were growing restless again. [85]

For centuries, eastern Turkey, Kurdistan and Azerbaijan have been not only an area of shifting military domination, but a field of struggle pitting Sunni orthodoxy against Shi'ite heterodoxy. The climax of that struggle came in 1514, thirty kilometers northeast of Van, near a dusty village called Chaldiran, when a powerful Shi'ite army led by Shah Ismail, the founder of the Iranian Safavid dynasty, clashed with an Ottoman force led by Sultan Yavuz Selim I, "the Grim."

Here, around this alkaline lake lies a field of virtual ruins unfathomable by the conventional means of contemporary archeology. In the intricate web of doctrinal complexities that streak and marble the world of Islam, far Anatolia stands out in its ramified heterogeneity. Shah Ismail, son of a religious family of Azerbaijan with more remote connections to the family of the Prophet, had united the fractious Turkish tribes that then ruled western Iran and Azerbaijan. The tribesmen were known as Qizilbash, or "red hats," for the red turbans they affected. Imbued with the fierce dedication and spirit of self-sacrifice characteristic of militant Shi'ism, Shah Ismail's red-hatted warriors rapidly extended their domain as far westward as the great Kurdish stronghold of Diyarbakir to the southwest. [86]

In Istanbul, Sultan Beyazit II dithered. A peacefully inclined man with mystical leanings, the Sultan may have harbored more than distant sympathy for the wild-riding Qizilbash warriors and for their Shi'a beliefs. But he had to contend with his youngest son, Selim. Tensions increased further when the Sultan's eldest son and favorite, Ahmet, donned the red turban and raised an army to attack Bursa, the first Ottoman capital. The Empire was at a crossroads. A continuation of Beyazit's reign or worse, the ascension of Ahmet to the throne, would have laid the imperial domains at the feet of Shah Ismail's heretical red-hats.

Faced with armed rebellion by his youngest son, Beyazit abdicated in favor of Selim, whose first act on taking up his sultanly duties was to have his two brothers strangled with a bowstring, a practice that was to become the traditional Ottoman vehicle for smoothing out the wrinkles of dynastic succession. [87] On the way back to his birthplace, Beyazit died of mysterious causes, possibly even from a dose of filial poison. Extirpation of the Shi'ite plague now became Selim's obsession. But before launching his forces against Ismail, the fanatically devout new sultan massacred some 40,000 of the Shah's followers in western Anatolia, an act that won him the honorific title of "the Just." The dead were the ancestors of the Alevis, the heterodox Muslim sect that I would later encounter in Istanbul. Over nearly five hundred years, their survivors had metamorphosed into nativist defenders of the secular state.

In the valley of Chaldiran, Selim's army finally encountered Shah Ismail's forces on the field of battle. Little could stand against the impetuous cavalry charge of the Qizilbash, brilliant horsemen who believed that God had granted them invulnerability. Were it not for the muskets of Selim's infantry, were it not for his artillery pieces, Van would not be the rampart of Sunni orthodoxy and the Turkish language that it has remained to this day. But the Ottomans' superior firepower overwhelmed the foolhardy red-hats. Victorious, they sacked Tabriz, and incorporated Kurdistan into the empire. Shi'ism, defeated, would never again raise its head in Anatolia. Not, at least, in overt form.

And yet, in 1913, the governor of Van had enrolled Said Nursi in a campaign to combat Shi'a propaganda. Had the good citizens of Van, and the villagers and mountaineers that populated the area, been something less than dedicated Sunnis? There is every reason to assume that some of the Shi'a heretics had escaped Selim's just mercies. They might well have taken refuge in the age-old tactic of dissimulation, only to reappear in the form of the Alevi sects that gradually spread across the empire and which—known pejoratively as Qizilbash—persist to this day. And, as I was to learn later, bad blood exists between them and the more "orthodox" Sunnis who populate the Nur movement and its periphery. Perhaps the bad blood had arisen from an uncomfortable sense of proximity, from the need to conceal.

Whatever the perceived ideological danger, it soon paled before the clear and present danger to the territorial integrity of the Empire. When World War I broke out in August, 1914, Russian armies thrust deep into Anatolia, guided and supported by Armenian irregulars intent on carving out an independent state. Van was to be the theater of confrontation, and Said Nursi was to play a hero's role, though ultimately he was unable to block the ultimate outcome: defeat.

\* \* \*

THE CITADEL OF VAN, a huge rocky excrescence jutting up from the marshy plain, overlooks to the south a scene of weed-clogged desolation. As the sun climbs toward the zenith, my guides and I clamber up the slippery path toward the summit. There, from among the cyclopean remains of Urartian fortifications dating from the beginning of the second millennium BC, we stare down at the remains of the old city, a landscape of hummocks, heaps of rubble overgrown with nettles, and the occasional shell of a mosque. Nothing here has changed since the brutal days of spring, 1915, my hosts tell me. Fearing deportation, poorly armed but grimly determined Armenian insurgents had barricaded themselves in the old walled city and fought off repeated attacks by the Ottoman forces. Their strategy was to inflict maximum damage on their Turkish tormentors, to hold them off until the arrival of the imperial Russian army. Their combativeness, and the early arrival of their saviors, spared them their lives, although it would cost them their homeland forever.

Van had been one of the jewels of Turkish Armenia. In the second decade of the twentieth century, Armenians outnumbered the combined Turkish and Kurdish population and were, in dress and behavior, like any urban population in Europe at the time. [88] But the encroaching Russian armies and the revolutionary agitation of the Armenian nationalist parties had created a tense and explosive climate. Few Turks were convinced by their protestations of support for the state. When, in mid-April, the new Ottoman governor, Cevdet Bey, the hard-line son of Tahir Pasha, ordered a call-up of 4,000 men for the army, the Armenians, fearing the conscripts would be murdered, declined and played for time, while reinforcing their defensive positions within the old city. Finally, when the governor issued an order for the extermination of the Armenians, the latter retreated behind their fortifications, determined to fight to the death.

From the citadel, atop which we now stand looking out over the lake, the railway docks, and the distant rooftops of the university campus to the northeast, the Ottoman garrison rained down gunfire, grenades and flaming projectiles on the town. Despite an unrelenting Ottoman artillery barrage, the Armenian defensive perimeter held firm. But food and munitions were running low.

The siege was lifted when the Russians marched into the ruined city in mid May, led by an advance guard of Armenian volunteers who promptly set up a provisional government. It was to last six weeks, when the Russians retired, followed by the Armenians of Van, never to return.

As the violent fighting in the spring of 1915 leveled the city and tore its once-sophisticated, cosmopolitan social fabric to shreds, so the tragic events of the war created another, more grievous casualty: historical truth. Perhaps to an even greater degree than in the Balkans, the history of high Anatolia is one of conflicting versions and irreconcilable claims. Historical accounts that favor the Armenians make little mention of the presence of Armenian officers and soldiers in the Russian invasion force, and say nothing of the mass killing of Muslims that took place when they finally captured Van.

The Young Turk authorities, and their Kemalist heirs and apologists, admitted—and to this day admit—neither to genocide nor massacre. The total number of Armenian dead throughout the region was not 2.5 million, they claim, but 200,000 who died not only of the rigors of forced evacuation from the combat zone, where they were regarded as a hostile fifth column, but of war, famine and disease. More than two million Muslims, they argue, supported by census figures, perished during those same years. [89]

Now a high-ranking operative in the Ottoman secret service and a confidant of the Young Turk leadership, Bediuzzaman Said Nursi had returned to Van in 1915, no longer with the aim of establishing his university, but of organizing the militia force which he was to lead in battle against the Armenians and the Russians on the shifting eastern front. The Horhor *medrese*, at the base of Van citadel, was transformed into a barracks, its walls hung with Mauser rifles and cartridge belts, swords, daggers and military cloaks. Within its walls lived the leaders of the Felt Hats, the militia that Bediuzzaman had commanded in the battle for Pasinler, near Erzurum, before falling back on Van, waging defensive skirmishes as they retreated.

The Russian forces accompanied by Armenian irregular units thrust deeper into Anatolia, killing civilians as they went. Elimination of the Muslim population, not capture of territory, had become the strategic objective of the invaders, whose goal was the establishment of an independent Armenia. The Muslim forces retaliated in kind. No mercy was given. Those were bitter times.

Said Nursi, claims his biographer, attempted to bring "humanity to the chaos of war" by ordering that a large group of captured Armenian women and children not be molested, but returned to their homes in Russian-held territories. The Armenians, in recognition, followed his example.[90] But the poorly armed and outnumbered Ottoman forces could not defend the city, let alone protect its non-combatant population. When Van fell, Said and his militia pulled back through the mountains toward Bitlis. There, he was to fight his final battle with gun in hand.

A FILMY CLOUD has veiled the sun as we scramble down the rough path from the citadel toward a dusty park at the foot of its northern flank. Here, the ruins of Van are invisible, hidden by the rock. While my companions adjourn for their midday prayers, I sip a lukewarm coffee in an open-air *çayhane*. A light breeze ruffles the willow branches, children are playing; in the distance I hear drums and *zurna*, as an army recruit is seen off to training camp. Down the dirt track that connects the park to the main road speeds an automobile, kicking up a plume of dust. Slowing only slightly it roars into the parking area, brakes violently and swerves into a power slide across the graveled surface. Then, engine whining, it races back down the road, fishtailing and spewing dust, to vanish as quickly as it had appeared, like the phantom racing cars roaring through the night streets of Rimini in Fellini's *Amarcord*. The settling dust coats the dry yellow leaves like a fine powder of melancholy.

My hosts reappear, blinking and drawing their hands downward across their cheeks as if to pull themselves back into the world of appearance. Making our way carefully, we clamber over the rocky spurs of the citadel and enter a lush willow grove sheltering beneath its south flank. The trees still cling to their last leaves, a chlorophyll fuzz of grass covers the spongy earth, and water trickles in rivulets toward an algae-covered pond. Here, from the base of the rock burbles a spring: "This was where Bediuzzaman set up his *medrese*," says Mr. K. "Listen! You can hear the sound the water makes. Horhor horhor …"

From several hundred meters away we catch the whine of oriental music. He perks up his ears. "This is not Turkish," he declares. "They are Iranian refugees; let us go and see." We pick our way across the soft ground toward a group of picnickers clustered around a Japanese boom-box from which cascades the sinuous cadences of Persian pop, the kind of music that, if played in any Tehran park, would earn them a lashing from the morality patrol. They are playing cards, slapping them down with whoops of glee or moans of disappointment.

Van lies astride the main refugee route from the Iranian border to the clandestine processing centre in Istanbul's Yenikapi district. This group, five men and three women, though only a few days clear of the Islamic motherland, seems already well into the Great Satanic mode, complete with baseball caps to match their aspirations. But despite breaking free of the mollahs, they remain suspicious. My attempts to strike up a conversation in Farsi elicit only monosyllables. Are you Iranians? I ask. From Tehran? They admit to no more.

Hasan K., in English, fares little better:

"You are refugees, yes?"

"Ummhh."

"You want to go to America?"

"Mnnhh."

Caution, with a slight tinge of hostility, has crowded out momentary curiosity. "They are passing through Van, thousands of them," adds Mr. K. as we move away. "There, you have the products of a tyrannical regime."

The Iranian religious establishment has founded a state where all public behavior is prescribed by God, and where the authorities must constantly combat evil and enjoin good. Laudable in theory, the system has become confused in practice. The lurking problem is less one of revelation than of interpretation. It was perhaps inevitable that those who exercise the monopoly of interpretation contrive to profit from their position, becoming not lovers of religion but, as the Iranian philosopher Abdolkarim Soroush has written, dealers in it.

We pause for lunch in a kebab house located in the heart of Van's market district, dodging fast-moving pushcarts heaped high with oranges, tangerines, cucumbers and tomatoes, and leaping over muddy puddles, nudging our way past plump merchants and scurrying waiters ferrying trays of Adana kebab and Urfa kebab, each one spicier than the one before. Then, replete, back into the car for a visit to a private residential high-school run by the Fetullah Gülen organization. None of the school's administrators are on the premises, but the caretaker agrees to show us the bright new facility. Though private, the school must respect the state curriculum. Nowhere on the bright, airy premises that overlook the lake, or amidst the clean, well-equipped labs, the spare classrooms and Spartan quarters where boarding students sleep four or six to a room, do we observe the merest sign of religion.

To the left of the entrance has been erected an altar to the Kemal adoration cult, complete with effigies and icons illustrating the great and heroic moments of the leader's life, primarily in his attributes as military commander. We see him conferring with his adjutants who stand, attentive and deferential, slightly behind him; we see him sleeping humbly in a snow-drift, wrapped in his soldier's cloak; we see him, in top hat, piercing gaze fixed on the far future, boring into the hearts and minds of the Turks; we see him, too, as great father, surrounded by mirthful children. You will trust and obey me as you do your own fathers, shouts the display.

As we sit down to wait for tea, Hasan K. whispers to me: "He is the Antichrist!" There is nothing either arch or ironic in his tone.

\* \* \*

FOR THE FIRST 40 years of his life, Said Nursi dreamed of and worked for the establishment of an institution of higher learning that would combine Western intellectual methods and disciplines with the traditional religious curriculum of the *medrese*. The school would be trilingual: Arabic, the language of the Qur'an, being compulsory, Kurdish permissible, and Turkish necessary.[91] The following morning, my two companions of the previous day pick me up for a drive north along the shoreline road to the campus of Centennial University.

"This," Hasan K. warns me with a rueful glance as we pull into the parking lot behind the main pavilion, "is not what Bediuzzaman had in mind at all." At Centennial U., the second language is English, not Arabic. Kurdish, through which Said Nursi's ideal institution would have reached out to the region's poor and relatively backward majority, is forbidden outright. While it may be spoken surreptitiously on the street and whispered in the corridors, no student, no professor would dare utter a single proscribed word in the classroom. The eyes and ears of the state are everywhere, ever wakeful, ever watching. And the long arm of the state is ever poised to lash out.

In the sociology department, in a tiny office whose furniture consists of a desk, two hard metal chairs and a filing cabinet, I encounter a man who encourages me to quote him. Professor Emir Yasir Demirci is a soft-spoken, articulate skeptic, with a wry sincerity that is instantly compelling. Emboldened by the atmosphere of confidence, I recount yesterday's reference to Atatürk as the Antichrist. He laughs: "From the fundamentalist point of view, that's exactly what he is. Atatürk stands for everything they fear and hate, for the absolute denial of religion. But the truth is that Atatürk really had no ideological commitment at all. He was neither for nor against religion. His only criterion was, did it fit in with his vision of Turkey or didn't it. His successor, Ismet Inönü, was 'Stalin' to his 'Lenin.' Inönü invented Kemalism as a vehicle for his own legitimacy after Kemal's death. Blame it on him."

"It's a paradox," he continues, "but the high point of the Atatürk cult came during the regime of the Democrat Party, under Adnan Menderes. During the single-party period, Atatürk's body was kept in a museum. The Democrat Party government built the Anit Kebir, the Atatürk mausoleum in Ankara. They had to, in a sense, to demonstrate their loyalty to the ruling establishment."

I have knocked on a propitious door. Professor Demirci is a specialist in the interaction of the Sufi tradition and the creation of the modern Turkish state, although I detect in him something more than the dispassionate observer of bizarre phenomena, more than the collector of intellectual butterflies. Said Nursi, he argues, is an enigma, a rational mystic, a quietist activist. "His faith draws upon his personal, internal experience, which is one characteristic of the Sufi tradition. The Sufi *tariqats* in the Van area are based on the local Kurdish tribal structure. But they are also consistent with Naqshbandi tradition in their critical view of the establishment."

Without an understanding of this tradition, one of the deepest-rooted in Turkey, he adds, it is impossible to grasp fully the peculiar phenomenon of Said Nursi, or of the Refah Partisi founded by Necmettin Erbakan. Although each is critical—and leery—of the other, they possess profound affinities and reach back to common sources.

The Naqshbandis, writes no lesser an authority than Hamid Algar, are, like every Sufi order, "a crystallization of a tradition that reaches back to the first age of Islam and the matchless person of the Prophet who, in the words of the Persian poet Fakhr ad-Din Iraqi (d. 1289 AD), is 'the Sufi in the hospice of the All-Compassionate.'"[92] But unlike almost every other Sufi order, the Naqshbandis trace their spiritual lineage back to Abu Bakr, the first caliph of Islam, and not to Ali, the fourth caliph and first Imam venerated by the Shi'ites. The Naqshbandis are hostile to Shi'ism, perhaps because their expansion in the Sunni world coincided with the rise of a militant Shi'a state in Iran.[93]

The order's founder, a saint called Baha ad-Din Naqshband, died and was buried near Bukhara, his birthplace, in 1389 AD. One of his most influential disciples, known as Ahrar, emphasized the crucial importance of the *Shari'a*. Under the impetus of his teachings, Naqshbandis went on to take up the militant and often armed defense of the holy law in places as diverse as India where they fought against the British, in the Caucasus against the Russians, in Indonesia against the Dutch, and in Turkey against the secularizing regime of Atatürk. [94]

The animating spark of this rejuvenated movement came from another extraordinary figure, Maulana Halid Baghdadi, a native, as his name indicates, of Baghdad who died in the Christian year of 1827. The Halidis, as his followers came to be known, spearheaded the fight against the imitation of westernism in the Islamic world, and against Western imperialism. For them, writes Algar, "the *Shari'a* was not, in the first place, an abstract spiritual value, or even the supreme element in the familiar Sufi triad of *shari'a-tariqa-haqiqa* [Law, Order, Reality], but the essential structure of Muslim society and the sole guarantor of its independence from foreign rule." [95]

As the influence of the Halidis grew, lodges were founded in the Kurdish cities and towns of eastern Anatolia, including Hizan and Bitlis, where Said Nursi was to study under sheikhs carrying on the Halidi tradition. Maulana Halid was known by his devotees as the Regenerator or Renewer of the Millennium. These high servants of religion, wrote Bediuzzaman, were "not innovators, but followers ... who proclaim the true and original meaning of religion ... through new methods of persuasion appropriate to the understanding of the age ..." [96]

It takes little imagination to realize that Said Nursi saw himself as such a figure. Even less to grasp that his followers did and do. While imprisoned in the western Anatolian town of Kastamonu, the wife of the prison warden gave him a hundred-year-old woven cloth robe, of the kind worn by religious scholars. The robe had been a gift to the woman's grandfather, a wandering Sufi who traveled to Baghdad, by the great Maulana Halid himself. Said, who as a matter of principle refused all gifts, promptly accepted the robe as though it were his own. [97] He took it as his mantle, but drew a distinction between the way of Maulana Halidi, that of Sufism—*tariqat*—and his way, the path of reality—*haqiqat*.

As I shake hands with Professor Demirci, carrying a copy of his Ph.D. thesis on Modernization, Religion and Politics in Turkey under my arm, pieces of the puzzle have begun to drop into place. The insistence on doctrinal purity and militant devotion that were so central to the life of the Naqshbandi order were present among the followers of Said Nursi. But where the more orthodox Sufis attached themselves to a living exemplar of the highest spiritual accomplishment, the Nurcus paid, they said, obeisance only to a text.

While in Van I have passed many days in a short time, as the Greek poet Odysseas Elytis put it. Now, at the crack of noon, my friends deposit me at the Otogar. The bus is already idling at the gate. Its final destination: Diyarbakir, the city of black basalt.

The Great Mosque at Diyarbakir, the city of black basalt.

*Photo by Fred A. Reed*

# VIII

## The Hour of Remembrance

Istiklal Caddesi—Independence Avenue—the thoroughfare along which I pass almost every day, fulfills a double, symbolic function: as a showcase of secular Turkey and as an unwitting illustration of a cultural surrender as complex as it is diverse. Here, far from the Anatolian hinterland through which I searched for traces of Said Nursi, on the cobbled pedestrian street that curves through Beyoglu, I encounter (this is the short list): self-assured suits in one big hurry barking buy and sell orders into cellular phones outside American fast-food franchises, lady shoppers of a certain age laden with make-up and designer shopping bags, transvestites (those darlings of Western writers hungry for cultural diversity and of gender studies specialists desperate for a subject), scruffy youths in skateboard chic or ultra-low-rise pants and unlaced sneakers, young people with assorted body piercings, little boys with close-cropped hair who dangle from the antique tram that grinds its way down the middle of the avenue with an insistent clanging of its warning bell, other children who hover after dark in lighted store entrances passing the glue bottle. Assaulting the ears of the passer-by, techno music from record shops wheezes like some demented carousel, and further up the street, arabesk street singers wail to the accompaniment of a thudding bass and an ear-splitting feedback whine, and from blue-jean emporia drone Christmas carols at all times of the year. The manifold delights, indeed, of the World Culture, adoption of which remains an article of faith with the faceless men who plot Turkey's happy course into the new millennium of modernity, oblivious—like the officers who serve the sailors the maggot-infested slab of beef on the Battleship Potemkin—to the rot.

But all is not the homogeneous bleakness of the post-postmodern affliction. At the quiet end of the street, down from Galatasaray Lycée—the Empire's first Western educational institution, which opened its doors to teach French to the imperial elite in 1868, when this was the district of embassies and the realm of extraterritorial privilege—a solitary fiddler sings languorous oriental ballads to his own accompaniment. In front of the lycée, every Saturday at noon, the Mothers of the Disappeared come to demonstrate in silence, holding photographs of their vanished loved ones beneath a looming outdoor photographic display commemorating the 75th anniversary of the Republic, their violent dispersion by the police a symbolic replica of this immense outdoor Atatürk shrine. The installation is sponsored by one of Turkey's largest banks which in turn is held by one of the country's powerful holding companies, whose interests and continuing profits are in turn guarded by those great and good protectors of public order, the Turkish armed forces.

Because it is the centerpiece of the modernist project, Istiklal Caddesi often metamorphoses into contested territory. Not only do aggrieved mothers come here to demonstrate—so do students, civil rights protesters and left-wing or Islamist trade unionists. At the far end of the avenue, the statue of Atatürk and his comrades-in-arms that dominates Taksim Square is a favorite spot for patriotic gatherings and wreath layings. When Turkish flags are prominently displayed, the police becomes attentive and solicitous and may even disperse overly curious onlookers. When the national symbols are in abeyance, and especially if the demonstrators are Kurd sympathizers or Islamists, out come the nightsticks and the plastic shields, the tear gas and the riot-control vehicles. Periodically, the shopkeepers must sweep up broken glass in the wake of rampaging or fleeing demonstrators. Such, they reason, is the cost of doing business on the street that stands for all that Turkey was to, and will not, if the population can help it, become.

Get thee behind me, Satan! The devout who pass through this valley of impiety and temptation must whisper as they move straight ahead, oblivious to the lurid posters of the Elhambra porno cinema, and the *raki*-houses of Cicek Pasagi, Istanbul's premier *mezze* palace where one can wile away an evening over a carafe of the milky, anise-flavored liquid powerful enough, as David Homel puts it, to stun an ox, while competing bands of fiddle, *oud* and clarinet players churn out raucous music that must struggle to be heard above the din of conversation.

Beyoglu's only concession to Islamic rigor comes when the call to prayer rings out at noon, and again at dusk. It is a grudging concession, no more. Music on that section of the street adjacent to the mosque comes to a momentary stop, and all one hears is the shuffling of feet and the nasal cadence of the *azan* reminding the shop owners and the office employees, the touts and the yuppies and the rappers, that here the immemorial hour of the Qur'an still prevails, its prayers marking dawn, noon, dusk and nightfall, alongside the invasive clangor of what Paul Virillio calls the globalization of time. [98]

Until five years after the establishment of the Republic, in 1928, time continued to be reckoned according to a system with roots deep in the past. The new day began at dawn, and both night and daylight were divided into twelve hours. As the seasons waxed and waned, the length of an hour, as articulated by the sundial, would expand or contract. Within this flexible, even organic framework, Islam, which is governed by lunar cycles, had need of precise calculations for the hour of daily prayer in an age when only the moon, the sun and the changing seasons marked the passage of time.

This dilemma was resolved by the establishment of time reckoning offices which were added to main mosques throughout the Empire. In them, time-keepers, using sundials and mechanical devices, would calculate prayer times, and the crucial fasting periods of Ramadan. Each day they would adjust their clocks according to the hours of sunrise and sunset. The *Muvakkithane*, as these offices were called, were convenient to passers-by, who would stop off to set their watches, check the long-term weather forecast and exchange pleasantries. In a wistful passage, the poet Ahmet Hasim evokes the life, and laments the sense of lost identity, that ebbed and flowed with all the cyclical predictability of the tide ...

"In olden times just as we had a way of life, of thinking, of dressing, which we could call our own, just as we possessed a sense of the beautiful which took its liveliness from religion, race and tradition, so too, we had control over our own "hours" and "days" which were in tune with this type of life. The beginning of the Muslim day was set by the glowing sunrise and the end by the evening's last rays. The hands of the old, innocent watches which were protected by their strong metallic castings would amble past their enameled numerals in a way more or less connected with the pace of the sun, and, in a gait that was reminiscent of the tired feet of insects, would inform their owners of the time with the precision of approximation. Time was an endless garden and the flowers therein were flowers whose colors were reflected from the sun and who inclined sometimes to the right and sometimes to the left. Before we became accustomed to foreign hours we did not know, in these climes, the twenty-four hour "day," black at both edges with the blackness of night, its back painted with various contrasting colors, with red, yellow or dark blue pigments, stretching like a large dragon from one midnight to the other. We had an easy, light day of twelve hours which began and ended with light, an easily-lived day. Times which had been times of happiness for Muslims were measured in such "days." The Muslims recorded events which instilled pride and honor in them in such "days." It is true that according to astronomical computations this hour was a false and primitive hour. But this hour was the sacred hour of remembrance. The acceptance of the Frankish hour in our customs and transactions and the fading away of the Alaturka hour into the mosques, ritual time-reckoning offices and tombs was not without its momentous consequences on our view of the world."[99]

These momentous consequences have not yet ceased working their way through Turkish society, each action producing, like the ancient and immutable law of the pendulum, a reaction. The Nur movement, which regulates itself by the Alaturka hour, lies at its core. Paradoxically, in order to penetrate to that core, I had to extend the scope of my investigation, to grasp the nature of the modern Turkish state. Here, on Istiklal Caddesi, I hoped to find answers.

\* \* \*

"ISTANBUL IS NOT TURKEY," proclaims Ersin Salman, founder and director of one of Istanbul's largest advertising agencies, over a table of *raki*, dried chick-peas and apricots, white cheese, olives and dark bread upon which several of his friends are nibbling as we speak. Mr. Salman is inebriated, and has tilted his crew-cut gray-haired head to one side as he points to a map of Turkey on the wall. "But," he says, thinking better of it, "Anatolia is in Istanbul, just like Istanbul is in Anatolia." His plaint was a familiar one. Cosmopolitan, intercontinental Istanbul, end-point of the Orient Express, has been overwhelmed by a flood of rustics risen up from the depths of the East. These people have brought with them their dress, their ways and manners, their beliefs. Some of them, spotting an opportunity, have brought more.

We are seated in Mr. Salman's office overlooking Istiklal Caddesi, where I have come to ask about the "civil initiative" that was to have revitalized Turkish politics in the late 1990s. Middle class, modern, secularist citizens had recoiled in disgust at the public revelation (though not the knowledge, for the identity of the curious bedfellows who make up the highest echelons of state power has been for years common, though unspoken knowledge) that the administrative apparatus and indeed the government had been infiltrated at the highest level not by communists or Islamists. Such miscreants can rely on summary justice, crippling trials and decade-long jail sentences for crimes of thought or belief. No, the infiltrators were the home-grown and flourishing Turkish Mafia, itself linked to the country's shadowy ultra-nationalist fringe. This fringe was, in turn, connected with the police and indirectly—came the whispers that spoke the unspeakable—the armed forces themselves. There was much indignation, much fluttering of hands, much anguished outcry.

On November 3, 1996, a traffic accident occurred near Susurluk, an undistinguished town on the main highway between Istanbul and Izmir. It revealed that Anatolia was indeed Istanbul, and vice versa. And not in the cultural sense that my host Mr. Salman intended. The Susurluk Incident, as the crash and political scandal that followed it are known, demonstrated that the Mafia-security apparatus nexus had penetrated to the heart of the secular state.

Perhaps, whispered some observers, it had become the heart.

Others, less startled, shrugged their shoulders as if to say: it has always been there.

Here are the facts, or the information that had the appearance of facts.

Just outside of Susurluk, a late model Mercedes sedan traveling at high speed collided with a truck driven by a man called Hasan. Three of its four passengers perished in the violent crash, which left smoldering wreckage strewn over the pavement. The identity of the victims set tongues wagging. They were: Hüseyin Kocadag, the deputy chief of the Istanbul police department, a man called Mehmet Özbey whose true name was soon revealed as Abdullah Çatli, an ultra-nationalist with strong connections to the security forces, and a beauty queen named Gonca Us, Çatli's paramour. The lone survivor, a Kurdish member of parliament, landowner and sponsor of the village guard movement from Urfa named Sedak Bucak, has been, to this day, unable to remember why the group had been traveling together in the Mercedes, let alone what he was doing there. The car also contained firearms, sophisticated listening devices, narcotics, and large sums of money.

Inquisitive journalists soon pieced together what details they could. The four had come from a meeting in Izmir with the Minister of the Interior of the day, Mehmet Ağar. The subject had been casinos, a revenue-raising device dear to the heart of the government which enabled it to look after its best friends in a style that would have shamed no sultan. Four months previous to the incident, the sultan of the Turkish casino industry, a dapper multi-millionaire named Ömer Topal, had been gunned down in Istanbul. Subsequently, members of the special police forces (which, let us recall, had been set up to combat the insurgents of Öcalan's PKK alongside the regular army) were implicated in Topal's murder, but were ordered released by the minister.

Mr. Ağar, who was forced to resign when details of the bizarre incident hit the headlines, was escorted to the door of the ministry and told, "Turkey is proud of you,"[100] a phrase that continues to accompany a man who rose through the police hierarchy and acquired something of a reputation as a torturer before becoming a member of Mrs. Tansu Çiller's True Path Party, then part of the coalition government of the day. The coalition leader, the Islamist Refah Partisi, failed to raise more than an eyebrow.

The most important victim—in all senses of the word, for some whispered that the Susurluk crash was anything but accidental—was "Mr. Özbey." Prior to the 1980 military coup, Abdullah Çatli had led ultra-nationalist youth groups affiliated with the Gray Wolves militia in Ankara, and was wanted in connection with the murder of seven leftist students. Those were times of social and political upheaval, of armed confrontations in the streets fueled by the paramilitary groups that were to give the Junta the pretext for intervention it sought. Captured and sentenced to prison, Çatli made a daring "escape," and was recruited shortly afterward by the security forces to lead the counter-attack against the anti-Turkish campaign being waged in Europe and North America in the '80s by ASALA, the Armenian terrorist revenge organization. As "Mehmet Özbey" he moved freely at the highest levels of Turkish society, and was rumored to be considering a political career when fate in the form of a truck overtook him.

The driver of the Mercedes, Istanbul Deputy Police Chief Kocadag, had a reputation as a "leftist" member of the security forces, and was known for his close ties with the Alevi sect, a heterodox Islamic group that enjoys the favor of the army. Meanwhile, a mysterious snapshot was produced that showed the late Mr. Çatli dancing in a nightclub with a certain Ibrahim Sahin, leader of the special police team that killed Topal, the Casino King. Imprisoned for his role in the murder, Sahin was released five months later, and showered with praise: "Turkey is proud of you."

The civil initiative campaign in protest against Security Forces/Mafia infiltration of the state culminated in a one-minute demonstration during which citizens were to switch off their lights. The night had come, the lights had been switched off, and the government had promised rapid action. Now, one year later, people like Mr. Salman were congregating over bottles of *raki* and tables of *mezze*, wondering not only what had gone wrong, but worse, what to do next. The task was daunting. The citizens' initiative reminded me of the chewed-over olive pits that littered the ash tray. Clearly, overcome by the malignant magnitude of the task, and dulled by drink, they were going nowhere. Subsequent events showed that it was unlikely that they ever would. There was, I reflected as I left the ad man's office, a fundamental flaw at the heart of the campaign. Where the murkiness of the malefactors could only be exposed by more light, and perhaps even by political heat, the well-meaning organizers had offered only more darkness.

But, with the "accident," the tight-knit fabric of official deceit had only begun to unravel. In December, 1997, a man named Akman Akyürek, the judge responsible for investigating the complex web of state, Mafia and police relations revealed at Susurluk, met an untimely end when his late-model Opel collided with a truck, also driven by a man named Hasan on the high-speed motorway west of Istanbul. Three months before, a high-ranking member of MIT, the national intelligence service, had also died along with his family in an accident involving a truck. That incident had gone unreported.

The death (no one was calling it murder) of Judge Akyürek drew attention for several reasons: his files detailing illegalities involving the state apparatus had vanished, while a wad of $10,000 (US)—possibly counterfeit—bills was left in the crushed vehicle which, though it had allegedly been struck from the rear, sustained damage only on the left side. Later, when police searched the home of the deceased, they discovered powerful explosives and three passports, two of which bore false identities. The judge, who was known as a leftist, was given a ceremonial burial by ultra-nationalists who chanted, "Turkey is proud of you."

The same curious coalition reappeared, in death rather than in life, at a heavily attended memorial service in Ankara, in April 1998, commemorating the natural death one year earlier of Colonel Alparslan Türkes, founder of the MHP, the Nationalist Movement Party which is today a junior member of the governing coalition. There, thousands of supporters, including influential political figures from all the major parties, chanted, "the Chieftain never dies." Many of them carried placards bearing photographs of none other than the late Abdullah Çatli.[101] Though no one said so, the message was clear: "Turkey is proud of you."

The mixture of dismay, outrage and cynicism that greeted disclosure of the identities of the Susurluk protagonists may have been ingenuous, designed to create surprise at the revelation that the forces of evil and disintegration had somehow wormed their way into the inner sanctum of the secular state. A more tenable hypothesis suggests that these very forces have been a key component of the Turkish Republic since its inception, an integral and essential part of the heritage of the Young Turk movement of which the current regime is the continuation.

The ideology of Pan-Turkism, as Hugh Poulton has demonstrated, has, from the beginning, been one of the core components of the state's identity. Under the Ottomans, the polity had been an Islamic one. As Islam distinguishes only between believers and non-believers, Christians and Jews were viewed as people of the Book whose status, though inferior to Muslims, was protected. There was no reason for and indeed no possibility of discrimination because of ethnicity. Ethnicity, in fact, is a social and ideological construct peculiar to a later age, and has little relevance in understanding the Ottoman *millet* system.

Whatever the origins of the system—some say it began with the appointment by Mehmet the Conqueror of Patriarch Gennadios as leader of the defeated Byzantines in 1453—the *millet* principle gained acceptance. These self-administering entities paid taxes and tribute to the Sultan, and managed community affairs with near-complete autonomy. Yet they contained a fatal flaw. Later, as a crude kind of proto-nation, they were to prove "ideally suited to the transmission of the new creed of nationalism penetrating from the West."[102]

The *Tanzimat* reforms, which reflected Ottoman concern that it was being left behind in the battle for imperial supremacy, speeded the process of the penetration of nationalist ideas, as the *millets* acquired nominal equality with the empire's predominantly Muslim population. The ostensible aim had been to create an Ottoman supra-nationality. Instead, the reforms touched off an unstoppable process of national retrenchment among the Greeks, Jews and Armenians whose participation in the affairs of state had been instrumental to the empire's power and prosperity. The same highly communicable nationalist virus rapidly penetrated Muslim consciousness, stung by arguments that its religion was a factor in the backwardness of the once-feared and puissant state.

Influenced by the Young Ottomans, Sultan Abdülhamid, at the same time he was promoting panislamic solidarity, made compulsory the use of demotic Turkish—and not Osmanli, the language of the imperial court with its expressive and sophisticated combination of Turkish, Arabic and Persian—in the schools. By the end of the nineteenth century, there were "three apparently exclusive principles being articulated: Ottomanism, Islamism and Turkism."[103]

These three principles, or ideological strains, found their fullest expression in the person of Enver Pasha, one of the members of the

Young Turk triumvirate of Enver, Talaat and Cemal, that seized power in the constitutional revolution of 1909, lost it during the Balkan Wars, only to regain it on the eve of the First World War, at which time it negotiated the Empire's alliance with Germany. Anxious to emulate the Europeans, the Young Turk authorities had set up a Boy Scout movement. Its emblem was the gray wolf, the mythical beast that, in Pan-Turkic mythology, had led the Turkish tribes out of Central Asia. [104] Later, under the Republic, the emblem appeared on stamps and bank notes, finally coming to rest with the contemporary heirs of Enver Pasha, the followers of Colonel Alparslan Türkes, whose mourners also mourned Abdullah Çatli, the slayer of leftists and Armenian terrorists, as they waved their hands in the "gray wolf" sign, first and fourth fingers extended, second and third pressed against an extended thumb.

Türkes had been one of the group of three dozen second rank army officers who called themselves the National Unity Council that overthrew Turkey's first democratically-elected government in 1960. He had read the notorious radio declaration that, on March 27, rang down the curtain on the career and life of Adnan Menderes, the "democratic dictator" whom the plotters saw as an obstacle to financial reform and rapid industrialization. They may also have considered Menderes to be "soft on Islam." Türkes and his followers on the NUC, argues Poulton, could not be described as radical nationalists when they were nudged aside by the generals who took over the military regime. "Things were different when they returned from their various exiles in the mid-1960s." [105]

From there, he went on to found the Nationalist Movement Party in 1969, and rose rapidly to the rank of deputy prime minister in the government of Prime Minister Suleiman Demirel, now president of Turkey. At the same time, he directed the paramilitary hit squads that were involved in violent fighting in the streets. There was a widespread belief that Türkes was attempting to create chaos, which would lead to martial law, direct military rule, and establishment of a fascist regime. He may have been emboldened by the initiative of the Greek colonels' junta several years earlier, which proved that the United States' NATO allies need not demonstrate any particular commitment to democracy. Part of the strategy worked; the army took over direct rule in 1980. Türkeş' leadership ambitions were thwarted, but the hyper-nationalist ideology he and his followers embodied was well entrenched deep in the military establishment.

* * *

SUCH WAS THE DILEMMA of the triumvirate of Enver, Talaat and Cemal when the First World War broke out in August, 1914. The Ottoman dynasty began its brilliant career as an army looking for a state. Now, as the lights were going off all over Europe, the trio were faced with an ineluctable conclusion: they ruled over a state whose army had all but ceased to exist. They reacted in two ways. First they concluded a pact with imperial Germany, the leader of the Central Powers. Since the early years of the century, Berlin had been extending its interests eastward—echoing imperial Austria's "Drang nach Osten"—along the trajectory of the Baghdad Railway, which was to link the German capital via Istanbul to Basra, where the Tigris and the Euphrates enter the Persian Gulf, nearly 4,000 kilometers to the southeast.

The reopening, along rails of steel made in the Ruhr, of the ancient overland trade routes that had linked Europe and Asia, under the impetus of the commercial revolution that shook late nineteenth-century Europe, not only expanded commerce; it heightened international rivalry. As the purchase of the Suez Canal had led to the consolidation of the British empire in the Middle East, and the completion of the Trans-Siberian Railway to war between Russia and Japan, the Baghdad Railway quickly became a bitter apple of international discord. [106] This discord would become one of the causes of the first great world conflict, in which the disintegrating Ottoman state was the prize.

From the Ottoman viewpoint, the tragedy of the Balkan Wars, and particularly the loss of Macedonia, following on that of Tripolitania and Albania, had driven home to Istanbul that the Entente Powers had only one, overweening design: to chew, swallow and digest the moribund empire—or, in the more modern idiom, to administer euthanasia to the "sick man of Europe."

For the desperate men who ruled the empire, there were other, equally excellent reasons for signing a mortgage with German capitalists. Germany, unlike Great Britain, France and Russia, was untainted by colonial adventures in the Middle East; it oppressed no Muslims and had every reason to provide support and succor to Sultan Abdülhamid's pan-Islamist revival program. In fact, Kaiser Wilhelm II had visited Istanbul, then Palestine and Syria, in 1898, where he offered pledges that "the German emperor will ever be their friend." [107] Germany's own imperial interests would have been well served by an eventual Islamic revolt against domination by the colonizing European Powers, France, England and Russia. [108]

At first blush, the Young Turk revolution and the fall of Sultan Abdülhamid hardly seemed to favor German imperial ambitions. Most of the members of the Committee of Union and Progress had been educated in France or England; there was little Teutonic steel in the slogan of "Liberté, égalité, fraternité, justice" that had rung from the balcony of Liberty Square in Salonica in July, 1908. The 1903 concession that established the railway had never even been published in Turkey. The nationalist reformers of the CUP were little inclined to tolerate restrictions on national sovereignty. As disintegration of the empire accelerated, Turkish nationalism and pan-Islamism found new life as political forces. But neither of these forces held the slightest menace for Germany, whose imperial interests favored a strong, not a weak, Ottoman state.

In the fashion typical of the diplomatic trade, the competing Great Powers talked peace as they prepared for war. As the fateful days of August 1914 drew near, Germany and England had all but concluded a comprehensive agreement covering not only the Baghdad Railway, but the assurance of British control over the oil fields of Mesopotamia. While the diplomats quibbled over concessions, however, the military strategists schemed and the armament factories hummed. As the European diplomatic system of balancing the conflicting interests of the Powers at the expense of everyone else—a situation that eerily recalls the rush to globalization under a single rogue superpower at the end of the twentieth century—began to fall apart, the rush for military alliances began. In October, 1913, General Liman von Sanders arrived in Istanbul at the head of a German military mission. Its task: to rebuild the Ottoman forces. At last, Enver Pasha, the self-styled military genius of the Young Turk triumvirate, would have his army.

The second prong of the Young Turk strategy was to resuscitate dormant pan-Islamism. In this enterprise, Said Nursi was to play a prominent role. On his first trip to Istanbul in 1896, the fiery young mollah from Kurdistan had made friends with the son of the Imperial Falconer. That man, Esref Sencer Kuscubasi, was to become the founder and head of the *Teskilat-i Mahsusa*, the shadowy organization whose principal task was to gather intelligence for the cause of Islamic unity, while opposing Abdülhamid's policies of repression. When Abdülhamid was deposed, his successor Mehmet Reshad transformed it into the empire's principle security agency. And when hostilities broke out, the Sultan not only appointed Enver Pasha as Minister of War, he also named him commander of the Special Organization. [109]

Three days after they joined the war, in November 1914, alongside the Central Powers, the Ottomans proclaimed *jihad*. Under the banner of the Caliphate, Muslims were summoned to battle to rid the Islamic lands of their imperialist occupiers. It was understood that the designated imperialist occupiers were France and England, both of whom had already established direct control over huge expanses of the empire and were ravenous for more. Germany, a benevolent European power, was seen as a friend.

Five men drafted the *fetva* that announced *jihad*: the first was the Sheikhu'l-Islam, the empire's supreme religious authority; the fifth was Bediuzzaman Said Nursi. While the proclamation was rapidly distributed throughout the Empire, its diffusion throughout the territories under British or French colonial rule was an entirely different matter. The task fell to the Special Organization, and to the empire's new-found allies, who "printed in Germany millions of copies of the proclamation in all the myriad languages of the Muslim lands."[110]

The proclamation had little effect, according to British historian Alan Palmer, who argues that it provided London with an ideal pretext to sever the remaining constitutional links between Istanbul and Cairo and declare a protectorate. But the timing of the British move may have had less to do with the *jihad fetva* and more with pre-planned imperial maneuvering. Cyprus had been formally annexed on the day that the Ottoman state joined the war on the side of the Central Powers, as had been Kuwait.[111]

The call to *jihad* gained an audience only in Libya, where the militant Sanusi brotherhood stood as a bulwark against colonialism and westernization. The proclamation's failure to mobilize the Muslim masses may have had something to do with the growing fixation on Turkish nationalism by the Young Turk overlords of the Empire. Bluntly put, the Young Turks were seen by many of their subjects as hypocritical manipulators who did not hesitate to rely on a Christian power to summon the faithful to struggle against other Christian powers.

Nowhere was this mentality more in evidence than in the episode of the *Göben* and the *Breslau*, two state-of-the-art German dreadnoughts which, having evaded the Royal Navy in an epic high-seas pursuit eastward from the straits of Messina, entered the Dardanelles on August 10, 1914. Two days later, the two warships dropped anchor in the Bosphorus and ran up Turkish pennants: they had been "purchased" from Germany, along with captain and crew, by the Ottoman government. In October, though, without the permission of their putative owners, the two battle cruisers bombarded the Russian ports of Odessa and Sebastopol, establishing German naval supremacy in the Black Sea. A week later the Empire entered the war, and King George V informed the Russian ambassador that "Constantinople must be yours," knowing full well that Russia's capacity to realize its desire had been crippled.[112]

But the depth of foolhardiness and desperation to which the Ottomans had sunk in the pursuit of their objectives was embodied in Said Nursi's audacious—and reckless—journey by German submarine from Antalya to Libya in the spring of 1915. In November, 1998, I stumbled upon the genesis of this daring episode of armed propaganda deep behind enemy lines when, traveling southeast from Diyarbakir, I visited the city of Mardin, the eagle's nest that overlooks the Syrian plain.

# IX

## City of Black

FROM VAN TO DIYARBAKIR the road winds down the southern flank of the Taurus escarpment, through wild, boulder-choked gorges and across late-autumn hillsides where black volcanic rock formations loom like phantom fortresses against the darkening sky. The bus, a gleaming Mercedes behemoth dubbed "Boing 999," and displaying a "Hilton" five star logo on its flank, lacks both the speed of a Boeing and the imagined luxury of a Hilton. Perhaps our vehicle is more powerful, newer, or carries a lighter load. Each time we manage to ease past the upstarts who dare to race us full out down the twisting, two-lane road, diesel engine whining and driver bent over the steering wheel, the passengers exhale as one with an audible "Allah-u Akbar."

Lest we forget that we are in the heart of the Special Emergency Rule Zone, there are seven roadblock-cum-checkpoints on this particular 300-kilometer stretch. At each one we must all clamber from the bus, show our papers and open our luggage to soldiers, gendarmes or police constables whose sullen faces perfectly match their limitless power over our transitory presence, and indeed, over all those who inhabit this in-turned, rebellious land. We are passing through the historic heart of Turkish Kurdistan. Spelled out in huge letters with whitewashed rock high up on mountainsides is the perpetual favorite quote from Atatürk: "I am proud to be a Turk," a reminder to the Kurds, as my hosts in Van had repeatedly taken pains to remind me, that the inscriptions made them, no PKK sympathizers, outcasts in their own land.

West of the Van Gölü rail ferry terminus at Tatvan, we enter the craggy hills that lie around Bitlis where, an hour later, the bus pulls up in the city centre and waits. Bitlis, at the foot of the steep cliffs crowned by the crenelated battlements of a Byzantine citadel, combines a location of high visual drama with the gritty, workaday atmosphere of an open-air bazaar. The sidewalks teem with Kurdish mountaineers in their traditional red-checked scarves; the women are dressed in baggy, brightly colored pantaloons and extravagant floral kerchiefs. Around the immobilized hulk of the Boing Hilton, vehicle traffic swirls and eddies with honking horns and impatient, vaguely threatening gestures. This, I knew, was one of the places in Anatolia most closely connected with Said Nursi's early career, first as a student, then as fighter for Islam and the Empire.

It was in Bitlis, we will remember, that Said first made his mark as an ambitious young mollah by challenging the authority of the provincial sheikhs whose word was religious law in these wild mountains. The fiery-eyed, wild souled young mountaineer from Nurs had the innate talent of the provocateur in his struggle to engage the attention of the powerful. His encounter with Ömer Pasha, the provincial governor, was no exception. Not long after Said had arrived in Bitlis, the Pasha's affection for the forbidden pleasures of drink reached his ears. In righteous anger he strode into the governor's offices at the Konak and, interrupting Ömer and his drinking companions as they were lifting their cups, admonished them for defying the Islamic strictures against alcohol. Under normal circumstances, the penalty for such lèse-majesté would have been summary execution: justice on the Ottoman frontier was rough, and greenhorn mountain mollahs were not expected to barge into the drinking sessions of the powerful and wag at them the finger of rebuke.

But Ömer Pasha, as Mustafa Pasha had been years earlier at Cizre, was sensitive to the influence of the local *ulama*, and restrained himself. Two hours later he sent policemen to summon Said, though not as a captive. Rising to his feet when Said entered his office, he promptly appointed the audacious young man his spiritual guide. [113] Said was to spend two years in Bitlis, living at the governor's mansion while he perfected his mastery of Islamic science. Whether or not Ömer held to his vow to cease drinking is unknown.

There too he faced the temptations of the flesh, in the form of the governor's nubile daughters. The situation was a delicate one: a young, vigorous, energetic and preternaturally charismatic religious prodigy—he had not yet been named "Wonder of the Age"—residing in the midst of six young ladies, three of whom were of marriageable age. In the town, tongues, perhaps jealous of Said's growing stature and influence over the governor, quickly began to wag. But their wagging was wasted. The devout young lodger refused the Pasha's daughters entry into his room and barely spoke to them. Later, he was to tell a visiting scholar that he could not tell the three older daughters apart, so intense was his concern for preserving the dignity of learning. [114] The incident—more properly, the total lack of incident—set the tone for a pattern of relations with women that was to last a lifetime. Said Nursi lived and died in fierce and determined celibacy, ill tolerating the proximity of the opposite sex. While later they would be drawn to his teaching and to his powerful personality women remained, if not peripheral to his vision—for the Qur'an draws no distinctions between the humanity of women and that of men—distant from the field of that vision. The Nur movement, constructed in the image of its founder, is a masculine universe. In my peregrinations through far Anatolia I had heard not a single woman's voice within the confines of the movement. Only when I returned to Istanbul was I able to meet and speak with a group of women affiliated with the community.

\* \* \*

As BEDIUZZAMAN'S Felt Hats fell back with the main army after the Ottoman defeat at Pasinler and the exodus from Van, they took up defensive positions in and around Bitlis. It was February, 1916, and the snow lay heavy on the mountains and in the deep gorges at the apex of which lies the town. As the ragged Ottoman forces took up defensive positions dominating the northern approaches, the civilian population was evacuated. But Armenian irregulars seized higher ground, and began to rake the defenders with machine gun fire.

Their blood fury was understandable. In 1915, as the Ottomans cracked down on the country's restive and increasingly rebellious Armenian minority, what most historians today identify as mass killings and deportations had spread to Bitlis. In June, 1915, many of the town's leading Armenian citizens were arrested and shot, the remainder were driven south toward Mesopotamia to join hundreds of thousands of other deportees. Sources sympathetic to the Armenian cause speak of 15,000 deaths in Bitlis alone.[115] Predictably, though, no mention of death and destruction among the Muslim population is available in these sources which in their single-mindedness, in the exquisite frisson of hapless victimhood, fail to see the explosive complexity of human conflict.

Demoralized, cold and desperate, the regular army broke and ran. Again. Said's volunteers, as was their custom, held on in a bitter rear-guard action, finally engaging the Russian cavalry in the snow-filled streets. The fighting was hand-to-hand, house to house. Wounded by bullets, one leg broken, Said was helped by four surviving companions into an underground culvert where they hid from the victorious Russians for 36 hours. Finally, weakened by hunger and loss of blood, they surrendered. After being interrogated, his broken leg in a plaster cast, Said was evacuated via Van and on to Russia, where he was to spend nearly two years in a makeshift prison at Kostroma, on the northernmost bend of the Volga.

\* \* \*

AT THE SIIRT JUNCTION, the intercity behemoths pull up at a roadside shrine to a local saint. Pilgrims bustle about in the cool evening air. Groups of women, headscarves tightly drawn, jostle at the main entrance while bearded theology students stroll back and forth, plastic soft-drink bottles under their arms, immersed in disputation. Entire families are picnicking, lounging on blankets spread out on the dirt. Beggars and ambulant vendors hawking sesame rolls, chewing-gum, soda and devotional objects work each newly arrived bus. The passengers shoulder their way past them to make a direct line for the toilets. Around the square, fruit stands and stalls sell roasted seeds, chick-peas, popcorn and grape-must taffy. Through the clouds of diesel fumes I catch the whiff of rose water and sanctity.

An hour, and two police checkpoints later, we pull up at Silvan. Here, in the town where "unknown assailants" had recently gunned down in broad daylight in front of a group of police officers a doctor who had dared express sympathy for the Kurdish cause, the electricity has failed. Acetylene lamps cast a stark, cadaverous glare onto the pavement. As the passengers stroll up and down in the darkness, two squeegee-wielding boys scarcely tall enough to reach the headlights swab road dust and crushed insects from the bus' windshield.

"When you arrive in Diyarbakir, call," were my instructions from Professor R. Within a half hour of phoning, I have been contacted by three men from the local Nur community. Several minutes later I am chatting with the unofficial welcoming committee over tea in an alcove of the Büyük Kervansaray, the restored sixteenth-century caravan stop that would be my lodging for the night. One of the three is an intense, inquisitive man connected by marriage to a high official of the state-run Water and Irrigation Authority. After an exchange of pleasantries, I outline my program. Of course, I hoped to meet members of the community. Even more, I wished to tour this ancient city of black basalt and, if possible, the hilltop town of Mardin, 50 kilometers to the southeast.

"We will arrange everything," they promise. "Tomorrow, someone will come to pick you up."

Next morning, to bright sunlight, I step out into the colonnaded passageway that overlooks the inner courtyard. The tendrils of climbing vines snake across the porous black stone walls, and in the garden beneath me a fountain tinkles amidst beds of roses. The paving stones of the court have been hosed down, and now they glisten with a black sheen in the oblique early morning light.

The further one travels from Istanbul, the better the bread. Breakfast in Diyarbakir only confirmed this fundamental law of Turkish existence. Fresh from the oven, breathing sweet steam beneath a crisp yet chewy crust, the small rectangular loaves with their yeasty, complex alveolar structure are the perfect foil for soft white cheese and tangy olives, or for butter and honey. Breakfast ended, feeling not far removed from euphoria, I lounge in the courtyard listening to the intense warbling of the resident birds, while I await my hosts for the day. Instead of last night's delegation, a man of medium height wearing a blue rayon shirt strides through the entrance and, with a broad smile, comes up to me.

"I am Ferhat S.," he introduces himself. "I am specialist in diseases of the nervous system." Dr. S., I would later learn, is a physician of high repute, whose large non-paying practice sets him apart in a venal trade where the patient's ability to pay determines the quality of treatment, or even its availability. After a call on the relative of one of the men I'd met the previous evening at the Water Authority, I follow the advice of my hosts and check out of the hotel. "You will take a room in the WA guest house," they say with a smile.

In southeastern Anatolia, the Water Authority ranks close to the army in the prestige that flows from the omniscience of the state. The walls of the guest house are lined with immense photographs depicting construction of the Greater Anatolia Project (GAP), the series of irrigation and hydro dams that, when completed, will cause the arid land to bloom and transform the poorest, most backward region of the country into a fertile garden producing cash crops, fruits and vegetables year round. Such, at least, is the plan.

(GAP will also control the headwaters of the Tigris and Euphrates, the two rivers that since antiquity have irrigated the bread-basket of Mesopotamia, now divided between the states currently known, with all the ephemeral certainty of the information age, as Syria and Iraq. Ankara has assured its two downstream neighbors that the flow will not be interrupted, but it is lost on no one that the complex of dams and reservoirs gives Turkey the power to turn off the tap at will, and, fear Baghdad and Damascus, to use water as an instrument of diplomacy. )

By the time we've made the rounds of the Water Authority, the lunch hour is upon us. This is not Istanbul: the pace is slower, more relaxed. As the doctor and I stroll back toward the guest house, I notice a table poised on the lawn beneath the boughs of a pine tree. Taking me by the elbow, he guides me toward it. The table, I see, is laden with salads and pilaf. Uncle and cousin soon join us, and a WA waiter brings bowls of soup. Diyarbakir traffic hums in the distance, but in this oasis of greenery with its alfresco luncheon centerpiece, birdsong alone impinges on conversation. "We are Kurds," my hosts assure me, placing hands to heart in the time-honored gesture of sincerity, "but we and the Turks are brothers. This is our religious belief. We are followers of Said Nursi; he teaches us that this is the road we must follow."

Had the founder of the Turkish state only followed the advice given to him by Bediuzzaman, how different would have been the outcome. But he did not, or, for reasons unknown to this day, would not.

Southeastern Turkey is crisscrossed, both figuratively and literally, by paths not taken. Since the founding of the Republic, the region has been wracked by three violent Kurdish uprisings. The latest, led by Abdullah Öcalan's PKK, has been unique, not in its brutal intensity, but in its sophistication and resilience. But it by no means exhausts the spectrum of Kurdish consciousness. Turkey's tragedy—and its shame—has been its rulers' refusal to accept that the exacerbated national sentiments of those quintessential non-beings and semi-citizens, the Kurds, are little more than a reflection of the dominant national dogma, a bitter negation of the slogans emblazoned across the mountainsides of Kurdistan like scar tissue from the mark of a red-hot iron on a forehead. In the unitary, totalitarian, national security state founded by Atatürk and perpetuated by his heirs in the military institution, the faculty of definition flows not from the free exercise of citizenship, a quaint Western concept applicable only in the prosperous capitalist heartland, and then only in the breech, lest it impede the flow of commerce. It derives from coercion, manipulation and brute force, the time-honored tools of human relationships.

As lunch beneath the trees slides into a free-ranging discussion that stretches into the golden light of the afternoon, I begin to appreciate how far these religious Kurds are prepared to go to preserve peace between the two communities. And how profoundly their sense of identity obeys not the nationalist, but the religious imperative.

The late November afternoon is already well advanced, and we are awash in tea, when Dr. S. and I finally climb into his car for a tour of the sights and sounds of the city of black basalt, punctuated by shorts visits to the mosques for his afternoon and evening prayers.

Everything is black in Diyarbakir, goes the proverb: the city's walls, its dogs and the hearts of its citizens. In the centre of the old town, we inspect the ruins of the Armenian cathedral, built too from the same black stone. It would have been destroyed in 1915, when the city had become an "inferno of torture and murder."[116] The roofless nave is clogged with matted straw, and shards of glass gleam among the heaps of dusty rubble. Inscriptions in Armenian survive above the main portal, now barred with a locked wooden gate.

A Kurdish refugee family has made the ruins of what must have been the presbytery their home. We follow a young mother down an alleyway where, with a huge iron key she unlocks a door. Behind her, we step into a tiny chapel, its altar and devotional statues lighted with bright-colored bulbs. This is a congregation of one, she tells Dr. S., who translates. Indeed, in the centre of the chapel, facing the altar, stands a single, wooden arm-chair. In Diyarbakir, then, at least one Armenian has survived to endure, in silence. Eventually he would die, and the last flickering candle of a community that had survived for almost two millennia would be snuffed out.

The geography of inner-city Diyarbakir is convoluted, spiraling in upon itself like a chambered nautilus. We make our way toward the centre, through narrow lanes between high black walls, catching glimpses of courtyards or rectangular minarets that reveal the presence of a mosque. Then, unexpectedly, we stand at the apex, the bazaar, where traders haggle unhurriedly, squatting around their cups of tea, and artisans fashion the objects of daily necessity, as if industrialized mass-production were nothing but an distant rumor.

Hard by the bazaar lies Diyarbakir's main mosque, built like everything else, of dark volcanic stone. Modeled on the great Umayyad mosque of Damascus, the Diyarbakir version boasts two fountains for ritual ablutions, one for the majority Sunni Muslims who follow the Hanafi school of religious jurisprudence, the other for those who follow the Shafi'i school, most of whose adherents, as was Said Nursi, are Kurds. This school claimed to have found the golden mean between the tolerance of the majority Hanafi'ite dispensation and the narrow rigidity of the Malikite school of Medina. Its founder, Mohammad ibn-Idris al-Shafi'i, developed the theological expedient of *ijma*—deference to public opinion—which enabled Shafi'i theoreticians to adapt their institutions and beliefs to a changing world. But like the Hanafi school, the Shafi'i rite sealed closed the door of *ijtihad*, the further interpretation of the Qur'an and the sunnah, judged to be immutable. [117]

Early darkness is creeping up from the stones of the city as we wind our way down another alley, then turn through an unmarked doorway and into a courtyard. Where few linger in the vast public spaces of the main mosque, here several bearded men wearing knit skullcaps are seated around a fountain on low stools sipping tea. Insulated from the hum of the city, we hear only the tinkle of falling water and the gurgle of turtle doves preening their feathers at the foot of a small tree in one corner. We've stepped into a *tekke*, a Sufi house of prayer, Dr. S. whispers, run by a branch of the Naqshbandi dervishes—the very order whose sheikhs once ranged the mountains of Kurdistan preaching submission only to God and resistance to irreligion, and had been Said Nursi's first teachers.

The *tekke* had arisen as an institution in the earliest years of Islam, in reaction to the ostentatious wealth and corruption of the Umayyad caliphs who ruled their far-flung empire from Damascus. In the first decades of the Islamic upsurge, under the Rightly Guided Caliphs, participation in the community's institutions had led toward God. But this direction was rapidly reversed as the ruling dynasty sank ever deeper into self-worship and the inevitable corruption of wealth. The *tekke*—a place of worship, contemplation and assembly—was devised by the first dervishes as a haven of refuge from the hypocrisy and venality of the world,[118] and later, in the hands of orders like the Naqshbandis, as nodes of resistance— passive or active—against worldly injustice.

The *tekke*, too, was the place of initiation, where the young postulant, called the *murid*, would undergo the three-day ordeal of endurance, known as the *chila*, under the spiritual supervision of the superior, the *murshid*. To demonstrate his steadfastness and gain admission to the order, the *murid* must sit motionless, with head bowed, on an animal skin, moving only with the permission of the *murshid*. For mature *murids*, the period of trial lasted 40 days.[119] In the Sufi courtyard at Diyarbakir, in an age and a place where profession of faith involves more than common courage, existence itself may be seen by these pious men as the ordeal, one which can be expected to last a lifetime. Though he disclaimed connections with Sufi doctrine, Said Nursi's state-imposed asceticism had all the attributes of a *chila* served without a *murshid* in the great *tekke* of exile and house arrest which life had become for him.

Night has now submerged Diyarbakir, obscuring the blackness of the stones with its more opaque darkness; dim lights cast a golden haze over the Sufi compound. As Dr. S. joins several of the bearded men in a closed prayer room off the courtyard, I take a seat on one of the low stools and absorb the enveloping stillness of the place. Those who have not joined the prayer shift themselves on their seats so as not to turn their backs toward me, and smile sweetly. A dove ruffles its feathers, then flutters up into the lower branches of the tree. All is slow, deliberate, meditative, as viscous as the hour itself.

At the close of prayer the *tekke* master invites us to stay on for the evening meal. To refuse is impossible, Dr. S. advises me, *sotto voce*. Who am I to disagree? "We give food to whomever comes to us," the master explains as the doctor translates. "And if someone, a traveler or a poor man, has no place to sleep, he is our guest as well." In fact, a young man was finishing his meal as we spoke, mopping the last drops of sauce from his bowl with a chunk of bread.

As we are finishing our humble fare—a piquant meat stew laced with the region's endemic red pepper paste, potatoes and chunks of Diyarbakir bread, as white and aromatic as the city is black and dour—we notice a man making his way out of the compound with a sack made of coarse fabric slung over his shoulder. "That man is taking used clothing to a needy family," says the master. "We take in clothing that people no longer wear and distribute it to the neediest."

"There is much poverty in Diyarbakir …" I venture, as the scenes of dirty, rag-clad children rummaging in garbage heaps that we'd encountered earlier that afternoon flash through my mind. He returns my comment with an expression of bitter acknowledgment. Yet at no time on my expedition into the inner reaches of Turkish Islam was I to find anything more than passing concern at the widening chasm that separates the poor—the little girls sifting through the garbage, the five- or six-year-old boys sleeping uncovered on their pushcarts outside the bazaar, the pre-adolescents toiling in the heat and din of a pumpkin-seed roasting shop—from the wealthy with their luxury apartments, their cell-phones, their Mercedes Benzes and BMWs. As the Nur community prides itself on the total absence of racial barriers, so at its prayer meetings laborers with frayed cuffs and worn-out socks rub elbows with prosperous merchants. I can detect no sign of class discrimination, no evidence of class awareness, though neither are missing from the broader social landscape of Turkey.

* * *

RECRUITING FOR THE TASK of escorting a visiting writer to Mardin could not have been easier—or more hectic. After the evening's reading session, young volunteers clustered around me, brandishing their imaginary petitions. I had two criteria: eagerness and ability to speak English. Finally I settled on a shy eighteen-year-old high school student named Nurollah. But hovering at his elbow, another young man was shifting impatiently from one foot to the other. "Take me too" his eyes implored, before he blurted out: "I am from village near Mardin, I can help you." His infectious smile radiated enthusiasm; his name was Kemal. I could not refuse him.

Next morning, the boys are waiting for me in the vestibule of the Water Authority guest house, primed for the excursion to one of Turkey's most curious cities—a place vital in my quest to follow not only Said Nursi's geographical journey, but also his spiritual progress.

Mardin perches on the flank of a hill overlooking the Mesopotamian plain that stretches south toward Syria. Nurollah, Kemal and I step from the minibus at the terminal, into the morning coolness. A high haze covers the land, and we can see no more than a few kilometers. The one-hour run from Diyarbakir to Mardin had given me a preview of the day: on one side, the studious Nurollah; on the other, his pal Kemal, giggling compulsively, rolling his wide-set eyes and grinning with a slightly crooked mouth. In his excitement, the words came tumbling out, slipping and sliding over one another, in an effusion of stammering and lisping. Kemal reminded me of a bumbling, gamboling puppy. As other passengers looked back over their shoulders at the bizarre trio occupying the last row of seats, he would strike up animated conversation, providing them with colorfully embellished information on the foreigner (I had long since learned to recognize the Turkish words for visitor, journalist and writer). And when we sped past the turnoff to his home village, everyone in the minibus knew it. Between bursts of staccato, rapid-fire questions and cheery banter, Kemal would open up the book he'd brought along, a collection of the writings of Said Nursi, from which he would quote chapter and verse to prove a point. Here was a young man teetering on a narrow crossbeam: on one side lay the depths of piety, on the other, the abyss of sanctimoniousness. It seemed inevitable that we would fall, but which way would it be?

Now arrived, we set out to explore the town. Accustomed to the sheltered life of the *dershane*, the two boys hardly know where to begin. They may well be my guides, but in this strange town I must guide them. Praise Allah, interjects Kemal, as we locate the tourist office. It is a peculiar one, predicated on a minimalist estimate of foreign visitor traffic. Neither the secretary, a charming modern woman, nor the director who soon arrives, speak anything but Turkish. The office offers no literature, no maps, no photographs, only a crudely drawn, photocopied schematic diagram of the town's main attractions, also in Turkish. So discountenanced are Nurollah and Kemal that their first reflex is to call for help, to the local Nur establishment. The prefect is not in; they leave a message. We wait for the call. Time passes; the call never comes. Frustration growing, I tell the boys we will strike out on our own. Reluctantly, they follow.

In the manner of hill towns, Mardin has only two horizontal axes; everything else is either up or down, often in the form of ancient, broad stone staircases that wind between high walls hewn from stone as blond as that of Diyarbakir is black. And, in the manner of most hill towns, Mardin boasts a citadel, perched high atop the crags thrust up from the plain by some ancient volcanic convulsion. As we make our way upward, my two companions gasping for breath (there cannot be much physical education in the Nur dormitory curriculum), we encounter a girl in high-school uniform sashaying down hill toward the town, satchel bouncing from her rolling hips.

"Merhaba!" she greets us.

"Is this the road to the citadel?" the boys ask deferentially.

"Yep, but you can't go there. It belongs to the soldiers," she laughs, with a note of mockery in her voice (has this secularist temptress intuited my two friends' identity?), and skips off down the steep path. We pause on a weed-clogged outcropping and stare out over the panorama of Mardin beneath us: a crazy yet coherent jumble of terraced roofs interspersed with minarets that mark the location of mosques. Then we turn downhill toward the town centre.

Every Turkish town has its Ulu Camii, or main mosque. Mardin's, like that of Diyarbakir, reflects the Seljuk influence. Like the Diyarbakir mosque, it too is built of the local stone, of a dusty golden hue. Nurollah and Kemal must offer their midday prayers; I want to visit the structure for another reason. While my two boon companions pray—Nurollah briefly and unassumingly, Kemal in a loud voice with elaborate ceremony, as if somehow doubting that Allah would otherwise hear—I wait in the courtyard beneath a vine-covered bower.

When the adolescent prodigy Said Nursi arrived here fresh from his near-disastrous encounter with Mustafa Pasha in Cizre, he took up residence with a distant descendant of the Prophet Job, Sheikh Eyup Ensari, who introduced him to the leading religious luminaries of the town and showed him the sights. One day, while visiting this very Ulu Camii, Said and a companion climbed to the top of the minaret, ostensibly to take in the view. Suddenly the young mollah leaped onto the parapet and, arms extended, began to circumambulate it, twenty meters above the ground, as a crowd of horrified and excited onlookers gathered below. [120]

Mardin gave him not only the parapet of the minaret from which to flirt with immortality. The city's charged intellectual atmosphere placed in his path a man whose ideas were to shape his views on the relation between religion and politics. His name remains unknown, but the individual was a student of Jamal al-Din al-Afghani—"the Afghan"—the Iranian Pan-Islamist pamphleteer and agitator who had sojourned in India, Mecca and Cairo, where he had lent his support to Colonel Arabi's armed insurrection against the westernizing ruling dynasty. Crushed by British forces in 1882, the uprising handed Britain a long hoped-for pretext to occupy Egypt, and touched off a fire-storm of resistance to the Western incursion into the world of Islam. [121]

Al-Afghani, a Shi'ite from the city of Hamadan who concealed his origins to avoid the hostility of his Sunni admirers, had early on identified Britain as the European power most inimical to the survival and prosperity of the Muslims. At once a dedicated modernizer, who urged his coreligionists to emulate the civilized nations of the West, and a fiery proponent of Islamic unity, al-Afghani was in Tehran at the time of the Tobacco Boycott of 1891. The following year, Sultan Abdülhamid invited him to Istanbul to lend his prestige to the Porte's pan-Islamic strategy. It was never clear, nor could it have been, whether this remarkable man was espousing a doctrine grounded in religious revivalism, or whether the Islam he sought to defend was a cultural construct shaped in reaction to the invasive West. [122] The ambiguity of his legacy can be seen in the wild disparity of his legatees: Imam Khomeini in Iran, and Bediuzzaman Said Nursi in Turkey, men whose only similarity lay in the single-minded intensity of their dedication.

Al-Afghani's influence also shaped the thought of the reform minded Egyptian scholar Mohammad Abduh, who, like Ibn Khaldun and Ibn Rushd (better known as Averroes), remains popular among Orientalists for his syncretic, Western-infused view of an Islam purified of the dross of tradition and dedicated to social happiness. Muslims "should take their place culturally and scientifically alongside the nations of Europe," he wrote, a statement that Said, who styled himself an admirer of Abduh, would have had no trouble endorsing. Putting his principles into action, Abduh returned to Egypt after the crushing of the Arabi rebellion, signifying his acceptance of British rule, and later rose to the rank of Mufti. Lord Cromer, British Consul General and de facto overlord of Egypt from 1882 to 1908 described him as an "agnostic."[123]

Said's sojourn in Mardin, so brief yet so eventful, produced a second encounter, this time with a member of the Sanusi *tariqat*, a militant Sufi order founded in 1837 by the Algerian Sheikh al-Sanusi. The eponymous order existed as a congregation-state in what was then known as Tripolitania, today's Libya, with clear-cut military and political, as well as religious, goals.[124] Among those goals, which it pursued with single-minded effectiveness, was that of resistance to Western colonial encroachment in North Africa. Sanusi-led fighters spearheaded the battle against the Italian invaders when, in 1911, Italy gobbled up the south shore of the Mediterranean. These were the same indefatigable Sanusis who, in the heat of World War I, responded to the call of the Ottoman caliph, waging *jihad* on the British armies of the Middle East, aided and abetted by their old friend Said.

Kemal's seemingly endless devotions had given me time to reflect on the past, still vivid in the luminous shade of the great mosque. Now, our midday hunger assuaged by some greasy kebab washed down with a glass of *ayran* in a basement *locanta* where the flies droned lazily in the sunlight, we hire a car to drive the seven kilometers of weed-clogged hills that lie between the town and Deyrul Zafaran, the Syrian Orthodox "monastery of saffron."

The rich yellow hue of the monastery's fortress-like walls, almost ruddy in the afternoon light, stand out against the washed-out grays and yellow-browns of the autumn landscape. We climb a flight of broad stone steps and knock at the massive, embossed wooden door. What seems like interminable minutes later the door creaks open and a squinting, wizened, waxy face peers around the edge. Nurollah, our designated spokesman, explains why we have come. The man, dressed in a beadle's black robe with a pillbox hat perched atop a bald head from which dangle wispy hairs, chews on his lip briefly, then with a downward wave of the hand motions us in. He reminds me of the dried herrings one could once find in village general stores throughout the Balkans; perhaps sixty years old, he could equally have been two hundred. But he treads nimbly as he leads us through the complex, chattering as he goes. Though we are being bombarded with information, processing it proves difficult. The beadle, Nurollah whispers as we make our way under a shaded portico, speaks Mardinese, the half-Turkish, half-Arabic dialect prevalent in these parts. His words must first pass through the filter of Kemal who, all atwitter, translates into Turkish for Nurollah, who then provides me with a twice-removed version. My questions follow the reverse order.

From the bright light of early afternoon, filtered through the trees in the monastery courtyard, we plunge into the darkness of the church built, explains the beadle, more than 1,500 years ago, pre-dating Islam.

The affirmation stops the boys in their tracks. This, Nurollah whispers, is their first visit to a Christian house of worship, and already their eyes are wide as saucers at the sight of holy images, with their rough outlines, elemental colors and crudely applied gold leaf, and the richly brocaded fabrics that drape the high altar. Here the faithful of another dispensation prayed years before the followers of Mohammad, the Seal of Prophecy, carried the Qur'an out of the desert of Hijaz.

In the church, a large fresco depicts the founder of the monastery. It is more than one thousand years old, croaks the beadle. The claim seems plausible: the portrait is encrusted with what can only be the accumulated soot and grease of centuries, the deposit of countless burning tapers and the exhalate of imploring mouths, the same unmistakable patina that coats the Byzantine icons I knew so well from the tiny churches of the mountainous triangle where Greece, Macedonia and Albania meet. Surrounding it are cruder, more recent paintings of familiar Bible scenes, bearing inscriptions in Arabic. My eye is drawn to a clumsy rendition of St. George slaying the dragon, at great remove from the gem-like inner glow radiated by the masterpieces of Byzantium.

As I attempt to interpret the icons for Nurollah, Kemal and the beadle are bantering and cracking jokes in Mardinese like long-lost friends. Kemal may have a touch of the school-master, but, with his rapid-fire delivery, energy and beguiling sincerity, he generates laughter wherever he goes. Now, the dome of the church echoes with his soprano giggle, and the nasal chortling of the ancient beadle.

From the church, the beadle leads us downward into the bowels of the massive structure, first to the burial crypt that contains the marble sarcophagi of the metropolitans who founded and guided the monastic community, then to a monumental baptismal hall, where I explain the rites of immersion to my astonished friends. Through a wooden door cracked with time, we enter a storeroom where the desiccated odor of dry wood rasps our nostrils. Here are kept the carved sedan-chairs in which the bishops and metropolitans would be born on the shoulders of chanting monks along the seven kilometer path to celebrate the holy liturgy in the churches of Mardin.

The Syrian Orthodox faith, one of the doctrinal peculiarities that survive in this three-pointed twilight zone of obscure belief systems whose apex is formed by the confluence of the Turco-Syrian border and the Mediterranean, and whose two legs point respectively north east and southeast into the barren mountains of Kurdistan, is neither Orthodox nor, strictly speaking, Syrian. It owed its existence to the convoluted religious politics of Byzantium, whose earthly empire once ruled these lands. The chronicles relate that in the mid-sixth century of the Christian era, the Bedouin monarch al-Harith visited the court of Justinian I in Constantinople. Nearly two decades earlier, al-Harith had defeated the Lakhmids, the Byzantines' main contender for power in the Fertile Crescent, and been rewarded with the title of phylarch, the highest rank behind that of emperor. In these years before the advent of Islam, the Syrian Arab tribes had adopted Christianity of the Monophysite variant.

So impressed were the Byzantines by the state visit of their powerful vassal that they appointed his nominee, the Monophysite bishop of Edessa—today's Urfa—a certain Jacob Baradeus, as prelate of the Syrian Arabs. "So zealous was this Jacob in the propagation of the faith," writes Philip Hitti in his monumental *History of the Arabs*, "that the Syrian Monophysite church became known after him as Jacobite." [125]

As it surged out of the depths of the Hijaz like spiritual lava burning and purifying all in its path, Islam swept away Byzantine rule and the Hellenistic culture that had put down only the shallowest of roots amongst the townspeople, and all but none in the countryside. Worse for the Byzantine overlords, their subject peoples were semi-heretical dissidents who believed that Christ had but one nature instead of the two officially recognized by the imperial religious establishment, a doctrine which had been adopted by the Synod of Chalcedon in 451. The Emperor Heraclitus' efforts to paper over the schism failed; most Syrians remained Monophysite. [126] When the new faith arrived, with its fierce insistence on the unity of God, the formerly restive provincial populations found it easy to accept. The Jacobites, Monophysites to this day, survived the Islamic flood in their mountain-top monasteries and in the oasis towns of the high Syrian plain, places like Mardin and Urfa, the city where I would seek out the empty grave.

In the bowels of the earth beneath the monastery lies a chamber whose walls and ceiling are formed by immense carved stone blocks fitted together with mortarless precision. The crypt, the beadle tells us, with wagging finger and breathless, croaking voice, is a place of greatest antiquity, built before, long before, the monastery itself. He does not say so, but it may well be one of the sacred sites of the Sabeans, the planet worshippers whose civilization was one of the most ancient to survive into the historical age in this, the cradle of urban culture.

By the time we return to Mardin daylight is fading. We are still in Emergency Rule territory, travel after nightfall is prohibited, and I am still traveling without an authorization. As the minibus speeds toward Diyarbakir, Kemal falls silent, unable to sustain his manic energy; then his head begins to nod. Speaking for the first time in normal tones, Nurollah relates how he came to the *Risale-i Nur*, the compendium of Said Nursi's writings that forms the core curriculum of the Nur community and the driving force of the movement.

"I saw a friend reading the books. Since I respected his opinion, I asked him to lend them to me. He did, I read them, and began to ask questions," he says, describing a process that repeats itself every day, in every corner of Turkey.

"I got answers that satisfied me," he adds. "And the people I met were honest and sincere."

They could also provide a solution for the most wrenching problem faced by the majority of prospective university students: how to continue on to a higher education when, in order to do so, they were often forced to travel to the ends of the country. Far from their families and friends, they are expected to survive in circumstances of extreme deprivation that can border on poverty. Nurollah's home town, Kastamonu, in the green and fertile hills south of the Black Sea littoral, lies far indeed from black Diyarbakir. But he was assigned to university here, in this hot and arid corner of Kurdistan. The existence of the Nur *dershane* made life bearable at first, he explains, then desirable.

"Now I've made friends, and I don't think so much about my home and family," he tells me, while our companion Kemal snoozes, his head bouncing to and fro as the minibus rushes toward Diyarbakir into the enfolding November dusk.

Tomorrow, at dawn, I leave for Urfa, my penultimate destination on the sinuous trail of Said Nursi. In Diyarbakir and Mardin, I had encountered less the material traces of the man, which had grown more evanescent the closer I drew, and more the subtle strength of his legacy.

# X

## Rum Millet

IN THE ANTIQUARIAN BOOK SHOPS that line the backstreets of Beyoglu, I would spend hours rummaging among old prints, photographs, maps and postcards; a kind of helter-skelter archeology of paper, a peeling away of successive onion-skin layers of the past. There, one rainy autumn afternoon, an image caught my eye. It was a postcard dating from the early years of the Great War, depicting the four Great Dinosaurs who, along with their empires, were soon to become extinct: Kaiser Wilhelm II of Germany, Tsar Ferdinand I of Bulgaria, Sultan Mehmet V and Kaiser Franz-Joseph of Austria-Hungary, surrounded by a steel-helmeted, square-jawed guard of honor which, in the end, availed them not a whit. Emblazoned on a scroll beneath their mustaches and medals are the words *Viribus-Unitis*—Virile Unity.

The war raised the curtain on the last act of the Ottoman tragedy, an act in which Said Nursi would be, once more, a prime protagonist.

The only empire to survive, though as naught but a hollow shell, was that still ruled by the dynasty of Osman. The arrangements were such that the new Sultan, Mehmet VI Vahideddin, pretended to rule, while the occupying powers, under the terms of the

Moudros Agreement, pretended to acknowledge his fiat. But they exercised the ultimate authority. Allied police patrolled the narrow lanes of Galata. Less than two weeks after the armistice had been concluded, an allied flotilla of 55 warships had steamed up the Dardanelles past the silent shore batteries of Gallipoli and dropped anchor in the Bosphorus off Istanbul. In blatant disregard for the armistice agreement signed in early October, four of those ships were Greek.

Conveying symbolically the new reality, Field Marshall Franchet d'Espérey, the French commander of the Army of the Orient, made a ceremonial entry into Istanbul in late November to a delirious welcome from the Greek and Armenian populations. The long-awaited signal had been given: now the parceling out of the moribund Ottoman state could begin in earnest.

Two months later, following the opening of the Paris Conference which was to seal forever the fate of the defeated empire, the same general made another triumphal entry into the City, this time astride a white charger presented to him by the notables of the Hellenic community. At a reception that night in honor of general Leonidas Paraskevopoulos, the commander of the Greek forces which had marched into Istanbul, clinging to the coattails of their French and British patrons, the president of the community raised his goblet of champagne in a solemn toast:

"Whet, O general, thine ardent blade, the brilliance and the fiery tongue—the greatest virtues of man, as once our immortal ancestors wrote—of the man in whose soul the very hands of God have deposited the sacred beliefs of the nation ..."[127]

To describe the Greeks as overconfident is to understate their *hubris*, that most poignant and persistent of the mortal weaknesses first identified by those selfsame immortal ancestors. Greek flags flew proudly from Istanbul's many Greek-owned businesses; portraits of the Greek Prime Minister Venizelos replaced those of the Sultan. Two weeks prior to Franchet d'Espérey's horseback ride, Venizelos had laid public claim to the Asia Minor littoral and for all of western and eastern Thrace, right up to the far suburbs of the capital. The Greek nationalists' pipe dream of the Great Idea, a state of "five seas and two continents," was but a signature and a brisk little pacification campaign away from realization. The Treaty of Sèvres, signed in 1920, was to fulfill their wildest dreams, and more. By establishing an independent Armenia and Kurdistan, the Treaty also whetted the dreams of those two ancient Anatolian nationalities. Little noticed in Istanbul, however, Sèvres strengthened Turkish national resolve, now running at flood tide through the hinterland to the east.

Rumors, not unfounded in the delirium of Hellenic territorial ambition, swept through the City. They spoke of reopening the great basilica of St. Sophia to the Orthodox Liturgy. Within two months, the seeds of the destruction of the *Rum Millet* had been sown. Turkish memories proved long. As the twentieth century now draws to an end, the once-proud heirs to the imperial purple of Byzantium have all but vanished.

* * *

OF ALL THE ADVENTURES of the body and of the spirit that marked the life of Said Nursi, the expedition to Libya, in its peculiar recklessness, best exemplifies the political naïveté and the daring of the man. When the *jihad fetva* was issued in 1914, the Ottoman Special Service, by then working hand in glove with German intelligence, was determined not only to distribute it among the faithful in the lands that had been lost to the Empire, but to rouse them to insurrection and armed resistance against the powers of the Entente.

The best submarines of the German navy were assigned to the task force. They would carry German and Turkish officers, including Enver Pasha's brother Nuri, and a small but select contingent of theologians led by Bediuzzaman, under the noses of the arrogant British fleet, and secretly put them ashore in Tripoli. [128]

After a night landing on the heavily indented Libyan coast near Benghazi, the raiding party with its bundles of Arabic holy war proclamations accompanied by a camel caravan bearing small arms, set out toward the interior, where the chief of the Sanusi order, Sheikh Seyyed Ahmet Sanusi, awaited them in his desert hideaway. While the Germans distributed arms to the overjoyed desert fighters, the scholars discussed, as an eyewitness later wrote, "both religious and worldly matters," and impressed their host with their eloquent Arabic. [129]

Wielding Mauser rifles, the Sanusis harassed British supply lines in western Egypt in the name of Islamic unity and solidarity with the Sultan-Caliph. But their close cooperation with the Germans, not to mention the increasingly overt Turkish nationalism of Enver Pasha, may have caused potential allies to turn away. No matter how bravely the lightly-armed Libyans fought, they were unable to turn the tide of war.

How long Said remained in Libya and where precisely he traveled is unknown. Eventually, however, he retraced his steps back across the desert, and by German submarine to Turkey, where he made his way east to Van to take up command of the Felt Hat militia in early 1915.

With the military defeat of the empire and the collapse of the Young Turk regime, Sheikh Sanusi sought refuge in Istanbul as the guest of Sultan Mehmet VI. The fiery Libyan was dispatched by the last sultan to Ankara in 1920, in an attempt to persuade Mustafa Kemal to abandon his opposition to the ruling dynasty and the institution of the Caliphate. Failing in that task, he remained in Ankara where he was appointed "General Preacher," and later traveled the southern, Arabic-speaking provinces exhorting the faithful to support Kemal's government in the national struggle. This was the very position which, in 1923, the victorious Kemal was to offer to Said Nursi, who promptly refused it. Meanwhile, in Istanbul, the defeated empire had now entered its death agony.

The collapse was as thorough as it was long in coming and—in the warm, reassuring glow of hindsight—predictable. While the Bolshevik Revolution relieved the pressure on the empire's north-eastern front, and the Ottoman armies swept into the Caucasus planting the imperial banner in places it had not been seen for three centuries, allied forces were closing in from the west and the south-east. In the Middle East, the "Arab revolt," that masterpiece of British treachery and cynicism, was sweeping northward through Egypt, Palestine and into Syria. The Arabs, gullible to the last, had believed Lawrence's promises of dominion in their own lands. Meanwhile, Mr. Sykes and Monsieur Picot had already redrawn, in secret, the boundaries of the region, guaranteeing future generations of conflict. (Sykes and Picot invented nothing, however. Their principles were those of the architects of the Bucharest conference of 1913 which divided and redivided the Balkans among the voracious mini-nationalist purifiers and their European patrons, charting the course to the First and Second World Wars and, latterly, the violent dismemberment of Yugoslavia.)

When they seized power in November, 1917, the Bolsheviks published the secret treaties. These documents revealed that Istanbul was to be incorporated into the now-defunct Russian empire. Details of the Sykes-Picot agreement gave proof of British and French designs in the region. The Balfour Declaration on the establishment in Palestine of a national home for the Jewish people added to the consternation.

Yet for all the evidence of western imperialist turpitude, the Young Turk establishment dithered, at odds with itself, paralyzed ideologically, unable to seize the strategic advantage. Enver Pasha, the supreme commander, cared little for the empire's Arab lands and—despite his support for the Libya expedition—less for its inhabitants. Turkestan, the mythical homeland of the Turks, beckoned. As British and Arab forces battled northward against stubborn resistance from troops commanded by Mustafa Kemal, Germany's ally Bulgaria crumbled, and Entente armies surged eastward across the Balkans toward Istanbul. The situation on the Eastern Front was equally grim. When, on October 1, 1918, the British marched into Damascus, the Young Turk government fell. One month later, an armistice was signed. The next day, the Young Turk triumvirate that had planned and led the empire to crushing defeat boarded a German submarine and sailed north into the

Black Sea, proceeding thence by train to Berlin where they were shown all the courtesy due to an ally in defeat.

* * *

SEVERAL MONTHS EARLIER, in June, 1918, Bediuzzaman Said Nursi had made his way back through Europe to Istanbul. In the turmoil of the October Revolution, he had escaped from his prison at Kostroma, at the far northern extremity of the Tartar lands, made his way across the river—apparently by walking on water, although it may have been late spring ice—and traveled from there to Berlin and on to Sofia with a passport issued by the German military authorities.

If the Libyan expedition exemplified Said's militant impetuousness, his Russian captivity had brought new depth to his beliefs. So, too, did his escape and return to Istanbul under German care demonstrate that he, like the Young Turk establishment whose policies he continued to support, remained convinced that Turkish-German friendship was the avenue of salvation.

But deep inside him the worm of doubt must have been gnawing. During the long dark nights of imprisonment, exile and despond, Said had despaired of his life and homeland. "I looked at my powerlessness and aloneness" he later wrote, "and my hope failed. Then, while in that state, succor arrived from the All-Wise Qur'an; my tongue said: *God is enough for us; and how excellent a guardian is He*." [130]

A transformation had begun, a turning away from political affairs, an awakening to the necessary primacy of belief over action in the world. The change was precipitated by the Ottoman defeat in 1918, and culminated seven years later in internal exile at the hands of the new republican government. On his return to Istanbul, Said refused Enver Pasha's offer of a military position, but accepted the General's offer to provide the paper—a rare commodity in a country at war—so that he could publish his Qur'anic commentary, *Signs of Miraculousness.*

Such signs, in the prosecution of day-to-day affairs, were rare. In those days of collapse and disintegration, few miracles were to be found. Though Said was appointed by the empire's supreme religious authorities to membership in the newly established Islamic Academy—the *Darül-Hikmeti'll-Islamiye*—the initiative was vitiated not only by events, but undermined by the Young Turks. Abandoned by his patrons, increasingly disenchanted with political action, he attempted to shape the fractious, impotent Academy into an instrument of resistance to the occupying powers. But such was not to be.

The centre of gravity of events had begun to shift eastward. On April 30, 1919, an imperial decree appointed Mustafa Kemal Inspector General for Anatolia. One week later, Lloyd George, Winston Churchill and Georges Clémenceau authorized a Greek landing at Izmir. Greek forces came ashore seven days thereafter, touching off a storm of outrage not only in the Aegean port city, but in Istanbul, where infuriated citizens demonstrated at the University, in front of the Bayezit Camii. As unrest wracked the City, Kemal sailed for the Black Sea port of Samsun. On the day of his departure, a British officer had spotted his name on a list of troublemakers and hastened to instruct the government to restrain the Inspector General in the capital. Too late. "The bird has flown," remarked the British military attaché. [131]

From Samsun, Mustafa Kemal made his way to Erzurum, then on to Sivas, where the National Pact of resistance was adopted. By the end of 1919, he had laid down the foundations of a parallel national government in Ankara. In Istanbul, the Islamic Academy fulminated against the debauchery of the occupation forces and chafed beneath the spineless acquiescence of the Sultan to the whims and commands of the foreign High Commissioners. A ruler of character would have decamped to Ankara to place himself at the head of the resistance. Instead, the pusillanimous religious authorities, at the Sultan's behest, proclaimed Kemal and his followers to be traitors to the *Shari'a*, as apostates who could be killed on sight. [132]

Among the few dissenting voices was that of Bediuzzaman Said Nursi, who thundered: "A *fetva* issued by a government and Sheihkhül-Islam's office in a country under enemy occupation and under the command and constraint of the British, is defective and should not be heeded. [ ... ] The *fetva* could have been issued after judgment had been passed on the assertions and counterclaims by a committee of politicians and *ulama* taking into account the interests of Islam. In fact, a number of things are being reversed these days. Opposites are changing their names and being substituted for each other: tyranny is being called justice; *jihad*, insurrection; and captivity, freedom." [133]

Said fulminated against the inversion of truth, but his rage was directed above all against the perfidy of the British occupiers who, at the behest of the Church of England, had asked the Istanbul *ulama* to answer six questions about Islamic doctrine. "They wanted a six-hundred word reply to the six questions. I said: 'I shall answer not with six hundred words, nor with six words, and not even with one word, but with a mouthful of spit!'" [134] But even as he did, the crisis was peaking within him. Its physical manifestation was an attack of what he termed "neurasthenia" that forced him to take leave of absence from the Islamic Academy.

His symptoms were perhaps more spiritual than physical, though the causes were rooted, inextricably, in the collapse of the state through which he had hoped to advance his vision of a revitalized Islamic commonality.

Within him the political Islamist was dying. A new vocation drawn from the religious faith of the community far removed from political structures was struggling to be born. Failure was the fertile seed bed in which it would flourish.

This redrawn persona he was to label the New Said; it would replace the Old Said of political action. From a primitive, tiny house in the hills on the Asian shore of the Bosphorus, he rejected an invitation by the authorities to set up an Islamic university with the words: "Do not call me to the world." [135] The crisis, which had begun in prison on the far bank of the Volga, culminated in 1921, precipitated by an unexpected betrayal by a close friend. It plunged him into a morass of helplessness, darkness and despair that was relieved only by a flash of illumination, the method by which he leapfrogged over the barriers of rote learning and to the essence of the Qur'an.

Natural phenomena, he had always believed, could only be explained by natural causes, as the tree produces the fruit. But in his despair he had been granted new insight. The effects—the fruit—as well as the causes—the trees—flowed from the direct, unmediated intervention of God, he now understood. Said Nursi's concentration on Final Causes, argues Serif Mardin, "was a natural outcome of the fashion in which philosophical debates had been carried out by the Ottoman intellectuals of his time. Both agnostics and conservatives had chosen biology, life and creation as the arena in which to wage the war of materialism against spiritualism." Said had fastened on biology in his refutation of materialism due to the peculiarities of the spread of Western science in the Ottoman Empire in the nineteenth century. The life sciences—biology, botany, physiology—had been incorporated early on into the program of the medical schools. Skepticism had grown as the life processes were shown to be chemical in origin. Standing the materialist argument on its head, Said turned to the processes of biology and botany as proofs of the creative forces of divinity.[136]

Concomitant with his break with materialism came a sharp critique of Western civilization which "takes as its point of support force, which manifests itself as aggression." To a culture he accused of encouraging lust and passion, that lower humans to the level of a dog, he opposed a radiant vision of Islamic civilization, founded in justice and equity, and based on "God's pleasure in place of benefit and self-interest."[137] There was a socio-economic aspect to his attack, as well. The deeper causes of the social upheavals that accompanied the apparent triumph of Western materialism could be summed up, he wrote, in two propositions: "So long as I am full, what is it to me if others die of hunger," and "You struggle and labor so that I can live in ease and comfort." The solution, he insisted, lay in the Islamic imperatives of *zakat*, the tax on wealth incumbent upon all Muslims, and the prohibition of interest.[138] Already Bediuzzaman Said Nursi had begun to swim against the raging current of westernization that would soon sweep over Turkey.

In the five years that spanned the defeat of the Young Turks, to whom he had looked as the vehicle of Islamic regeneration within the Empire, and the rise of Mustafa Kemal, upon whom he would come to look as a betrayer of the faith, Said's movements are difficult to trace. It is known that he returned to Van where his Horhor *medrese* now lay in ruins. It is also known that his mood, scarcely unaltered since his illness in Istanbul, was bleak—as if embodied in the ruins over which he strode in the city where he had spent the years that shaped his intellect and spirit.

Though he had by now all but abjured politics, the epic resistance of the Turkish nationalist forces to the British and French sponsored Greek invasion won Said's respect. At the same time, Mustafa Kemal, now firmly in charge of the new army, was aware of the fiery mollah's denunciation of the *fetva* that had branded him an apostate. A consummate manipulator of men, Kemal summoned Said to Ankara, where the national government was preparing to rule the country. After several refusals, Bediuzzaman finally yielded. In late July, 1922, on the eve of Eid al-adha, the Feast of Sacrifice, he arrived in the new capital.

Final preparations were underway for the Great Offensive that would sweep the invaders from Anatolia. Its supply lines over-extended, its morale undermined by the whisper of defeat, its ammunition in short supply, the Greek expeditionary force broke and fled across western Anatolia with the Turkish troops in hot pursuit. Converging on Izmir and other coastal cities, the erstwhile restorers of Byzantine glory fought the grim battle of despair and panic for a fingerhold on ships waiting to evacuate them. The conquering Turks exacted vengeance that was Tolstoyan in its sweep and cruelty—and no doubt motivated by the atrocities committed by the occupying forces. By the end of September, more than two thousand years of Asia Minor Hellenism lay in ruins and more than one million refugees had fled. The empire's Greek-speaking citizens had paid for the adventurist temerity and greed of the Athenian political establishment. Those of Istanbul would take longer to feel upon their skins the delayed but inevitable response to Franchet d'Epérey's white charger.

* * *

HARD BY THE VISCOUS, sewage-clogged waters of the Golden Horn languishes the enclave of Fener. Trapped on a narrow stretch of flatland between the derelict waterway that was once the heart of maritime Istanbul and the hills of the militant Islamist enclave of Fatih, Fener—Phanar, "the Lantern," in Greek—is a microdot upon which is encoded both the history of empire and that of its surviving subjects. Hidden from passers-by, and surrounded by mosques the better to delimit its otherness and its submission, the Rum Patrikhane of Istanbul bravely carries on the supermillennial tradition of the Byzantine Empire as the seat of Eastern Orthodoxy. Here resides, in circumstances sorely reduced but still glittering, as if in the reflected, burnished faint gold light of centuries, the Ecumenical Patriarch. From Fener he ministers to the spiritual needs of the world's some 250 million-strong Orthodox believers, and to those of a tiny, steadily diminishing flock of some 2,500 souls, the last surviving Greeks of Istanbul.

On a blustery winter afternoon on the eve of Ramadan, and not long before Christmas, I share the patriarchal antechambers with several local petitioners. They trade small talk about the weather, complain of being kept waiting as they might complain about a parish priest, and cluck disapprovingly about the latest attempts by the Turkish government to interfere with the administration of community institutions. Although I had hoped for an interview, and even submitted a list of questions, my audience will be a short one, whispers the head of the patriarchal library whose kind intercession has brought me this far. Two days earlier he had called to tell me: "Granddad will see you this Thursday. Can you come?"

Now, my turn come, I step into "granddad's" office. With a rustle of black vestments, the Patriarch strides forward to greet me, the gold medallion hanging from his neck gleaming. The man who sits atop the patriarchal throne, when he is not seated behind a more mundane gilded work table receiving petitioners and guests, is an ethnic Greek from the tiny Aegean island of Imbros, baptized Dimitrios Archondonis, and known throughout the Orthodox world today as Bartholomeos I.

We exchange pleasantries in Greek. His All-Holiness' voice is richly inflected and resonant, his bearing vice-regal, as befits a Lord's vicar, even in such reduced circumstances as these. His long white beard, while wispy, betrays no faintness of resolve. Behind Bartholomeos' fatherly, or should I say brotherly manner (for he is by a few months the younger of us) lies a politician's keen sense of the possible and the probable. Looming above that sense like a black curtain hangs unthinkable (and possibly ineluctable) reality.

Unless the attitude of the Ankara authorities toward their protected minority changes, he may well be the last holder of a post that had emerged as imperial Constantinople asserted its own claims to primacy as against those of the Pope of Rome. Turkish law requires that the man who would be patriarch be a citizen of the Republic, born and educated in Turkey. As the Greek Orthodox population shrinks, the pool of potential candidates for the highest office in Eastern Orthodoxy has all but dried up. Soon it will cease to exist, and with it will perish an institution that has endured in the City for more than 1,500 years.

When Mehmet II conquered the City in 1453, he had abrogated the Patriarch's worldly powers, but confirmed and enhanced his ecclesiastic prerogatives as the head of the new empire's largest protected community, henceforth to be known as the *Rum Millet*: the "Community of the Romans." Only with the demise of the Ottoman state, nearly 500 years later, was the *millet* system abolished, to be replaced by an aggressive, assimilationist Turkish nationalism that left no room for expressions of ethnic otherness.

As with all questions arising out of the drifting apart, then the schism that rent the Western and Eastern churches asunder, the precise date of foundation of the patriarchal institution is impossible to determine. As Rome slipped into cultural and political decline, the new, eastern imperial capital, Constantinople, grew in importance. Accorded "precedence of honor" by the Second Ecumenical Council of 381, the city on the Bosphorus was to become, ruled the Council, the "New Rome."

Seventy years later, the Fourth Council held at Chalcedon, confirmed in ecclesiastical terms the new political and economic reality: Constantinople had become the centre of an eastern Empire. Meanwhile, the men who held the title of archbishop of the City of Constantine had gradually begun to use the title of "Ecumenical Patriarch" with no recorded protest from the papal establishment in Rome. [139]

Were modern, secular and Westward-gazing Turkey a modern, secular and Western-oriented state, instead of an ersatz one, the dilemma of the patriarchal institution would simply not exist. Standing outside of time, central to no immediately apparent Machiavellian political strategy, the Ecumenical Patriarchate should be, Bartholomeos tells me in plangent tones, an asset to the Turkish regime.

"We are strong supporters of Turkey's admission to the European Union," he says, as I discretely lick sweet vanilla toffee from a spoon offered to me in a glass of water, a traditional offering of hospitality. The table in front of me is submerged with a tasteful though slightly lurid arrangement of fresh-cut flowers.

Look at the question of the theological seminary of Heybeli (once known as Halki), he continues. "Now there's where you should visit!" And it was as though he had said: there you will understand the creeping tragedy of our community.

I have visited the place, I interject as the Patriarch nods with approval.

It had been a cloudy Sunday in April. The eastward crossing from the steamer dock at Eminönü into the diffuse sunlight filtering through the high cloud cover had been smooth, as though steaming through a sea of yogurt. The Princes Islands stood dark against the horizon, their wooded slopes taking on contour only as the boat eased around rocky headlands to land briefly, then steam off. Once the passengers might have been prosperous Greeks, the men in Panama hats and ice-cream suits, the women in full skirts, and blouses that displayed their ample breasts to greatest effect, off for a picnic among the pine groves that overlook the inland passage across the Sea of Marmara toward the shoreline suburbs. Once arrived, they might have sung sweet ballads about the flowering almond trees. But today all were Turks, snoozing or leafing through sporting newspapers, studying the day's soccer lineups. "Çay, kahve," intoned the white-coated steward as he ambled through the passenger cabin like a walk-on in someone else's dream.

Listing slightly to port, the steamer nosed around the pine-clad north cape of Heybeli, then shuddered to a halt at the dock. From the quay, at one end of which stands a Turkish naval academy, I walked through the somnolent town, noting the rusting, padlocked gates of an Orthodox church. As the road curved inland and upward, I passed abandoned villas surrounded by jungles of tattered palms and overgrown with vines, and blocks of new holiday villas. At the top of the hill I could see my destination through the wind-sculpted pines. Turning off the road, I worked my way through the grove, feet crunching in the bed of pine-needles. Soon, the academy's buildings loomed before me, windows vacant, a faint breeze barely audible in the boughs that hung about my shoulders.

Before I could see the guard dog it had sensed my presence. As I came up to the gate the animal leaped at me, slavering and wild-eyed, barking and growling in a paroxysm of fury from behind the bars. The ruckus awakened the watchman, who sidled suspiciously up, gesturing, "what do you want" with upturned palm.

"I've come to visit from Istanbul," I say in Greek.

Surprise.

Do I detect a lessening of the dog's ire? A few more words of explanation spoken in the language of Kazantzakis and Seferis and the gate creaks open, after the watchman has lashed the dog securely to an iron post next to the guard-house. Dimitro is his name, and he is one of the last Greek Stambouliotes.

"I work here on Heybeli [he uses the Turkish name] six days a week, and once a week I go back to town to visit my family," he says.

The Academy was founded in 1848. Those had been better days. Yes, the plot by the Phanariots, the Greek merchant princes who congregated about the seat of Orthodoxy, to capture the Empire from within had foundered on the shoals of Pan-slavist perfidy, but the *Rum Millet* had preserved its strength and its influence, which reached directly into the antechambers of the Sultan. In fact, the Orthodox Church had not yet been suborned by anything so petty as Greek imperial ambition, and could claim itself the faithful shepherd of an obedient and hard-working flock. From the great school at Halki strode popes and theologians sworn to uphold and propagate Orthodoxy within the legally established confines of the *millet*.

For the last quarter century the corridors that once echoed with the voices of theological disputation have fallen silent. Dimitro leads me through the empty hulk of a building. We peer into empty classrooms and walk, with reverberating footsteps, down long dark hallways. Dust and melancholy hang in the air, undisturbed by our passage.

Though the institution survived the fall of the imperial establishment, its relations with the Republic quickly grew strained. Under the Lausanne Treaty of 1923, Greece and Turkey had exchanged populations—the first great modern experiment in ethnic cleansing. In the bilateral accords that followed, full Treaty protection was accorded to the Christian Greeks of Istanbul, Imbros and Tenedos and the Princes' Islands, including Halki, and to the Muslim Turks of Thrace. With one fell swoop, the number of candidates for the Seminary shrank, from thousands to hundreds. Still, the school continued on, until in 1974, its doors slammed shut when Turkish troops landed on Cyprus to protect the

Turkish-speaking minority there against a *coup d'état* fomented by the colonels' junta in Athens.

Not a word of Greek is to be seen in these dusty premises. Portraits and busts of Atatürk glare down from every wall and alcove, fixing the visitor with a blank and piercing gaze. "What can we do?" shrugs Dimitro. "It's the regulations."

Suddenly we hear a door slamming shut. There are two monks living here, Dimitro informs me. And the Prior, along with a small staff who look after their needs. "Sometimes the Patriarch comes for the day, to rest and meditate," he adds, as we peer into the communal dining room, where three places are set at a long refectory table. Further down the hall, sheets are heaped in a wicker laundry basket illuminated by sunlight slanting through dusty windows. It is as if we have intruded into a seventeenth-century Dutch still-life, as if the painter's brush has interrupted the creeping pace of humdrum life and brought a secret existence to a halt, capturing the imprint of hands on half-folded bed linen. Behind closed doors lurk the final survivors, removed from a world that ignores them. Perhaps they exist only in the minds of old Dimitro and his midday visitor.

The day has turned overcast and damp, with rain in the air. Below, on the forested slopes, holiday makers are playing pick-up soccer or firing up their charcoal grills for the afternoon meal. As I meander back toward the dock to catch the early afternoon steamer back to Istanbul, boys on bicycles zigzag at high speed down the streets, and horse-drawn carriages hurry through narrow lanes beneath the fresh green leaves of springtime. Heybeli yawns and stretches, indifferent to the banal tragedy unfolding up there, amidst the pine trees.

"INDEED," SAYS BARTHOLOMEOS I, "the seminary has been closed for 27 years, without any justification. Every year in this country new schools are opened for training Muslim men of religion. We are Turkish citizens. Why is it that we are deprived of the right to do the same?"

Kemalist historiography, that of the historical victors, casts the fall of the Empire and the destruction of the Caliphate as a revolutionary upheaval that brought the old order to its irrevocable end. In fact, as Hugh Poulton has demonstrated, the Ankara regime that expelled the Greek invaders and consolidated Turkey's frontiers at Lausanne, was little more than an extension of its predecessors, the Young Turks. Eighty-five percent of the Ottoman Empire's civil servants, and 93 percent of its staff officers retained their positions in the new republic.[140]

The continuity was ideological as well. Where the Empire had at first been multinational and, in the broadest sense, tolerant of its minorities, the introduction of Turkish nationalism as one of the pillars of the regime rapidly shifted the terms under which the state's subjects might seek legitimacy. As, under the Young Turks, then Atatürk, Turkishness became the dominant characteristic of the new society, the public space in which the historical *millets*—the Greek, Jewish and Armenian communities—could operate began to shrink. They were seen, not without some historical justification, as foreign, as not partaking of the newly forged national entity.

To buttress the national state, its ideologues propounded a doctrine called the Turkish History Thesis. The Turks, they claimed, were the descendants of the founders of civilizations in Iraq, Anatolia, Egypt and the Aegean. Soon it would became the official truth. An accompanying linguistic doctrine, the Sun Language Theory, asserted that as the Turkish race had shown its predominance in world history, so too did its language form the matrix of all other languages. It was an ambitious project, a synthesis of Bolshevism and Fascism, the two competing totalitarian ideologies that emerged from the ruins of World War I. For the Kemalists, Turkish nationalism would be the monolithic solution to all social, political, economic and cultural problems.[141] Turkey became a country exclusively for the Turks, as defined by a series of racial criteria reminiscent of Nazi theories. By the late

1930s, professions like law and medicine were closed to all but those who could prove their "Turkishness."

When the Second World War began, the male members of the country's Greek, Jewish and Armenian communities were mobilized and shipped off to work camps in the Anatolian interior. Though it had been Germany's ally in the First War, Turkey had declared its intention to remain neutral, which ill-pleased Hitler. Though the feared German invasion did not take place, the country plunged into a severe economic crisis fed by the need to maintain adequate forces of dissuasion near the borders. The minorities were perceived as wealthy parasites who could be made to pay. And pay they did. In November 1942, a Draconian capital tax law was enacted. The criteria that defined what each person was to pay were religion and ethnicity.

Two lists were set up: one for Muslims, the other for non-Muslims. Defaulters were deported to labor camps. [142] Though the tax was presented and justified as an extraordinary measure for extraordinary times, its effect was to further weaken the influence of the non-Turkish merchant class of Istanbul. For it was here that Greeks, Jews and Armenians still wielded economic power well beyond their numbers. Still, the tax did not entirely eliminate them.

The day of reckoning for the Greeks would come more than twenty years later, in the fall of 1955. To describe the social and political atmosphere of the time as "complex" hardly begins to exhaust the possibilities.

In Cyprus, still a colony of Great Britain, a guerrilla movement known as EOKA led by George Grivas, a former Nazi collaborator, had taken up arms in the cause of *enosis*, unification of the island with Greece. The British, argue Greek sources, recruited members of the island's Turkish minority community into a special constabulary, on the Ulster model. The Turkish minority, say Turkish sources, had long known itself to be part of the larger Turkish nation, and could only protect itself by allying with its powerful countrymen. Intercommunal fighting erupted; an international conference was convened in London.

Early in September of that year, rioting broke out in Istanbul. Historian Feroz Ahmad suggests that the demonstrations of high-school and university students may have been organized by the government to convince the London Conference that the Turkish people strongly opposed *enosis*. They may also have been, as Ahmad claims, an explosion of the pent-up social and economic tension in Turkey's cities. Whatever the cause, "the demonstrations spontaneously degenerated into a riot—the rebellion of the Istanbul 'lumpenproletariat,' the bootblacks, porters, apartment janitors and mendicants—ex-villagers barely subsisting amidst the relative luxury and wealth of the city. This mob pillaged both Greek and Turkish stores in a fit of 'merciless hostility to wealth.'"[143]

The Greeks saw matters differently. In the course of the rioting, religious institutions were vandalized, Greek-owned businesses destroyed. Angry mobs gathered in the streets outside several of Istanbul's Orthodox churches and bombarded them with stones. In Salonica, a bomb blast damaged the house in which Atatürk was born. That same day, students demonstrated in Taksim Square, then set out, accompanied by "other elements … howling like wild animals" toward those districts where most Greek stores were located, and toward the Patriarchate, smashing, burning and beating those unfortunates who happened to fall into their clutches. To cries of "Cyprus is Turkish!" they swept down through Beyoglu, and converged on Fener, where only determined action by the Turkish Armed Forces, now acting with a martial law decree, prevented mass bloodshed and the destruction of the patriarchal quarters themselves.[144]

In the end, it mattered little whether the events of September, 1955, had been intercommunal rioting or a state-sponsored pogrom. The cumulative effect of the Capital Tax law of 1942 and the smashing and burning of 13 years later had been to undermine, then destroy the fragile equilibrium established by the Lausanne Treaty. When the Turkish authorities point to the mistreatment of Greece's ill-loved and often besieged Turkish Muslim minority, their Greek counterparts are quick to riposte: "At least the Turkish minority in Greece still exists." And while, as right-thinking, liberal-minded advocates of impartial justice and unfettered human rights, we are quick to admit that the malfeasance or cruelty of one side cannot justify the same behavior on the other side, deep down we must acknowledge that our standards, and our moral indignation, are debased currency in the great counting house of rancor and retribution that is the human condition.

I left the Patriarchate feeling glum. Not, God forefend, from my meeting with Bartholomeos I, who proved courteous and attentive to a fault, even though it was late in the day, at the hour of the stifled yawn, and dozens of petitioners chafed impatiently in the anteroom. No, as I wandered homeward through the drizzle, my mind had also wandered off, toward the all-but-forgotten denizens of this place, the Phanariotes, whose ambition and cohesion had begotten a scheme—a plot, perhaps?—to resurrect the Byzantine Empire. Unlike the Greek nationalist Great Idea, the Phanariot strategy was to capture the Ottoman Empire from within. Few groups could have been better suited to the hopeless and exalted task.

Scions of the wealthy merchant class of Christian Constantinople, the Phanariotes drew their name from the new Patriarchal enclave. Encountering few obstacles, they made their way in a social, economic and political environment where "national" identity was secondary to skill, intelligence and financial acumen, and where religious qualifications were honored in the breech. While the Sultan's highest ministers must be Muslims, his physicians, interpreters and bankers might be from any of the protected *millet*, and most often were.

From the first days after the capture of the City by Mehmet II, the surviving dignitaries of Byzantium bent to the will of the conqueror, and sought ways to integrate themselves into the new regime, which they perceived as a much lesser evil than the Church of Rome. Memories of the sack of Constantinople by the Frankish mercenaries of the Fourth Crusade were still raw. The Roman schismatics were far closer to the Devil than were the new Muslim rulers, whose erudites often knew Greek, and whose philosophical inquiry drew extensively on Aristotle and the Neo-Platonists.

Once the Empire had reached the limit which it could not exceed without overextending its military and cultural supply lines, it entered into a period of consolidation and internal economic development. As it did, the European powers came to see the Sublime Porte less as an enemy, more as a customer. Economic development also brought with it the rise of a new elite class in Orthodox society: the sons of the nobility were packed off to Europe to study medicine, which rapidly developed into an Orthodox monopoly. The Sultan's physician would, after all, have the ruler's ear. [145]

The young princes who had studied in the West returned imbued with the spirit of the Enlightenment, itself drawn like a lustrous carp from the limpid waters of the classical revival sweeping Europe. Early on, argues a Greek historian, they acquired the certainty that they were the heirs to the creators of that glorious classical civilization. This certainty, in turn, conferred on them a sense of superiority, of destiny. Byzantium, they became convinced, had been the emanation of ancient Greece and Imperial Rome. [146] Now, they reasoned, it was theirs to revive.

Though they lurked, like the Patriarch's petitioners, in the antechambers of the Sultan, the Phanariotes aspired, not to a reform of the imperial edifice which would bring the Orthodox community closer to power, but to the consolidation within the Ottoman state of a new, reborn Byzantium, half Ottoman, half Greek.

By the end of the eighteenth century, the plan had foundered, like a boat wrecked on the twin shoals of the Napoleonic adventure and Russian imperial ambition. But not before, in the Ottoman Danubian provinces, a succession of enlightened Phanariotes had seized the opportunity to demonstrate in practice their lofty ambitions. There, in what is today's Romania, the Hegemons, Hospodars and Voïvodes of Moldavo-Wallachia lorded it over their rustic subjects, discoursing and rhapsodizing in pseudo-archaic Greek on the Grand Principles of the Enlightenment, translating

Molière, establishing libraries and writing novels, while they administered captive territories in the name of the Sultan, earning themselves the resentment and the grudging admiration of their Romanian vassals.

The ambitions of Catherine the Great may have caused them to compromise their ideals. In 1774, the Treaty of Kuchuk Kaynarja sealed the first defeat of Ottoman arms in the Balkans, laid bare the weakness of the once-unassailable giant. It provided guarantees of fair government and worship for the Christian population, and implied rights of protection for the Empire's Christian subjects. [147] It also brought Moldavo-Wallachia under Russian influence, and the Phanariot project into direct contact with messianic Russian pan-Slavism. Moscow, the Third Rome, yearned for Constantinople, the Second, in a swoon of imperial ambition.

A Phanariot historian dolefully concluded: "If therefore, at the time appointed by the oracles, and upon such victories of the Russians over the Ottomans and in circumstances so favorable, the Romaioi have not been delivered, it is difficult to contemplate the later recovery of the Roman empire ..." [148]

But what really scuttled the Phanariot scheme was not, as the chronicler moaned, the accumulated sins and transgressions of the rulers for which God was now punishing the Greek regents of Moldavo-Wallachia.

No, the cause lay not in the stars, but embedded in the doctrine of the Enlightenment which they had assimilated and helped diffuse. Its product had not been a Byzantine revival, but Greek nationalism, a heady blend of archaism and romantic fantasy, projected onto an ill-defined cohort of half-Albanian, garlic-chewing klephts and brigands. Within 25 years the prospect of seizing the Ottoman empire from within and reconstructing upon it a revitalized Byzantine state had given way to the siren song of the ex-nihilo creation of a new sovereign state, which would be a tiny perfect replica of the Athenian republic of Pericles. Unlike the takeover plot, the new entity would have to fight for its existence; it would have to enlist the assistance of Europe. It would not and could not live in symbiosis with Ottoman structures, but only against those structures; could not function in symbiosis with Islam but only against it. Ever resourceful, the Phanariotes abandoned their dreams of imperial grandeur, and flocked to rule the fledgling state, upon which they would imprint their mindset and which they would subdue to their oligarchic ambitions. But that is a different story.

* * *

THOUGH THE AUTHORITIES in Istanbul continued to govern nominally, the armistice that ended hostilities between the defeated Greek invaders and Mustafa Kemal's forces was signed by the Ankara regime. On November 1, 1922, the Grand National Assembly voted to abolish the Sultanate. Istanbul acquiesced. Its foreign protectors, thwarted, sat on their hands. Two weeks later, Mehmet VI, the last in the glorious lineage of Osman and Orhan, crept by night from Dolmabahçe Palace and boarded the British cruiser H.M.S. *Malaya* for the long voyage to oblivion. Three days after the Sultan had decamped, the Lausanne Conference opened. Unlike Sèvres, Turkey now came to the table with arms to bargain.

There, on the western shores of Lake Geneva, the Turkish delegation led by Mustafa Kemal's devoted lieutenant Ismet Pasha, concentrated entirely on secular, national issues. Ismet's job was to convince the delegates and plenipotentiaries of Britain, France and Italy that the new government in Ankara desired nothing more than a homogeneous Turkish state; that it wanted nothing of the Arab lands that it had ruled under the empire. His approach proved congenial to the powers. It also proved a useful bargaining chip in inducing them to relent in their demand to restore the system of Capitulations that had crippled the Ottoman state.

The mood in the new capital dismayed Bediuzzaman. He had put Istanbul behind him and come to Ankara to urge those in power to establish a government based on the Qur'an and the *Shari'a*. The Turkish forces had won their glorious victory over the Greeks and liberated their land through Divine intervention. The Great Leader Mustafa Kemal had himself invoked God's assistance. The moment was propitious, Said reasoned, to transform the infant Republic, where the spirit of consultation so dear to his heart had finally triumphed over despotism, into a centre of Islamic values and Islamic civilization, to bring about an Islamic renaissance. True to form, he had mistaken his ardent desire for reality.

"When I went to Ankara in 1922," he wrote, "the morale of the people of belief was extremely high as a result of the victory of the army of Islam over the Greeks. But I saw that an abominable current of atheism was treacherously trying to subvert, poison, and destroy their minds. 'O God,' I said. 'This monster is going to harm the pillars of belief.'" [149]

Victory had laid upon Kemal's shoulders the mantle of invincibility. Having used religion to rally the population of Anatolia to the anti-crusade, he turned upon it. Elected in 1923, a docile assembly raised hardly a peep. What opposition existed remained faint and divided. Said Nursi saw his duty as one of exhortation. Were the deputies to heed their religious duties they might turn back from the precipice. With his characteristic audacity, he published a ten-point circular to be distributed to the members of the Grand National Assembly. "Hold fast all together to the Rope of God," he enjoined them, quoting from the Qur'an, for "the present is the time of community. The collective personality of a community, which is its spirit, is firmer and more capable of carrying out the ordinances of the *Shari'a*. [ ... ] If a collective personality, the spirit of the community, is righteous, it is more brilliant and perfect [than that of an individual]. But it it is bad, it is exceedingly bad." [150]

Then, as though addressing Kemal directly, he went on: "The instrument of your victory and the body which recognizes your services are one, they are the community of believers, and in particular the lower classes who are solid Muslims ... And it is therefore incumbent upon you to act in accordance with Qur'anic injunctions." [151]

The circular earned the ire of the Mighty One, who shouted angrily at Said in full parliamentary session: "We called you here in order to benefit from your elevated ideas, but you came here and immediately started writing things about the prayers, and have caused differences amongst us."

No man to flee from a challenge, Bediuzzaman got to his feet and pointed his finger directly at Mustafa Kemal: "Pasha, pasha!" he thundered. "After belief the most elevated truth in Islam is the obligatory prayers. Those who do not perform the prayers are traitors, and the opinions of traitors are to be rejected."

With these words the mollah from Nurs had challenged the unquestioned master of the land, something no mortal did with impunity. The confrontation had laid bare the arguments which would be invoked in the suppression of Islam under the secular Republic, and which would sustain the dogged campaign of resistance waged in the name of faith by Said Nursi and his followers.

Simit sellers at the Halilürrahman Dergah, Urfa.

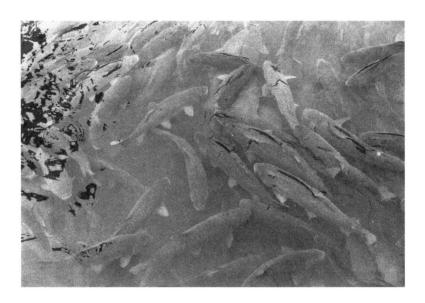

Carp in the sacred pool, Urfa.

*Photos by Fred A. Reed*

# XI

## The Fish and the Fire

WHAT IS THE TRAVELER'S CONSOLATION? A glass of cool water on a hot day. Pungent, frothy Turkish coffee at the nodding hour. Companions who need not be knowledgeable but must be sincere. A bench beneath a tree beside clear waters teeming with fish. Narrow streets that wind among ancient carved stone walls then give, abruptly, onto courtyards whose paving blocks are worn by the diagonal trajectories of men and women moving without hurry and yet with purpose. The faithful hastening to prayer.

Urfa is, at first glance, a dusty oasis town that does double duty as a burning, fiery furnace in the summer months. But its past is complex, mysterious. As the bus from Diyarbakir pulled into the Otogar, oblique afternoon sunlight filtered through a high atmospheric haze fell across the cream-colored jumble of houses that cover the hillsides like scattered building blocks, their geometric regularity broken by jutting minarets and palm trees. And when I stepped from the intercity bus onto the asphalt, the late-November air was soft and enveloping. From afar sounded the call of the *muezzin*. I knew then that Urfa was the destination I had been seeking. A gritty town that could pass in this golden hour for a corner of the heavenly garden.

Where the language barrier is greatest, the traveler's imagination is most free to wander, to impute near-prophetic profundity and sudden illumination to what might be a banal discussion about the weather or the price of eggs. By then, too, my quest for the elusive shadow of Said Nursi, who always seemed to be disappearing around the corner a few steps ahead of me, had become, by a process of intellectual and emotional osmosis, something of a pilgrimage.

Professor R., who had been monitoring my progress from Istanbul, had issued instructions for Urfa as well. I was to contact a man called Necip Bey, the local Nurcu community leader whose last name I never learned. He would see to my material comfort and spiritual well-being, the professor had assured me. At the bus station, Necip Bey's son was waiting to greet me, along with a friend, a lecturer at Harran University. "Necip Bey is busy now," they tell me with broad smiles. "You will come with us."

Several hours of daylight remained. We climbed a gentle hill, pausing to inspect a great Armenian church converted to a mosque; from the terrace, the town lay at our feet: a succession of low, rolling, sandstone hills, the citadel and, directly below us, a curious depression thick with trees in which lay a complex of religious buildings, the sacred precinct that lies at the city's core and at the heart of the legend of Urfa.

IN A TIME ANCIENT almost beyond memory, Ibrahim al-Khalil, also known as Abraham the Prophet, passed this way along the road to Canaan. The town, known then as Hourri, was ruled by Nimrod, the great Assyrian hunter king who looked with a mixture of disdain and unease upon this bold man who challenged the idols from which he drew his power and legitimacy.

We may choose to understand, as do most Western interpreters of the Qur'an, that the confrontation that was to ensue gives mythical embodiment to the struggle between monotheism and polytheism that raged among the Semitic peoples of Palestine and the Arabian Peninsula, itself a mythic overlay on the deeper conflict between the matriarchy of the region's earliest hunter-gatherer cultures and the patriarchal agriculturalists who supplanted them. In this reading, both Abraham and Nimrod are taken as archetypes. Or we may choose not to adopt the interpretive approach.

The account that follows partakes of neither the rigors of theological scholarship, nor the fragmentary discipline of archeology or anthropology, both late comers to the field. It has telescoped decades, perhaps centuries, and cast epic confrontations that may have taken place far away in this charged place. In my own defense at such license, I invoke the lesser deities of narrative coherence, but pass no judgment on the veracity of the events the Qur'an relates. Urfa, seen at this golden hour, renders credible if not the argument of literality, at least the veracity of revelatory diction which itself is all safe literality.


Spoke the Prophet from whose loins were to spring, through Isaac and Ismail, the tribes of Israel and of Arabia, forebears of the Jews and the Muslims, to Nimrod: "My Lord is He who giveth life and causeth death."

The king, to whom Allah had given the kingdom, replied: "I give life and cause death."

"Lo!" said Abraham, "Allah causeth the sun to rise in the East, so do thou cause it to come up from the West."

"Thus," comments the Qur'an, "was the disbeliever abashed." [152]

The debate now engaged, the Prophet enjoined the king to forego his idols.

Stung, Nimrod responded: "Bringest thou unto us the truth or art thou some jester?"

"Nay," Abraham retorted. "But your Lord is the Lord of the heavens and the earth, Who created them; and I am of those who testify to that. And, by Allah, I shall circumvent your idols after ye have gone away and turned your back."

Those assembled at the King's court said: "Is it thou who has done this to our gods, O Abraham?"

"He said: But this, their chief hath done it. So question them, if they can speak. [ ... ] And they were utterly confounded, and they said: Well thou knowest that these speak not. [ ... ] Fie on you and all that ye worship instead of Allah! Have ye then no sense?"

"They cried: Burn him and stand by your gods, if ye will be doing."

"We said: O fire, be coolness and peace for Abraham."[153]

Thence led to the pyre and lashed to the stake, Abraham was rescued by God, who made the king and his courtiers "the greater losers." As the fire licked at the Prophet's legs, it was suddenly transformed into cooling water. And the burning logs were transformed into fishes. From the escarpment atop which stood Nimrod's throne the water flowed down to the basin below, where it collected to form a pool, ever replenished, and where the fish thrived and multiplied, the former logs becoming glossy carp in their millions, swimming peacefully in remembrance of him who was saved.

NOW MY GUIDES AND I are strolling quietly along the cut-stone walkway that surrounds the pool of cool liquid fire. Couples meander through the colonnaded courtyards of the mosque and *medrese* complex that nestles among the plane trees and cypresses. As we walk, swift swimming schools of fish follow us, roiling with a flash of glistening scales toward the surface, eyes agleam with anticipation. We purchase a tin of special fish food and, as if sowing seed, scatter it across the surface. Suddenly the carp gather with a thrashing of water, and we see the insides of their mouths, pink and luminescent.

These precincts, which the citizens of Urfa call Gölbasi, have been impeccably restored and maintained, in stark contrast with public spaces throughout Turkey; the lawns are green and well-manicured, and even now, in late November, roses are still blooming in flower beds laid out on the gentle slopes that surround the pond and sanctuary. In the oblique light of late afternoon, the whole complex seems to glow with the luminosity of golden sandstone.

And in starker contrast with other public spaces throughout Turkey, no litter is to be seen, no beggars, bootblacks or perambulating vendors work the broad stone esplanades or the quiet, tree-shaded pathways. Voices are muffled, almost whispered; people move slowly, bending over the clear, deep water to appraise and admire the fish. Across the pool from the esplanade is the Abdürrahman Medresesi, dating from the twelfth century of the Christian era; adjoining it stands a condolence room to which mourners may repair after one of the funerals that are frequent in these parts, for to be buried in the holy precinct brings God's favor upon the deceased. Someone has died, for the courtyard is full of dark-clad men wearing expressions of grief and solicitude. Such would have been the expression on the face of the mourners who crowded this very sanctuary beneath a gentle rain on the afternoon of March 24, almost 40 years ago.

\* \* \*

NECIP BEY, the man into whose hands I had been entrusted by Professor R., seemed to shape the Urfa community of the faithful. I never ascertained what he did for a living. In his early sixties, of substantial girth and utterly unassuming appearance, he resembled some of the wealthy bazaaris I'd encountered in Iran over the years. Men with frayed cuffs and well-concealed fortunes, much more concerned with piety than with ostentation. Men who were the secular pillars of the religious establishment. He spoke no foreign language; my Turkish was fragmentary. Yet in his good-natured expansiveness he not only transmitted his sorrow at the wall of non-communication that stood between us, but contrived to make me feel, though my presence might well have importuned him, a sought-after guest. These are not small gifts, and he shared them with prodigality.

No meeting was too small, no question too insignificant for Necip Bey. He would stride confidently into a room, smiling benignly, settle at the strategic corner of the sofas that lined the walls, whence he would control the room, and, with a subtle gesture, cause the reading to begin.

Bediuzzaman, who mastered Turkish only in his early twenties, had first written in Ottoman, strongly influenced by Arabic and Persian. There is, confirms Serif Mardin, "something evocative of the Qur'an in his rhetoric. [ … ] The incantatory style of Said Nursi still plays an important part in attracting a clientele to the order. The magnetic effect of [his] arch, convoluted style and the import of what often amounts simply to ungrammatical phrases is difficult to understand for persons who come from the clerk-subsidized orthodox Muslim elite establishment, i.e., the Faculty of Divinity at Ankara. [But] the allusive and superficially obscure style of the sage has had an undeniable power in winning over disciples."[154]

At the end of a passage, the reciter would fall silent and Necip Bey would launch into a commentary, circling back to the key point, identifying the core argument, bringing to the text examples from the daily life of the community. The exegesis would be followed by another excerpt, more elucidation, then a brief prayer. Finally, the senior prefects of the *dershane* would pad through the crowded room bearing trays of tea, and for several minutes the only sound in the room would be that of spoons tinkling against the sides of glasses as sugar was stirred into the pungent red liquid.

By now I had lost track of the hour, of the date, perhaps of the year, and the place. I, like the rapt audience, had been transported to an ethereal and insubstantial realm far from the hue and cry of partisan politics and the meanness of the market place, and into a timeless brotherhood that seemed poised, like the proverbial dervish, between eternity and infinity.

The hour of the clock, however, was late.

Tomorrow I would be accompanied by Murat, an English student who was my designated interpreter. What he lacked in English skills, Murat more than compensated for in his eagerness to oblige. We both carried small dictionaries, and I had long since mastered the phrases required for asking the names of things in Turkish. We will meet in the morning for breakfast, Murat told me, repeating in the language of signs and gestures.

After the morning meal, Murat guided me along Urfa's main street. We turned left down a narrow alley lined with greengrocers and fruit stalls overflowing with mandarines, apples and tiny cucumbers, then right into a dead-end street. "Here is Ipek Palas Otel," he announced, "where Ustad died." When Said came here in the spring of 1960, the Ipek Palas was Urfa's finest, boasting contemporary conveniences and running water. Today it smells like a flophouse, the rancid air thick with ammonia. Ill-shaven, swarthy men lounge in the vestibule, smoking, playing cards and glancing idly at a television set that whines with *arabesk* music. After a word with the desk clerk, he leads us up to the second floor and along a corridor to Room 27. Every other room in the Ipek Palas has been renovated, using the meanest and flimsiest of plaster board, polyester and fast-warping plywood. As we move down the hallway I glance through half-open doors into the rooms with their sagging beds and wrinkled, yellowed sheets, tiny sinks, cracked plaster walls and stained fake-gossamer curtains. Not so Room 27, to which nothing has been done. The original wooden door remains, the original window frames. A clock on the wall has been stopped at 2:50, the hour of Bediuzzaman's death.

I flash back to the late-Ottoman rococo of the Dolmabahçe Palace in Istanbul, with its immense chandeliers, massive gilt-inlaid furniture and dusty brocaded draperies, where the hands of the clocks have all been immobilized at 9:05, the hour of Atatürk's death, on November 10, 1938.

Several months earlier, in the unlikely venue of Skopje, the capital of Macedonia, the fateful hour had once again impinged itself upon my consciousness. As part of the 75th anniversary celebrations of the Turkish Republic, the authorities had commissioned two plays. About Atatürk. One depicted the youth of the Founder; the other, entitled "9:05," his last hours on earth.

That night, this play was being performed by a group of Turkish traveling players. I had just ended a meeting with Ljubisha Georgievski, Macedonia's ranking theatrical director and former presidential candidate.

"As resident director at the National Theater, I have to attend the performance," he told me with a sigh of resignation. "Why don't you join us."

I did. From the balcony, we look on uncomprehending as actors Mr. Georgievski dismisses as little better than amateurs struggle to bring life to a recitation of the life and times of a man as amenable to the human touch as Lenin. We see Atatürk's elderly and devoted mother, his nubile wife, his obsequious subalterns, his servile yet ruthless successor Inönü, dictator in waiting, and a smattering of lesser characters from the past.

"You know, every play is also the portrait of the regime under which it is written," Georgievski said at intermission. He should know, having forged his directorial skills under the Tito regime in the former Yugoslavia.

No play entitled "2:50" has been created. As I sat cross-legged in the tiny, sunlit room at the Ipek Palas Otel, I began to understand the chasm that separated the two frozen clocks, and the deepest resonances of the hours they chimed. The true drama remains to be written but, given the realities of modern Turkey, can never be. For it would breathe life into the confrontation between the two protagonists whose epic struggle for a people's soul continues beyond the grave.

\* \* \*

LIKE MOST OASIS TOWNS, Urfa is compact and in-turning. Oh, there are peripheral concrete block bedroom communities springing up now to house the Kurds who have been driven from their mountain villages, but the life of the city is still centered on the buzzing bazaar and the quiet, tree-shaded paths of the Gölbasi. Slowly Murat and I make our way toward it, passing through the courtyard of the Ulu Camii, with its octagonal minaret that seems to be slightly tilted, austere in its Umayyad lines like its larger model at Diyarbakir, its dusky sandstone seeming to radiate from within even at the near-meridian hour indicated on an ancient sundial. As in any Islamic community, the membrane between mosque and bazaar is porous, mercantile exchange and piety flow in both directions, sustaining the fabric of the city, enforcing the inviolability of contracts sealed with a handshake, and respect for the norms of social behavior.

Small, compact, pungent, multicolored, the Urfa bazaar percolates with porters bent double under their loads, slow-moving merchants, women dressed in bright headscarves and bejeweled with brilliant baubles gesticulating with the kind of insistent hand movements that one does not encounter in Istanbul or Ankara. Their language is not Turkish either; like Mardin, Urfa boasts a prominent Arab minority. After all, the Syrian border is less than one-half hour away.

Murat leads me through dark passageways, through arched portals and around blind corners; we enter the bazaar as we would a labyrinth. In one section we examine and price kilims, in another silk scarves; down yet another corridor, copper ware. A few paces further along a smith is hammering out red-hot iron rings of the kind used to tether cattle or horses, then plunging them with a whoosh of steam into a bucket of turbid water. Around us, push-carts jockey for position. Several of them are veritable mobile toiletry emporiums, sagging beneath the weight of everything a gentleman could possibly need or desire for impeccable personal grooming: mirrors, shaving brushes and soaps, razors straight and not, tweezers and nail clippers, scissors for the unruly zone where mustache meets nostril, styptic pencils, soaps and lotions, kerchiefs and socks, tissues and colognes or tiny vials of alcohol-free scents for the pious.

Feeling mildly fatigued, we turn into the Gümrük Han, a sixteenth-century caravansary preserved intact. In the shaded courtyard, around a fountain, Turks in skullcaps, Kurds in checkered headcloths, and voluble Arabs of prosperous girth and indeterminate occupation are sipping tea, playing cards, and perusing the small merchandise being offered for sale. At a nearby table, a dark-skinned man is rearranging his display of *tasbis*, watch-bands, cigaret holders, lighters and engraved silver cigaret cases in front of him, perhaps for the tenth time today. Two tables over, an ambulant dentist is kibitzing as two prospective patients finish their hand. He has arrayed his wares at one corner: a complete set of false teeth in a plush-lined box. They can be bought as a set, or by the tooth, depending on need. Am I interested? he asks. No, I smile, as toothily as I can. In the courtyard of the Gümrük Han, the concept of interactive shopping hailed as revolutionary by the snake-oil salesmen of Internet stocks, has long been superseded. No need to visit the crowded stalls of the digital marketplace, no need to click through publicity-ridden web sites and endure recalcitrant search engines, no need to encrypt precious personal data. All you need do is sit down in the shade, order tea, and listen to the birds as they chirp and flit overhead. Everything your heart desires will come to you.

As we made our way back to the street and toward the Gölbasi, the call to prayer rang out. "Pelease excuse me," Murat smiled, inserting a vowel between the two consecutive consonants to obtain the euphony required by Turkish, and hastened into the mosque of Abraham, the largest in the complex known as the Halilürrahman Dergah which marks the Prophet's birthplace. I sat down on a bench to wait.

The Dergah is a sanctuary within a sanctuary, wedged among the plane trees beneath the cliffs that rise to the citadel on one side, and the limpid waters of the Gölbasi on the other. Perhaps because we are of feeble faith we accredit only with difficulty the legend (or truth) that worshippers flock here to attest: that this tiny grotto carved into the foot of the rocky precipice is the birthplace of the great patriarch of the Semitic tribes. Neither the Old Testament nor the Qur'an confirms Abraham's birth in this place. Such considerations cannot sway the pilgrims who congregate around the mouth of the cave, men on one side, women on the other, waiting to step inside and pray.

Murat and I enter in our turn, bending almost double beneath the low ceiling of rough-hewn stone. Through a coarse screen we look down into a recess, lighted by a dim bulb, which is reputed to be the birth chamber. At the bottom of this cleft a small electric pump whines, pumping out the accumulating seepage.

Since midday, the sky has been growing darker. In this bone-dry climate a sudden shiver of humidity wafts through the air. As we step from the cave, the sun shines through the clouds; around it has formed the halo that presages rain. Murat leads me across the courtyard, away from the throng of supplicants. Between the courtyard and the waters where the sacred carp swim stands a small rotunda whose open walls are formed of wrought-iron grill-work.

We say nothing, for this is what I had come to Urfa in search of and, having circled around it for three days, viewing it obliquely, had finally reached. Through the filigreed wrought-iron work of the barrier I look down upon a long rectangle outlined by a low enclosure of polished marble. One end, where a head had once lain, points southeast, in the direction of Mecca. At its foot stands a green potted plant.

It is the empty grave.

A marble plaque on the wall, engraved in Turkish, English and Ottoman, reads: "This is the place of Master Bediuzzaman Said Nursi (His Excellency), the author of the epistles of divine glory (*Risale-i Nur*). He died in Urfa joining his all-merciful Allah on the 23rd of March 1960. One day after his death he was buried here. But on the 12th of July 1960 some administrators of the time removed his body and buried it in an unknown area."

Murat and I linger silently, perhaps for a half hour, perhaps longer, at the shrine. As we walk away, a light rain has begun to fall. Overnight it turns to a drizzle, transforming the dust of Urfa into mud. There is a chill in the air the following morning as Necip Bey and the two university lecturers drive me south to the airport where the plane to Ankara, then Istanbul, awaits. Urfa, I believed, would be the last stop on my Anatolian journey. It was not.

The human chain demonstration, Istanbul, October, 1998.

*Courtesy of Yeni Safak*

# XII

## Of Headscarves and Mystics

A FTER NEARLY A MONTH in the Anatolian hinterland, I felt like a sailor on shore-leave when I returned to Istanbul. Around me roared the big town: streams of workers and office employees, shopkeepers and students, yuppies and traditionalists, the frantically busy, the indolent and the underemployed, the bright shiny face of Turkish modernity and its gray, gritty, clenched-tooth mirror image of frustration and resentment. Fishermen on the Galata bridge braved the slanting rain, their breath misting in the damp cold, as they waited for a nibble. Ambulant vendors were doing a brisk business in umbrellas, knit caps and mittens now, along with cold remedies and pocket-sized packages of tissue. Behind the fogged windows of cafés, pedestrians in from the cold rubbed their hands together and drank hot *sahlep* to ward off the chill of winter as it plunged down the Bosphorus like a rogue bulk carrier about to run aground on Seraglio Point.

I had some unfinished business to attend to. My pseudo-pilgrim's progress through the Nur community had revealed to me the movement's strength, breadth and resilience. And also, I thought, its vulnerability. The universe through which I'd traveled was an exclusively masculine one. Men had been my constant companions.

In this parallel constellation, women seemed to exist—if they existed at all—in a space beyond, an intergalactic black hole made up of anti-matter. They were invisible, their existence all the more troubling for not being evoked. In Van, in Diyarbakir, in Urfa, I had wondered how a community could so visibly exclude half the human species? Was the systematic separation of the sexes a function of the innate conservatism of these Turkish Muslim believers, or a peculiarity of the Nur movement, the peculiar legacy of Bediuzzaman's own relationship to the opposite sex? Was the community, despite its vehement protestations, really a contemporary *tariqat*, a late twentieth-century Sufi order that has learned to conceal itself behind the doctrine of a governing text while preserving and perpetuating an informal yet emphatically existent hierarchical system? Did the brotherhood, of which I'd seen and felt such powerful evidence, exclude sisterhood?

When I met Professor R. a few days later, I raised the question. "Because you cannot see them do not think they are not with us," came the reply. Well then, if the Nur community indeed operates a parallel structure of residences and study centers for women, could he arrange for me to visit such a place, to speak to them? To see for myself?

Several days later I found myself wedged into the passenger seat of a small car driven by one of Professor R.'s friends, on the way to Bagcilar, a middle-class suburb with bright new shops and parks that nestles as cozily as an Istanbul agglomeration can around one of the hills to the west of the city centre. There we were to visit a *dershane* run by and for young women, in this case students at several of Istanbul's universities. The difference between it and the movement's all-male establishments was palpable as soon as we stepped through the door. The premises, modestly furnished and barely decorated, gleamed with the kind of impeccable luster that no group of young men, however devout, could either imagine or produce, whatever the combination of scrubbing and devotion. Doors closed swiftly and silently at the end of the corridor as we removed our shoes.

As male visitors we presented a challenge and, perhaps, a moral dilemma. This would be the reason that I was accompanied by the father of one of the young women I was to meet; later, the father of another of the residents would join us. If I were to judge by Said Nursi's stay at the house of Ömer Pasha in Bitlis, the community would be extraordinarily sensitive to any unsupervised contact between its daughters and what, for want of a better term, we must call "strange men."

Though I was on high alert for signs of coaching or guidance by their fathers, my discussion with the young women took place directly in English which they, as members of this first generation of Islamic students up from the humble classes, had mastered, unlike their fathers. By the end of my two-hour visit, it seemed more likely that these strong-willed, articulate women would soon be coaching and guiding their fathers though, within the traditional family hierarchy, such forwardness would be unthinkable.

"I was 15 when I met friends in the movement and began to read Islamic books," explains Nuriye, a student from the Anatolian city of Sivas. "Our biggest problem is how to believe. You have to do more than pray and profess your belief. After I read Said Nursi's books I understood my belief wasn't enough. You must see the existence of God in every living creature."

From the beginning of the Nur movement, she explained, women have been drawn to its peculiar blend of fervor, removal, devotion and resistance. But the circumstances they faced in the first decades of the Turkish Republic made it all but impossible for them to function at anything more than the domestic level. It was only under the presidency of Türgut Özal that women wearing *hijab* (traditional Islamic dress that covers the hair and conceals the contours of the body) were allowed to attend university—to return, gingerly, cautiously, with infinite precaution and immense pride, to the public sphere from whence they had withdrawn or been excluded when their head-covering was, metaphorically, ripped from them by the Kemalist "reforms." Now, however, the window of opportunity opened by Özal was closing again.

It had all happened so suddenly, or so it must have seemed to the country's secularist rulers who had endorsed Özal's policies of privatization and liberalization out of fealty to their American mentors, but never accepted his recognition of the Kurdish fact, nor his rehabilitation of Islam.

Seemingly out of nowhere, women in *hijab* had flooded the streets. They were not only plump Anatolian housewives in flowery pantaloons carrying plastic shopping bags or balancing packages on their heads. They were slim, scrupulously groomed girls and young women wearing colorful headscarves and smartly-cut long coats, hurrying to class, wearing the sign of their religious identity boldly, like a flag.

With the rise of the Welfare Party, consciousness—and affirmation—of the Islamic presence burst upon the country. Entire families thronged to the public parks they had once avoided, now that outdoor consumption of alcohol had been restricted by the many religiously inclined municipal administrations. Most of all, young women in headscarves had marched into the universities as if they owned them, into the medical, engineering, fine arts and social science faculties. It was poor evidence of the old bugbear of a fundamentalist conspiracy to relegate them to a shadow world of domestic toil and polygamy. In fact, alleged the government, prodded by the military, there seemed instead to be evidence of a fundamentalist plot to overwhelm the secular institutions so dear to the heritage of Atatürk by flooding them with alert, intelligent young women who seemed invariably to earn better marks than their jean-clad, smoking, and alcohol-imbibing secular sisters. Paradoxically, what was once derided as a badge of submission and ignorance now took on all the colors of an intellectual and moral movement.

Terrified, the authorities struck back. Instructions were issued to university rectors. These men, owing their situation to the Ministry of Education, were hardly in a position to decline. Henceforth, girls wearing *hijab* as inoffensive as a headscarf were to be banned from university campuses. Then-Prime Minister Mesut Yilmaz remarked in what must be counted as one of the classics of double-speak, that freedom of conscience would be respected, but in the fight against fundamentalism no quarter would be given. The authorities, so hard-pressed to deal with secret police death squads and Mafia-connected media barons, would deal harshly with these headscarf-clad trouble-makers.

On October 11, 1998, at 11 o'clock, a human chain made up primarily of women demonstrating against the anti-*hijab* edict stretched across much of Turkey. In Istanbul alone, hundreds of thousands massed on the access roads to the Bosphorus bridge despite police efforts to stop them. The protesters used a strategy developed several decades earlier by Iran's Islamic revolutionaries in their fight against the Shah. Women in head-scarves peacefully challenged the police, who were reluctant to press the issue. After a few moments of tense negotiation, thousands of women streamed hand-in-hand onto the bridge, meeting their sisters from the Asian shore at the mid-point. It was, noted observers, the largest demonstration ever held in Turkey. Estimated participation ranged from two to six million. These same observers also noted that although women wearing headscarves were perhaps a majority of the demonstrators, they were accompanied by their husbands, brothers and children, as well as by thousands of women in western dress who felt they had a point to make about democracy.

They had been supporters of Refah, Muslim women and their friends and families intent on staking a claim to public awareness. Not the young women with whom I now spoke in the Bagcilar dormitory. A ruling by Fetullah Gülen that permitted women to discard their *hijab* if they thought it best for their careers or welfare had sown confusion. What counted? Short-term political advantage, or the eternal pleasure of God?

For Nuriye's friend Zeynep, a doctoral student in physics at Marmara University and nominally a follower of Mr. Gülen, the high oracle of Üsküdar, the debate was over before it began. "They asked us to remove our *hijab*, but we did not. Of course there is uncertainty over our future. But we believe this is a test for us. Perhaps we are not worthy of the *hijab* we wear."

It was not the first time, among the Nurcus, that the policies of the state had been, through some curious metamorphosis, transformed into an instrument of punishment or sanction seemingly moved by divine, not human, agency. It was as if the bodies of women had become the battleground upon which the primal, eternal war between belief and disbelief would be fought. So they would be, and so it would be.

"Islam," says Zeynep with a smile of assurance as her father beams, "does not offer laziness to women. Everything we do should be in the name of God."

"Does that include *hijab*?" I ask, pressing the point. A discussion in Turkish follows.

"The Prophet Mohammad, peace be upon him, ordered women to cover their bodies except for their faces and hands," Zeynep explains. In fact, no such precise injunction appears in the Qur'an, and I am about to say so when she continues.

"We understand its meaning through our interpretation of the Prophet's own life and actions. Conditions are far different, of course, so we must understand his aim."

The notion of "political Islam"—as it was expressed in the human chain—is, I'd well learned by then, anathema to the Nur movement. The authorities, runs the argument, are politicizing religion and the religious parties are falling into the trap. Not Said's followers. But I wonder, as cups of steaming tea and plates of sweets arrive, if it is legitimate to deduce rules of dress code from the example of Mohammad himself, why cannot the Prophet's clear and indubitable action in founding a state not also be interpreted in the same terms? For "Islam was not simply a spiritual community. Rather, it also became a state/empire. Islam developed as a religious-political movement in which religion was integral to state and society."[155]

Not so for Nuriye, Zeynep and the other young women I met at the Bagcilar *dershane*. Each individual, they argue with an unshakable conviction, must strive only to become a more complete believer. As these believers form families, then ever-larger social groups, a community is created. Islam will come, carried by a rising tide of exemplary individuals. Whether or not that community would then constitute a state becomes a matter of conjecture.

"Injustice will end one day," Zeynep says when I ask her what she will do if she is not permitted to continue her studies. "We're no longer bound by Turkey. The world is open to us. I am a Muslim. Nothing else."

* * *

SEVERAL DAYS LATER on a cold, rainy afternoon in a basement tea-room in the heart of Fatih, I encountered another group of young women in the company of my friend Nazim. Like him, they were students in the literature faculty at Istanbul University. Unlike him, their academic careers have now been destroyed by the government crack-down on *hijab*.

"Now I see the true face of the system," says the young lady I will call Aysel. She is slight, fine-featured, wears a tightly knotted headscarf with a floral motif, and speaks in a soft voice that barely disguises her anger.

"Before, we were studying, preparing for our working lives. Now I understand that they have drawn a line we cannot cross. I used to be tolerant, but now I realize they do not tolerate us, so I've lost my patience."

Her friend Serife (not her real name) interrupts: "The system needs democracy that doesn't conflict with its interests. It sees that Muslim ladies wearing *hijab* are in conflict with it. So they force us to leave our beliefs at home. They want to drive us from public life. What does this have to do with democracy?"

The third member of the trio, Ebru, joins in: "Now what are we to do? We cannot continue our studies, and we won't discard our *hijab*. The problem for us is that our political organizations, our youth organizations are weak, and the system is doing everything it can to weaken them more. But do not mistake our reaction for acceptance. No."

The actions of the state have been predictable. After all, what more can be said about a regime which closes what was then the largest political party in the country (Welfare/Refah), incriminates its leader, and takes punitive administrative action against women who dare to wear the overt sign of their faith? But they feel even more bitter, betrayed by Fetullah Gülen, the man who claims to stand aloof from politics while surreptitiously giving aid and comfort, they allege, to the regime. "I think Fetullah Gülen is afraid of losing his benefits," says Aysel. "He thinks that if he doesn't issue a *fetva* on *hijab* he'll lose the leadership of his community, and maybe even more in future."

"We don't want to attack him," adds Ebru. "What we don't like is his attitude. He has a position to protect; he's become a conformist."

What will you do? I ask, without leadership, without a movement, without an organization?

"Leaving school does not mean leaving education. We're hopeful that we can rescue ourselves, react to these impositions, and be successful," says Aysel, who has emerged as the catalyst and spokeswoman for the group. "If we abandon our *hijab*, we will be in conflict with our deepest beliefs."

Are there women in Turkey today you can look to as an example? A moment of silence. "With God's help, we will be those women," Aysel says. "Insh'allah," her friends nod gravely. Nowhere in our hour-long conversation over a cup of fast-cooling tea did I find the slightest reason to doubt her.

IF *HIJAB* IS A FLAG, not all Muslim women are prepared to wave it.

When a friend handed me Nuray Mert's mobile telephone number, he gave me no warning about what I would encounter. Several days later, I stepped down a short flight of stairs and into the lighting boutique in Istanbul's toney Nisantasi shopping district, the tastefully dressed, impeccably coifed woman in her mid-thirties who greeted me with a frank and vigorous handshake could have been a living advertisement for all secular Turkey claims to be: bright, well-educated, open to the wider world through her fluency in English and German. In fact, a copy of the previous week's *Guardian* airmail edition is lying atop a stack of German newspapers on her desk.

With an ironic smile, Ms. Mert defines herself as a free-lance intellectual. Not entirely by choice. "My academic colleagues could not tolerate it when I accepted Islam," she says.

My eyebrows shoot up in barely concealed astonishment. I had been prepared to meet yet another of the glib, busy secularist intellectuals who pullulate along the interface between the republican establishment and Western sensibilities. She, like them, would rattle off the usual fashionable clichés, then see me politely out. This was different. Spoken in a cozy atmosphere of designer lamps casting a subdued glow, Ms. Mert's sudden assertion thrust me into acute cognitive dissonance. From Iran to Istanbul and beyond, Islamic women have taken *hijab* as an external signifier of their adherence to the faith. Here was a woman who had not, yet still claimed her faith.

"I've committed the ultimate betrayal," she laughs again, revealing a personality that is far from adverse to provocation. "People from my background, the well-off secularist classes, are assumed to share the same ideas about religion and society. That included me. So when I told my friends and family I've become a born again Muslim, they were stunned."

"I don't wear the headscarf," she continues. "It wouldn't be possible for me to look after my sister's boutique if I did. There are zones, like this part of Istanbul, that 'Islamic' people simply cannot be seen in. *Hijab* is seen as declassé, you know."

More insidious than the February 28, 1997, *coup d'état* against the Welfare Party, worse even than the economic discrimination against the vast majority of the country's citizens, is the psychological suppression of Islam in Turkey, she continues. So pervasive is this oppression that Muslims, and even Islamist intellectuals, have internalized the dominant discourse about themselves.

(Ms. Mert would have known that the same phenomenon affects the Islamic world as a whole, where generations of intellectuals have internalized the self-serving truism that Western knowledge subsumes all other knowledge.)

"Of course, they're reacting to the elite society's response to Islam, which is really a class reaction when you get right down to it."

"But what I wear or do not wear does not change my beliefs. I'll even go out for a drink of *raki* from time to time, which irritates my more orthodox friends. But I think God will forgive me these small sins."

If we are to judge by the number of men who can be seen in smoky cafés of an afternoon or evening, knocking back tiny glasses of the milky white liquor while nibbling on bits of cheese and olives, God already has much to forgive.

* * *

THIS STORY WITHIN A STORY lies embedded in the broader history of Islam in Turkey. Alongside the dominant, law-bound (some would argue, hidebound) doctrinaire orthodoxy of the imperial Sunni establishment had flourished sects, cults, Sufi orders and heterodoxies. Some of them, like the Whirling Dervishes of Konya still exist, albeit as folkloric relics, preserved by the state like a box of frozen cultural pudding in the freezer compartments of the great global supermarket, all but voided of its religious content of radical divine love, the better to be consumed by western media celebrities in their boundless existential boredom.

Others are still alive.

Nazim and I had made our way one December night to Istanbul's western suburbs. We were late to our appointment for the *sema*, the dance and prayer ceremony of the Alevis, Turkey's religious odd men (and women) out. "Let us off here," Nizam instructed the cabbie. We had stopped several hundred meters beyond our destination. "No need for the driver to know where we're going," he explains as we trudged along the roadside past empty lots and leafless trees, heads bent against the wind-driven sleet that had begun to fall. Taxi drivers are encouraged to report suspicious passengers and their destinations to the police. Turning up a driveway, we arrive at the headquarters of the Cem Vakfi, the religious foundation that guides the Istanbul Alevi community.

Wearing no headscarf, Ruhsen Fer, a woman in her forties, paces back and forth at the entrance. A former refugee from Bulgaria, where the late and unlamented communist regime, in one final paroxysm of nationalist pathology, had attempted to force that country's Turkish minority to Bulgarize itself, Ms. Fer will explain the evening's proceedings to Nazim, who will translate for me. We hurry up the stairs to the third floor where the *sema* is about to begin.

In mosques, the worshipper's attention is focused on the *qible*, the sign of orientation toward holy Mecca. In Iran, for instance, the proper direction is indicated in all hotel rooms. Devout Muslims carry tiny compasses that determine the precise cardinal point toward which they must prostrate themselves. But here, tonight, in the Cem Vakfi *semahane*, we find ourselves in a large indoor amphitheater; the faithful are seated on cushions in semicircular rows sloping toward a circular space at the centre. Men and women, some wearing headscarves, some not, are seated together. Such boldness, such unisex worship, would be unthinkable in any mosque. On a bench along the back wall of the colonnaded room, directly across from a low stage, sit perhaps a dozen elders, bright-eyed men with luxurious mustaches wearing the proletarian cloth caps that Atatürk decreed must replace the fez when he imposed western dress in the late '20s. Leaning toward me, Nazim whispers with a smile, his fingers forming a tulip-like gesture of high appreciation, "these old men, they are sugar!"

The musicians, five venerable men wielding the long-necked stringed instruments of devotion, the tambours and the sazes that resonate like the voice of God, are seated cross-legged on sheepskins. The walls are hung with portraits, some of whom I recognize. First among them, the bearded, shining, idolized face of Imam Ali, to whom the Shi'ites look as their spiritual ancestor closest after the Prophet to God, and whom the mildly heretical Alevis consider as partaking himself of the Godhead.

Close by is a smaller depiction of an elderly bearded Sufi, recognizable as Hajji Bektash Veli, the founder of the Bektashi order, and further along, Nazim whispers, a likeness of Yunus Emre, the Turkish mystical poet. The last was a photographic likeness of Mustafa Kemal Atatürk in military garb. That portraits should appear in a Muslim place of worship was surprising enough; that a photograph of Atatürk should be hanging alongside the semi-sacred images of Ali and Hajji Bektash Veli was breathtaking.

"I told you these are heterodox people," laughed Nazim as he followed my eye to the Atatürk portrait.

The hum and bustle of conversation stills as the musicians strike percussive chords from their instruments. The eldest, who is seated upon a sheepskin, intones a passage from the Qur'an, first in Turkish, then in Arabic, followed by a prayer to the glory of the Turkish army. The ceremony had begun strangely, indeed. What had the army, that implacable opponent of the "Islamic threat," done to merit the praise and prayers of a religious order? The answer lies embedded in yet another story, a story of dissimulation and survival closely linked to the history of the only Ottoman institution to have outlasted the Empire itself—the army.

\* \* \*

PERHAPS A KILOMETER due north of Taksim Square, in the heart of the most westernized section of Istanbul, stands a block of fine late

Ottoman buildings. Built in 1834 by Sultan Mahmut II in the wake of the *Tanzimat* reforms dear to his heart, they housed the Military College he established to train the Empire's European-inspired officer corps. The *Harbiye* (War College), like its sister academy for training civil servants, was modeled on the Grandes Écoles created to perpetuate the centralizing bureaucracy of republican France. When the military academy withdrew to Ankara, the *Harbiye* became the Military Museum.

The Republic claims for itself the *bona fides* of European-imported modernity, and presents itself as a clean, dramatic break with an Asian past. But the history of the army gives the lie to this amusing little fiction. Here, in the echoing corridors of the *Harbiye*, the visitor encounters but a single continuum: that of the tradition of Ottoman arms, from Osman and Orhan to the present. Nowhere does there appear a sharp dividing line of the kind that should distinguish the never-to-return imperial past with the ever-glorious republican present. If anything, when compared with the accomplishments of the Ottoman war machine, the latter-day achievements of the Turkish army seem like small beer.

Then, the massive, well-drilled armies that struck terror into the European imagination, twice bore the Ottoman horse-tail standards to the gates of Vienna, having long before defeated the Serbian nobility in the epic battle for Kosova, the Hungarians at Mohacs, subjected the Balkans and established the Empire as the military and political power of the age.

Today, this once invincible force burns villages and expels citizens from Kurdistan in the name of the fight against Terrorism, but could barely mobilize a fraction of its forces to deal with the aftermath of the crushing earthquake of August, 1999.

One could speculate with endless poignancy on the reasons for this. One could make the usual arguments about the technological backwardness of Islamic civilization, the slowness of even such a sophisticated warrior class as the Ottomans to adopt the Western invention of firearms. Even when they finally did, writes Bernard Lewis, "the Ottomans ... continued to rely on outsiders for the science and even the technology needed to produce it."[156] The modern Turkish army, no less than its Ottoman forebears, perpetuated this dependence on outsiders: the martial Prussians, the French, and latterly, the Americans, who today provide the equipment, the ammunition, and the strategic guidance for the war against the Kurdish insurgency.

But one might also argue that the decline of the military establishment which neither Mustafa Kemal nor Said Nursi, each in his own way, was able to halt, had begun far earlier, with the corruption of the spiritual force that lay at its heart: the Janissary Corps. A Janissary presence lurks at the heart of the museum, in the form of a musical diversion of the kind calculated to attract tourists hungry for oriental exotica. Twice daily, a military band known as a *Mehter* performs in a capacious indoor amphitheater: to this venue I now turn my steps.

I've just slid into my seat in the steeply banked hall when barn-size doors behind the stage slide open to reveal the inner courtyard of the *Harbiye*. There, a group of musicians dressed in seventeenth-century Janissary garb comes marching in closed ranks straight toward, then into the amphitheater. Over a throbbing bass line of kettledrums sounds the bright metallic clash of cymbals, the braying of shawms and the whine of trumpets. Once inside the semi-enclosed space of the auditorium, the noise is ear-splitting, and all acoustically produced.

At its prime, the *Mehter* provided the musical model for the *Alaturka* style that had fascinated European composers as disparate as Lully and Gluck, as close as Mozart and Haydn. In the brassy, nasal blare, the thudding and the clashing I detected echoes from the wildly stirring, faintly parodical music that evokes the violent, threatening, yet ultimately empty tantrums of Osmin in *The Abduction from the Seraglio* by which Mozart signified to his eighteenth-century European audience that the "Turkish threat"— once dire—had now become a matter for laughter.

But on the battlefield, the *Mehter* would strike terror into the hearts of the enemy, and set the tone and pace for the advance of those redoubtable Janissary infantrymen for whom the Sultan's will was God's command.[157] Like his father Murat I, who died a hero's death on the Field of the Blackbirds, Beyazit intended to create an elite corps devoted to his person. The Janissaries were the first through the breach in the land walls of Constantinople on that fateful day in May, 1453. They became the spearhead of the conquering armies of Soleiman Kanuni, known in the West as "the Magnificent."

Even as the Janissary Corps constituted the heart of the Ottoman military machine, it concealed within it yet a deeper heart:

"The *Mehter* music you heard at the Military Museum used to begin with the recital of a poem in honor of Hajji Bektash Vali," lets drop, almost as an aside, Professor Izmettin Dogan of Galatasaray University, and head of the Cem Vakfi, whom I encountered in his office on the shores of the Bosphorus on a humid day in April.

If anyone would know, it would be the suave, polished French-speaking Professor Dogan, whose portrait graces the entry hall of the building in which Nazim and I had found ourselves that frigid November night.

In ways unknowable and mysterious, the doctrines of Hajji Bektash Vali, the holy man from Khorassan who may have been Turk, Arab or Iranian, became those of the Janissary Corps. Perhaps this was because Hajji Bektash believed that "those who have been martyred for Islam are more exalted than those whom Islam regards as prophets."[158] Others claim that Orhan, the founder of the Ottoman dynasty, was himself a follower.[159] So strong was the connection between the dervish order and the elite fighting corps that being a Janissary was synonymous with being a Bektashi.

The Bektashis, over time, had evolved from the relatively conventional Sunni beliefs of the founder into an antinomian, syncretic sect which came to believe in a godly Trinity composed of Allah, Mohammad and Ali, a concept that would cause orthodox Muslims to cringe. Strange contradictions abounded. The

Bektashis, almost alone among the Sufi orders, allowed women to participate in their ceremonies; their followers were allowed to drink wine, in violation of one of orthodox Islam's sterner prohibitions. About them floated a whiff of sulfur and free thinking. Yet the Janissaries were committed to celibacy, sworn to defend the Sunni orthodoxy of the sultans they served. This they did and did not do.

By the dawning of the *Tanzimat* era, the Janissaries had fallen into decay and disrepute, the common fate of closed, conspiratorial organizations—the same fate which had befallen the Assassins of Alamut, and later, the followers of the great false messiah, Sabbatai Sevi, the Dönme of Salonica. Once the terror of the Sultan's enemies, the invincible fighters had become the terror of the Sultan himself, deposing viziers and even rulers who displeased them or sought to restrain their insatiable thirst for power and privilege, and perhaps their crypto-Bektashi leanings. Finally, with one stroke of the pen and many strokes of the sword, Mahmut II, the builder of the *Harbiye*, abolished the mutinous Janissaries by the simple expedient of mass murder, an archetypal Night of the Long Knives. After all, in a royal house where the sovereign, on ascending the throne, would strangle his brothers with a bowstring to forestall dynastic quarrels, the elimination of tens of thousands of once proud fighters weighed no more heavily than the autumn leaves falling from the plane trees.

The Bektashi order's fall from grace was sudden and wrenching. Their *tekkes* were confiscated, and their property turned over to the Naqshbandis, their rigorously Sunni adversaries in the struggle for the Sultan's favor.[160]

Resilience, though, has always been the prime characteristic of Turkey's Sufi orders. While Mahmut's swordsmen were decapitating the Janissaries, the Bektashis went into hiding, and began rebuilding their organization in the rural areas of central and eastern Anatolia. It was here, one hundred years later, that they won the attention of Atatürk, on his journey to the East, on the eve of the War of Independence, and rallied to the nationalist cause.

Having fought beneath the nationalist banner and shed their blood on the battlefield, the Bektashis were rewarded with the banning of their *tariqat* by this selfsame Atatürk, in November, 1925. But the *tariqat* proved resilient. Mahmut had been unable to break it. Neither could Atatürk. Unlike Bediuzzaman Said Nursi, who realized that the essential quality of the Great Leader was his enmity toward religion, and paid for that realization with a lifetime of prison and exile, the Bektashis were able to trade a pledge of fealty and harmlessness for tacit recognition by the secular republic.

Stranger still is the story of the Alevis, whose contemporary doctrine is a mixture of Shi'ism and modern Turkish nationalism laid over an accumulation of beliefs that can be traced back to Central Asian shamanism, Zoroastrianism, Manicheism and Nestorian Christianity, to name but a few. "People believe that Islam in Turkey is the Sunni variant," explains Professor Dogan. "But Sunnism is Arab Islam; Alevism is Turkish Islam. We are followers of Sheikh Ahmet Yesevi, the spiritual father of all Turkish Islamists."

In fact, he argues, Atatürk was the first Turkish ruler since Beyazit II—"a great Alevi sultan"—to nurture and protect the Alevis. Alas, sighs the professor, that was Beyazit's undoing. He was forced from the throne by the Janissaries at the instigation of his son Selim, who went on to acquire the sobriquet of Yavuz, "the Grim," to destroy the Qizilbash armies of Shah Ismail at Chaldiran.

That battle, and the massacre of the innocents that preceded it, eliminated the last vestiges of organized Shi'ism as a force in Anatolia. But in their isolated villages, those who had escaped with their lives secretly nurtured their beliefs. So persistent did they prove that "Qizilbash" became the accepted term to describe the followers of Beyazit II. Finally, after four centuries of suppression, they have reappeared, in the guise of Alevis, metamorphosed into faithful defenders of the secular republican order.

To claim a common origin for the cult of Ali, the patron saint and demi-God of the Alevis with their Shi'a-inspired customs, and the Bektashi dervish confraternity would be incautious in the extreme.

But in the bizarre netherworld of the clandestine, the semi-clandestine and the state-manipulated into which Turkish Islamic heterodoxy has been driven, their curious merger makes a kind of convoluted, inverted sense. It was precisely this convoluted sense made flesh that I encountered at the Alevi *semahane* that winter night.

Lurking deep in the cell structure that gives form to the historical orthodoxy of the Military Museum, I intuited a hidden connection: the battle for the soul of the Turkish army. The practice of dissimulation may well be repugnant to high Sunni Islam, in its doctrinal rigidity. But it is the defense of the downtrodden, the weapon of the weak. Beneath the icy and austere demeanor of the army commanders, what concealed heresies struggle for influence and seek the favor of the state, the better to subvert it?

\* \* \*

IN THE *SEMAHANE*, the invocation to the army has ended and 40 members of the congregation, waists girded with green ribbons, have stepped from their seats and are now squatting on their knees, on the floor. Tonight they will symbolically re-enact, as they do every Saturday night in Alevi *semahanes* across Turkey and the Balkans, the heavenly voyage of Mohammad that culminated in the Banquet of the Forty. Intoxicated by the juice of a single grape which the Prophet caused to be pressed and fermented, the Forty had risen to their feet, wrapped their waists with the turban that God's Messenger had let fall to the ground, and begun the dance of heavenly ecstasy. [161]

Tonight's worshippers, modestly dressed people with hard-working hands and creased faces, clad in ill-fitting jackets and knit sweaters, some of them wearing Kurdish dress, look on as the forty contemporary stand-ins begin to sway slowly from side to side, calling out "Allah! Allah!" in answer to the shouted invocation of the *Dede*, the chief elder. Facing the mustachioed musicians at the centre of the stage, they segue into incantatory chanting of the holy names of Allah, Mohammad and Ali, followed by those of the Twelve Imams and the emblematic figures of the Bektashi order.

"We take the Imams and the Saints as our model," whispers Ms. Fer as Nazim, himself fascinated by the spectacle, translates fast and furiously.

So complex is the allegorical structure of the ceremony that I have my hands full keeping up with Ms. Fer's exegesis and watching at the same time. A man, accompanied by a young woman wearing a green headscarf held in place with a red ribbon—green is the color of Islam, red the color of the flag that flies atop the golden dome of the shrine of Imam Hossein at Karbala—advances carrying a basin and a ewer. The ablutions are symbolic, she explains. "This is another difference between us and the Sunnis," against a rising whine of microphone feedback making suspension of disbelief difficult.

The ceremonial ablutions completed, the tempo of the music gradually increases, and the forty men and women rise to their feet and begin to revolve slowly in a circle, rotating like planets around the sun. Stillness falls over the hundreds present, their necks strain forward as the dancers break into a fast-shuffling cadence, bending forward then straightening up. Now the atmosphere in the hall is dense with a spiritual excitement that is as palpable as it is invisible.

Raising their right hands close to their faces, the dancers stare at their palms as if into a mirror, while they clasp their left hands to their hearts. A crackle of energy radiates out from the fast-turning circle, sweeping over the worshippers like the concentric rings of force that ripple outward across still water when a stone breaks the surface. I can feel my own pulse thrumming, my breath shortening, Nazim stares, fascination quivering at the corners of his mouth.

Now, on the raised platform, one of the elders begins to twitch, his head thrown back as though in a convulsion, the veins in his neck tense like twisted-wire cables. At once the source and the focus of the spiritual energy being emitted by the whirling human generator, his back arches in an ecstatic trance as a sharp intake of breath sweeps the hall. He has achieved the transient state that, among some Sufis, is characterized by loss of sanity and self-control, that point at which "the soul becomes intoxicated, expansive with the wine of knowledge of the Divine, enraptured by the contemplation of God."[162]

Soon the ecstasy and the rapture are exhausted, as exhausted as the musicians who have been playing and chanting for two hours. The revolving dancers gradually slow their pace, their movements now free of the near-epileptic jerkiness of divine inspiration. In the hall, too, the onlooking faithful relax their intent gaze; the low buzz of conversation returns. The ceremony has ended. Coats slung over their shoulders, the men file out accompanied by their wives. Nazim and I make our way back to Istanbul, nibbling the dried fruit and crackers we've gleaned from the Alevis.

It had taken me little time to become aware that what Westerners mistake for the monolith of Islam was, in fact, a rich and complex mosaic. Side by side with the high Sunni doctrine that, since Yavuz Selim, has constituted the established religion, have endured not only the *tariqats*, but entire full-blown heresies and heterodoxies. Most of them endure to this day, deep in the hidden recesses of the country's soul. No one knows how many Alevis exist in Turkey today. Some say 20 or even 30 million, nearly one-half the population. The figure is apocryphal in the extreme. Experts on the subject estimate their number at no more than ten million.

The worshipful attitude of the Alevis toward Atatürk can be understood, both as the gratitude of the beholden to the self-proclaimed protector, and as a reflex of survival. What is less easy to grasp is the filiation of ideas that leads, in Alevi iconography and theology, from Hajji Bektash Vali through the Janissary Corps to the founder of the Republic. While one can easily grant the plausibility of a reincarnated sense of deity in the spiritual lineage of Ali, through Hajji Bektash, and Ahmet Yesevi, how this might extend to the agnostic Mustafa Kemal is another matter entirely.

Predictably, the orthodox Sunnis are suspicious of the Atatürk-Alevi connection. They believe that the Alevis, those ultimate dissimulators, have infiltrated the highest echelons of the state and the army. On the other side, the Alevis accuse the Sunnis of discrimination. Anti-Alevi pogroms have occurred, both in Istanbul and in the Anatolian hinterland.

In a letter written in 1935, before he was again arrested for exploiting religion and religious sentiments in a way damaging to the security of the state and hauled off to prison with more than one hundred of his followers, Said Nursi had warned both the Sunnis and the Alevis that "the atheistic current which is now so influential will make one of you a tool against the other. And after defeating the one, it will destroy the tool."[163] In the cold light of contemporary events, Bediuzzaman's injunction seemed invested with uncanny accuracy.

From the summit of Pine Mountain, overlooking the battlefield of Myriokephalon.

Said Nursi's treehouse in Barla.

*Photos by Fred A. Reed*

# XIII

## A Metallic Gold Chevrolet

Early December is call-up time in Turkey. All across the country young men set out for their compulsory military service. More than a rite of passage, induction into the army bonds male citizens to the only institution that can make, and enforce, a serious claim to stability. "We are the state" has always been the implicit, clinching argument of the military. The young men and their families who have congregated at bus and railway stations from one end of the land to the other have been told they are perpetuating a proud tradition, the only one unsullied by the baseness of partisan politics, above the swirl and corruption of parliamentary democracy.

A fine rain was falling as I climbed aboard the midnight bus to Isparta at the Istanbul Otogar for my last foray into the Anatolian hinterland. The bus station was seething with conscripts and their families. Kerem, my seat-mate and fellow traveler, and I looked out the window at the cheering, shouting, clapping throng. On the far edges of the compact crowd musicians beat on drums and huffed into *Zurnas* that squealed like aggrieved pigs. From the multitude closely packed around the bus rose a rhythmic chant. "No soldier is as brave as our soldier!" translated Kerem, a fluently bilingual eighteen-year-old Australian-born Turk, in his down-under twang.

In Turkey, the invocation of bravery is more than a figure of speech, and induction into the army more than a dry formality. Any one of the youngsters now bidding good-bye to their families might end up dead in the mountains of Kurdistan. I thought back for an instant to a former foot soldier I'd met in Istanbul several months before, a glib, street-wise young man who had suddenly broken into tears as he described how his best friend had died in his arms after a skirmish with the Kurdish insurgents. "What were we doing there anyway?" he wanted to know. "My friends and I never had any quarrel with the Kurds." I took his feelings for those of most of the Turkish soldiery: frightened young men forced to kill their own countrymen for reasons known only to their commanders, and perhaps only to the shadowy few who issued the ultimate orders. But the army was a machine for obedience. Theirs was but to do or die.

With a flick of the steering wheel the driver maneuvered the Mercedes-Benz coach through the crowd as the conscripts clambered on board, many of them red-eyed. Our destination, Isparta, was one of the country's main induction centers. The extended hands of mothers, sisters and girl-friends stretched up toward the windows. From the periphery, little boys hoisted onto shoulders waved. The bus accelerated up the exit ramp and onto the access road to the motor way, the drumming and chanting faded, and soon the heads of the recruits were nodding. Dawn would come soon enough, and with it the electrical clippers, the rough wool uniforms, the barked commands and the discipline of a thousand-year-old institution.

For Kerem and I, sleep would come much later. Earlier that day I'd gotten a call from Professor R. "A young man will be accompanying you to Isparta and the other places on your journey. He will help you and make sure you understand everything," he told me. The eighteen-year-old, who had come back to Turkey to seek out his religious roots, turned out to be Professor R's master-stroke. Though he may have been from the West, little marked him as a member of that coveted marketing segment variously defined as teen-aged or adolescent for which movies are made, music assembled, electronic diversions created, soft drinks promoted, clothing designed, behaviours charted. Bright, polite, and articulate, Kerem wore a neatly-knotted tie and carried a briefcase, smiled carefully and laughed less. As a young man searching for the connection between his life in the fleshpots of the West and the austerity of the Nur movement, he had little time for idle joking, much for concentration on matters of the spirit. His self-abnegation was all the more touching in its contingency and fragility. At any moment, the tentacles of the sordid, lurid, pounding world might reach out and ensnare him, like a depth-dwelling giant squid pulling a proud ship down into its watery realm.

As the bus sped along the Istanbul-Ankara motor way, gliding by the grimy industrial towns that line the Gulf of Izmit that would crumble to dust in the 'quake of July 1999, Kerem told me his story. This was his second visit to Turkey. The first had taken place six years before when, as a twelve-year-old, he had been sent back by his father, a member of the Nur community, to attend a *medrese* and become a *hafiz*, someone who can recite the Qur'an by heart. The experiment had been a terrible failure. Overcome by homesickness, and by the utter strangeness of his new environment, he returned to Sydney and to his family. Now he was back, of his own accord, to pick up those dropped threads though, he admitted, he had hardly expected to be accompanying a Canadian writer to Isparta, a place so remote from tourist itineraries that guide books, if they speak of it at all, devote to it no more than a paragraph or two, to mention its rose-water, a precious ingredient in perfumes and cosmetics.

For different, though converging reasons, Isparta for Kerem and me was a prime destination. In this small city and its environs, Said Nursi had lived out many of the last years of his life, in conditions of extreme duress, under house arrest, banishment and prison. And it was in Isparta, on a bitter moonlit night on a graveyard high on a hillside that I would be led to yet another empty grave.

* * *

ON APRIL 17, 1923, Bediuzzaman boarded a train at the Ankara station. Its destination was his beloved Van. Accompanying him to the station were a number of members of the Grand National Assembly, and Mustafa Kemal himself. The two men exchanged words, sharply. The soldier who would soon consolidate his absolute power over the new country had asked the mollah his opinion of statues. The Qur'an, replied Said, holds no brief for idols. "The statues of the Muslims are monuments like hospitals, schools, orphanages, mosques and roads."[164] So saying, he climbed into the carriage and began a voyage out of his former self, a voyage of withdrawal from the maelstrom of politics and into the bitter, lonely battle to preserve his vision of religion and its place in society. On that fateful journey the man he now called the Old Said passed into eclipse, to be replaced by the New Said.

In its desolation and destruction, Van mirrored the bleakness of his inner world. He had put aside the tribal costume he long affected for simpler homespun robes. From Van he withdrew to a cave in the mountains from which he would venture every Friday to give the sermon at the city's main mosque.

Events quickly overtook him. The life of prayer, contemplation and preaching to which he now looked forward was soon to be shattered by the first great convulsion to wrack the newborn republic: the Sheikh Said revolt. The upheaval, led by the eponymous Naqshbandi holy man had broken out in 1925 among the devout Kurds of southeastern Anatolia. Hugh Poulton, always perspicacious, somewhat understates the issue: "The Sheikh Said revolt of 1925, which was more a religious and tribal revolt than a national uprising, suggests that Islam was definitely the main component of group identity for large numbers of Kemal's new subjects."[165]

Several of the insurgent leaders, all Kurdish mollahs, had come to see Bediuzzaman, and to exhort him to take up arms against the Ankara government. Kurdistan was seething with unrest; the local dignitaries had massed horses, weapons and ammunition. Though they had joined the *jihad* against the illegitimate and corrupt authority of the Sultan, and fought under the banner of Islam, the Kurdish tribal leaders now realized that they had been used, their religion betrayed. In Ankara, the republican authorities accused the rebels of complicity with Britain, which, unhappy with the Lausanne Treaty, was allegedly stoking the fires of discontent.

(Little direct evidence of British involvement in the Sheikh Said revolt has come to light, but London could have plausibly been interested in weakening the fledgling state. Though the Foreign Office and the colonial authorities had wished to dismantle the Empire, they preferred the toothless, sub-imperial entity in Istanbul to the mercurial Atatürk.)

Pressure on Said Nursi mounted, as delegation upon delegation sought his endorsement for their cause. Sheikh Said himself wrote to Bediuzzaman, promising victory should he join the movement. Bediuzzaman's reply was short, swift and unequivocal:

"The Turkish nation has acted as the standard-bearer for Islam for centuries. It has produced many saints and given many martyrs. The sword may not be drawn against the sons of such a nation. We are Muslims, we are their brothers, we may not make brother fight brother. It is not permissible according to the *Shari'a*. The sword is to be drawn against external enemies, it may not be used internally. Our only salvation at this time is to offer illumination and guidance through the truths of the Qur'an and belief; it is to get rid of our greatest enemy, ignorance. Give up this attempt of yours, for it will be fruitless. Thousands of innocent men and women may perish on account of a few bandits." [166]

The letter was a succinct and elegant summation of the New Said's convictions. Had Abdullah Öcalan paid heed to the words of Kurdistan's most illustrious mollah, the region might have been spared the campaign of devastation unleashed upon it by Kemal's self-proclaimed heirs, the generals, more than fifteen years ago. Had Sheikh Said heeded Bediuzzaman's warning, the fate of the Kurds might have been less tragic. But both he and Öcalan possessed an ample share of the quality of bullheadedness. They plunged ahead, certain of victory. In both cases the result, for Kurdistan and for Turkey, was tragic.

In February, 1925, the uprising broke out. It handed Mustafa Kemal the pretext he may have been waiting for. One month later, the Ankara government set up what were euphemistically called "Independence Tribunals," and assumed unlimited powers to pursue the policies it had concealed from all but its closest allies. Soon after, another law banning all the *tariqats* and closing down their lodges and the *türbes*—the shrines of holy sheihks at which the common folk worshipped—was promulgated: it was "a move to smash the localized folk cultures and replace them by a unified national culture, as well as removing a perceived reactionary countrywide alternative power network."[167]

Religion had united the population in the struggle against internal and external enemies; now it was to be discarded, to be supplanted by an amalgam of Turkish nationalism and hard-line secularism. Said Nursi's open opposition to the revolt, which had flared like a prairie fire, then quickly died out, availed him little. The authorities had begun rounding up the leading religious and tribal leaders of the region, and sending them into exile in western Anatolia. A detachment of gendarmes was sent to arrest him in his mountain cave. Though his followers quickly gathered around him and could easily have overwhelmed the gendarmes, Said offered no resistance and followed them back to Van. There, hundreds of others had already been concentrated in the high school from which they set out on a winter journey by foot and horse-drawn sledge across the snowy wastes of high Anatolia.

Moving from town to town, the cortege finally arrived in the Black Sea port of Trabzon in early spring. From there, the deportees were transported by boat to Istanbul. In the capital, Bediuzzaman reiterated his non-participation in the rebellion. Meanwhile the ringleaders, who had been apprehended, were delivered to Diyarbakir where they were given summary trials and hanged. After three weeks in Istanbul, Said was once again put aboard a ship for the trip to Antalya, then made his way inland until he finally came to rest at Isparta.

When it settled on Isparta as his place of exile, the Ankara government was betting that, removed from his natural surroundings, Said Nursi would wither and die, at least as a potential threat, if not in actual fact. The greenhorn secular fundamentalists had, in fact, delivered him into a spiritual environment that would respond to his extraordinary personality and talents in a way that surpassed their darkest foreboding. Nor had they grasped the mettle of their adversary; his epic stubbornness and will to persevere against all odds.

The chief town of a remote, mountainous religion, Isparta had specialized since early Ottoman times not only in the production of rose-water, but of spiritual sensibility. As the Empire began to totter, the region's fertile land had drawn to it large numbers of Greeks, who rapidly set up educational establishments. The effect on the local population was the same as it had been in Bitlis before the turn of the century: resentment of the success of the outsiders, coupled with a sharpened sense of their own religious identity.

The banning of the *tariqats* had succeeded only in driving them underground, increasing their effectiveness as centers of passive resistance. At the same time, the structural changes taking place in Turkey had drawn the rural population into the wider social communications network. Even in remote towns people had become aware of the world beyond. [168]

No Greeks remained in Isparta after the mammoth exercise in ethnic cleansing known euphemistically as the "population exchange" of 1923-24, the events still mourned in Greece as the "Asia Minor Catastrophe." The town's Muslim inhabitants, however, flocked to hear Bediuzzaman's sermons and to sit at his feet in the town *medrese*. The authorities were alarmed, and promptly resolved to send him to a place even remoter and more obscure, a place where he would be deprived of civilization, of company itself. That place was Barla, a tiny mountain village overlooking Lake Egridir, as beautiful and as lonely a place as a mystic caught in the bulldog jaws of illumination could have hoped for.

* * *

AT 7:30, AS DAWN WAS BREAKING, the bus pulled into the Isparta Otogar, minus the contingent of conscripts. They, after sleeping their last sleep of civilian innocence, snoring, heads lolling onto the shoulders of their seat-mates, had clambered shivering from the coach on the outskirts of town, just outside the entrance to the military camp. Kerem and I, shivering like the conscripts, now strode diagonally across the outdoor concourse where we were intercepted by three brothers from the Nur community. One of them, Mustafa—a prefect at the Isparta dormitory—would be our host and guide.

The briskness in the air seemed to have insinuated itself into the demeanor of our hosts. Their pace was purposeful, their mood one of resolute good humor. The *dolce far niente* of the southeast had given way to a sense of moderate urgency. There was much to see, and little time in which to see it. As I was soon to certify, while there was indeed much to see, little could be seen. The subject was missing: an absence structured by a handful of artifacts, a car, a middle-aged man's tale, and a breeze so gentle as to barely sway the branches of a mountain pine.

After an hour or two's snooze and a bracing breakfast of the kind I'd come to crave, Mustafa, a friend of his called Cemal, Kerem and I shoe-horned ourselves into a dented Mitsubishi pickup truck for the ride up-country toward Barla and beyond, to Pine Mountain, the lofty aerie where Bediuzzaman—harking back perhaps to his boyhood in the mountain valleys of Kurdistan—would spend so many of his days and nights in contemplation of the universe and of his own fate.

For several kilometers the road skirted the shore of the lake, as slow-moving cloud reflections played across the surface. There was a softness about the countryside, in contrast to the brute-edged peaks mirrored in the alkaline blue of Lake Van. But the elements were similar, and must not have entirely displeased Bediuzzaman when, in the early spring of 1925, a fisherman's craft deposited him, accompanied by a gendarme, at the tiny Barla jetty. The solitude he had voluntarily cultivated in the caves and ruined monasteries above Van would now be his once more, and would serve him well. His own injunction to his followers—"Do not call me to the world!"—must have crossed his mind. But there were two capital differences: his exile from the world was no longer voluntary, and it would last for all but the last few years of his life.

Instead of turning off at Barla, we continued for several kilometers before coming to a stop in front of a metal gate barring access to a gravel track that wound upward into the hills. Secured by a heavy padlock, the gate would not yield. Mustafa's efforts to locate the man with the keys, a local farmer, proved fruitless. Several hurry-up calls to Isparta followed. (Though the movement may cultivate a certain doctrinal archaism, it does not forego the utility of cell phones, not to mention e-mail and web sites.) Technology was, however, of no avail. "The students of Nur must be resourceful," Kerem translated for me as, with a grin and a grunt, Mustafa smashed the lock with an ax retrieved from a box in the truck bed.

The gates swung open and, wheels spinning merrily in the dust and gravel, the Mitsubishi slithered its way uphill, throwing up behind it a fantail of dust. I recalled my visit over equally abominable roads in a pickup truck to the desolate lair of the Assassins of Alamut, in the mountains of northern Iran, several years before. The followers of Hasan Sabah were purists, as were the Nurcus, but there ended all resemblance. Antinomian to a fault, the men of the Eagle's Nest had perfected the art of political murder in the name of spiritual purity. But Said Nursi preached withdrawal from the political world, and salvation of the world of belief. Far from confronting the iniquitous rulers of the corrupt and corrupting State with paradigmatic violence, he avoided it. Distant ideological descendants of the Assassins may lurk in the complex depths of modern Turkish Islam, but not surely among Bediuzzaman's acolytes, who live in society and teach by goodness that is just as paradigmatic and, in the long run, certainly more effective.

Switchback upon sharp curve, the dirt track climbed through scrub forest until, across a narrow valley, a summit peeked from the clouds. "Çan Dagi!" exclaimed my guides, pointing to the peak of Pine Mountain. At the summit, up a two-hundred meter path, stood an ancient, gnarled, wind-sculpted cedar. In its branches Said had built one of the platforms that provided him refuge, proximity to the birds and the wind, and perhaps a sense of freedom from the pull of the earth. We pulled off our shoes and scrambled up a ladder slippery with dew until we stood on the rough-hewn planks where he would perch, studying what he called the Great Book of the Universe or composing in his mind the random collection of essays and Qur'anic exegesis that would later be fashioned into the *Risale-i Nur*.

A few meters down the slope, on a rock shelf poised over a precipice, loomed the hulk of an ancient, lightning-blackened pine. Far below, Lake Egridir gleamed dark turquoise beneath the shifting cloudscape and from the valley floor, came the echoes of human activity: a vehicle speeding along the road, a tractor tilling a field. Had I been standing in this place some 800 years before, I would have heard the distant clash of arms as a powerful Seljuk force led by Sultan Qilij Arslan of Konya met and overwhelmed a Byzantine host under the Emperor Manuel Comnenus. Then the field was known as Myriokephalon; the Byzantine defeat destroyed the Eastern Orthodox Empire's last hope of expelling the Turks from Asia Minor. Some historians argue portentously, as is their want, that the battle decided forever the destiny of the East. [169]

The destiny of the East was still at issue, I thought, as I stood looking out over the plain far below. My three companions had withdrawn a few paces uphill and, begging my forbearance, had pulled out a red-bound book to recite a passage from Ustad's work. Halfway between prayer and expostulation, in the strange, elevated sing-song style unique to Bediuzzaman, the reading set off an eerie counterpoint to the rustling of the wind in the cedar boughs and the distant whisper of earth-bound life. It set me to wondering, too, if there was more in this place than the wind.

* * *

LITERARY BIOGRAPHY can be a perilous enterprise. The biographer must often reckon with the inaction of the subject, as all creative energy flows toward, and from, the *oeuvre*. The classic injunction to the writer is to show, not tell, but the biographer knows that the author's despair or illumination, the forces that generate the work and shape the style cannot be shown, only approximately described and documented. How, in the film *Immortal Beloved*, which relates the great love of Beethoven's life, could the truculent genius' deafness be reconciled with the imperative of making his music audible? How, in *Amadeus*, can the wellsprings of Mozart's creative genius be even suggested by the jealous hack narrator, Salieri?

A similar dilemma awaits the writer who would presume to find in Said Nursi's eight-year exile in Barla a notion of causality. It certainly awaited me.

His exile from Van and arrival in the village had brought his life of action in the world to an irrevocable halt. The days and nights, months and years spent in lonely meditation, prayer, supplication and privation, are difficult for a replete Western reader to imagine; the long climbs to the summit of Pine Mountain, the hours seated cross-legged on flimsy platforms erected in the high branches of trees, outposts in the realm of the birds. The Old Said, who bestrode two continents, the dashing warrior who fought at the head of the Felt Hat militia, the agitator and secret agent who traveled by submarine to Libya, waged open polemics with the mighty of the Empire, rubbed elbows with revolutionaries and wagged the finger of admonition at nation-builders had vanished. Worse, the man himself had been uprooted from his native Kurdish soil and from the spiritual climate of Anatolia that had been to him like the air he breathed.

Said was a poor writer—he often termed himself a semi-literate—who composed his Qur'anic commentaries, an ongoing, accretive process of sudden insight and brilliant outburst, in his head, then dictated them. But for the work to take its final shape, he needed an interlocutor, a pupil, a scribe, a disciple. Even in Barla, against all hope and probability, such individuals found their way to him. Here, the lay intellectuals and *ulama* with whom he had once discussed the future of Islam in Turkey were "replaced by peasants, craftsmen, small traders and their sons."[170]

These were the resources now at Bediuzzaman's disposal; with them he would work. To the simple folk he attracted by his strange and exemplary manner of living and speaking, he now addressed his arguments, and beyond them, to what he must have intuited as a multitude, waiting as the thirsty crave water, for the words that would defend and ennoble their endangered beliefs.

For all the isolation and impoverishment he endured in Barla, he contrived in a short time to establish a loose, ad hoc structure that could not yet be termed an organization (such would have been rooted out mercilessly by the authorities in any event), but that secured the transmission and diffusion of his words. These would then be sold for a pittance; the revenues were all that kept Bediuzzaman alive and financed wider distribution.

His immediate aides may have been lower level religious scholars or pious laymen, but their devotion far outweighed their lack of theological sophistication. They were the people—men and women—who copied down Bediuzzaman's dictation in the Arabic script still then in use. This original version was then handed to him for corrections, which he often performed in one of his treehouses, then copied again by the volunteer scribes and passed on clandestinely to others who would write out still more versions. Thus did the first work composed in Barla, known as *The Words*, find its way from village to village, from town to town, and from one end of Turkey to another. It was not until the late '40s that a primitive duplicating machine was first used. The *Risale-i Nur* itself, Bediuzzaman's *chef d'oeuvre*, was first printed in 1956, in Latin characters, under the Democrat Party government of Adnan Menderes. Up until that time, an estimated 600,000 hand-written copies of either the whole or the parts of the *Risale-i Nur* were in circulation. The number of readers would have exceeded that many times over. [171]

Westerners dazzled by Mustafa Kemal Atatürk's reforming boldness may have trouble appreciating the magnitude of the task that lay before Said Nursi and his growing group of scribes, "postmen," and followers. Even as the War of Independence was drawing to a victorious conclusion, plans were being drawn up not only to sever the new Republic from its Ottoman past, but to attack and destroy the Islamic commonality which had been the ultimate legitimating symbol of the Empire. [172] Then, with all power concentrated in his hands, Atatürk unleashed his modernizing project upon a country still in shock.

The first step had been to close the religious schools and ban the *tariqats*. Soon religious dress was proscribed, and the wearing of European hats imposed on pain of death. (Bediuzzaman steadfastly refused to obey the new law, claiming before a court, "this turban comes off with this head!") Then, the regime struck at the living heart of Islam, when, in 1928, it banned the Arabic alphabet, effectively ending the traditional teaching of religion—and severing the people's link with their past. It was that same year that the traditional time system was abolished, to be replaced by Western time.

"No more tradition's chains shall bind us," we can hear the pseudo-Bolshevik Kemal humming under his breath as he signed the first decrees. For Arabic, the language of Divine revelation, was substituted a Turkish language which the secular intellectuals of Ankara were busily purifying of its foreign words. The crowning indignity came in 1932 when the *azan*, the call to prayer, was replaced by a Turkish version, causing immense popular resentment.

By then the CHP, Atatürk's Republican People's Party, had captured the Turkish state apparatus. The Party's principles were written into the Constitution in 1936, and the CHP launched a program of mass education designed to bring to every corner of the land the new truths of nationalism, secularism and Western culture. Taken together, this amalgam was called laicism, in its rigidity and self-righteousness a sombre parody of the late eighteenth-century French revolutionary invention. This, then, was the many-headed Hydra that Bediuzzaman Said Nursi and his raggedy band of followers set out to challenge from their humble headquarters in Barla.

* * *

FROM PINE MOUNTAIN we wound our way downhill, wedged the gate closed, and retraced our path to the Barla turnoff. Set in the folds of the hillside overlooking Lake Egridir, surrounded by orchards, the village today shows signs of prosperity. Vacation villas dot the approaches, the dwellings of the Nur community faithful, explains Kerem after a brief consultation with Mustafa, "people who want to be close to the place where Ustad spent so many years of his life."

In the heart of the village stands the immense plane tree with the platform where Bediuzzaman meditated and composed, and beneath it, the house in which he lived. Today the modestly restored building houses a small prayer room, with a selection of his books on display in the vestibule. Across the street the movement has built a guest-house supervised by a resident caretaker, former air force sergeant Hayati Mansuroglu, a grizzled Korean War veteran with a salt-and-pepper beard, powerful hands and a booming laugh who long ago traded his pilot's cap for the knit skullcap favored by Turkey's Muslim believers.

Through the windowed balcony I looked out across the deep ravine that separates the village from the slopes of Pine Mountain. "Look," said sergeant Mansuroglu, touching my elbow, "there is the pathway Bediuzzaman followed when he would climb to the summit." In the fading early December light, a flock of sheep was making its way down that path with a faint tinkling of bells.

Although we were expected back in Isparta that evening, sergeant Mansuroglu insisted we stay for dinner. While summer brings a constant flow of visitors, in winter guests are few, and his must be a life of quiet monotony. Swift-flitting conviviality, like the lustrous pearly gray hybrid doves on offer at the Istanbul pigeon market, can be captured only in a finely woven net of hospitality. We were easy prey, and within minutes the food lay steaming before us on the floor: bread, bowls of red lentil soup, and "Barla balcony pilaf" made from cracked wheat, followed by sweet local apples and hot *sahlep*. Then, hastily taking our leave of Barla balcony and its jovial, lonely caretaker, we crammed ourselves into the Mitsubishi, and plunged headlong into the growing dusk.

Straight past the bright lights of downtown Isparta, which consists of a few hotels, kebab salons, pastry emporia and many bank branches, we drove, and headed for the house on a winding side-street where Said Nursi lived his last nine years—with many interruptions for court appearances—before the fateful journey to Urfa. As at Barla, the house, a traditional Ottoman lath and plaster structure with an overhanging timbered second floor, has been restored. Padding in stockinged feet across the cold wooden floor we visited the Master's bedroom with its stark iron bedstead, the prayer room, the study and the kitchen, now transformed into a bare-bones museum. A handful of surviving artifacts are on display: a tea-pot, some dented tin ewers and two tiny pots for brewing Turkish coffee; torn, frayed, patched and re-patched clothing; and a glass-enclosed showcase containing manuscript copies of the *Risale-i Nur*. One of them is bound in brightly colored woven cloth from a woman's dowry, Mustafa explains, evidence of a subtle feminine component in the austere masculinity of the community.

The familiar stink of coal-smoke filled the air as we stepped out onto the sidewalk. Night had fallen. We walked a few paces and paused before the locked doors of a garage. Mustafa twisted a large key in the antique padlock, swung open the doors and flicked on a light-switch. There before us, its metallic gold paint gleaming in the faint light of the bare bulb, stood the 1953, four-door Chevrolet, the vehicle that had carried Bediuzzaman across Anatolia on his final, fateful journey to Urfa. Adamant in his refusal to accept any gift, no matter how small, Said had eventually reimbursed, from the proceeds of his writings, the faithful students who had purchased the car.

\* \* \*

FOR THE FIRST-TIME foreign reader of Bediuzzaman Said Nursi's voluminous output, perhaps the most striking feature is its almost mechanical, near-obsessive sense of order. Though composed in a state of high incandescence and dictated *pèle-mèle* to the scribes he recruited among the villagers of Barla, the essays that make up his first collection, *The Words*, reveal an internal classification system as complex as it is ramified, a structure that seems to partake of both the organic and the industrial. *The Twenty-Fourth Word*, for instance, "consists of Five Branches from the luminous tree of the verse, *God, there is no god but He; His are the Most Beautiful Names.*" The Third Branch is broken down into Twelve Principles which explain "certain figurative Hadiths" while the Fourth lists the "Four Categories of workers in the palace of the universe."[173]

Embedded in this expository method of systems, sub-systems and subsidiary, secondary systems themselves made up of "words," "flashes," "thoughts" and other classificatory and mnemonic devices, lies a near-dialectical encounter between the mechanistic Newtonian view of the universe that had insinuated itself into the Islamic discourse of the day, and the venerable mystical tradition of the Sufis. For all Bediuzzaman's abjuring of mysticism, for all his warnings to his followers against it, his perception had been shaped by its methods and procedures, by his encounters with the Naqshbandi sheikhs of Bitlis, and by his own readings of Ibn al-Arabi, the mystical master from Andalusia.

What Bediuzzaman and the Sufis shared was the need for a system that would facilitate access to knowledge and would order that knowledge. Sufi speculation led away from phenomena and towards the mystery of Being. Said Nursi's originality was that he turned the Sufi point of view on its head. He would mobilize the tools, the symbols and the apparatus of the mystic orders to redirect the attention of believers away from conduct and ritual and toward a picture of the physical universe as bodying forth, in its extraordinarily complex yet regular processes, the presence of a supreme Maker.

Like the Sufis, Bediuzzaman did not scorn the use of hermetic language, even when describing the physical world that he regarded as conclusive evidence of the presence and existence of God. As for Muslims the Qur'an is one with the Arabic in which it was written, so, to a lesser degree, is Said Nursi's work inextricably connected with the lofty, eloquent and often oblique Ottoman diction it embraces.

In the austere surroundings of countless meeting rooms throughout Turkey, the rich, flowery and, for modern Turks, barely comprehensible complexities of Bediuzzaman's prose generates an imaginary total environment of evocative images, moral imperatives and intellectual injunctions in which, like the Qur'an, form is indissociable from content.

The *Risale-i Nur* recreates nothing less than society and the world; it provides the pious with both a microscope and a telescope. Given the spiritual barrenness imposed by the secularists who ripped Turkey from a past of immense richness, Said Nursi's *oeuvre* unfolds with the same organic abundance, order and luxuriance that he exhorts his readers to find in the universe itself, where "the cosmos is seen to be a vast and infinitely complex and meaningful united book describing its Single Author." [174]

* * *

SHORTLY AFTER SUN-UP the next day we depart Isparta for Emirdag, Said Nursi's last of many places of exile. Instead of the pickup, Mustafa has borrowed a late-model Toyota: we shall cover the 200 kilometers in style. Another senior member of the Isparta community whom I shall call Salih, has come along for the ride. As we hurtle at top speed along the near-deserted highway that runs due north, Kerem interprets as I bombard the two with questions about the lives of the young men under their care.

Beyond certain privileged enclaves in Istanbul, Ankara and a handful of other big towns, what we term youth culture does not exist in Turkey, except in the form of television images. The young people I encountered were at home in and conversant with the real world, were already exercising personal responsibility, already thinking for themselves and building strategies for integrating themselves into a society that they expected to change. What Turkey's westernizers cannot grasp is not only the alienation that affects youth in the West, but the rejection by many young people of the model drummed into them by a system they can recognize only as a purveyor of falsehood. The Nur community draws much of its strength from its ability to channel this rejection. But in a broader sense, the movement's ability to draw young people to it also reflects the failure of the republican educational system's attempt to restrict young people to the current Western understanding of adolescents as isolated from the mainstream of day-to-day adult concerns. [175]

Students from traditional religious families tend to gravitate naturally to the Nur community, explains Mustafa as he hunches over the wheel of the speeding Toyota. But the movement is not above fishing for souls. Not only must it maintain its membership, it must expand. "We visit the universities and talk to the students about our movement," he says. "If they show interest, we invite them to visit us. And if they like the visit, we invite them to move in."

Prospective residents need not be religious, "but they must agree to live by our rules." The rules are strict: neither television nor radio is permitted, nor are newspapers. Smoking is forbidden, alcohol consumption is unthinkable. Relationships with girls are out of the question. Only religious books may be brought into the dormitory, and only the voluminous works of Said Nursi are truly encouraged.

"One of the youngsters in the Isparta dorm was being called regularly by a young lady," Salih volunteered, with a hint of a grin. "Instead of giving him an ultimatum, we raised the question in an indirect way, and gradually worked to dissuade him from continuing. 'Here, our focus is on love for God as it is expressed in the Qur'an,' we told him."

(Back in Istanbul, I mentioned the conversation to Professor R., who gave me another reason for the community's success in maintaining celibacy. "We keep 'em hungry," he said, with a booming laugh. "All they have time to think about is food. There's plenty of time for marriage later." Indeed, no Nur dormitory student I encountered on my journey was anything but slender, nor did I ever witness the merest scrap of food left on any plate.)

At the end of nearly a month spent traveling through the Nur archipelago, I had found something almost monastic in the other-worldliness of the *dershanes*. To avoid feeling excluded, a young man would have little choice but to enter into the routine of prayer and ritual readings that set the tone and rhythm of existence within the walls. Conversely, the evils of the world—primarily politics and sex—are not allowed even the tiniest foothold. The struggle for purity is not an easy one. For all the interdictions, the world is everywhere, lurking just outside the door, hovering in the shadows, blaring from the radios of passing cars, flickering in store windows, screaming in heavy black type from the headlines of newspapers displayed on the newsstands, sashaying down the streets in the form of modern young women dressed in short skirts and platform shoes, tight-fitting pants and, most provocative of all, scarfless heads.

"Our aim is to train true Muslim believers," says Mustafa. As I asked myself, train them for what? Later, I realized that to ask the question was to make assumptions that revealed more about the questioner than about the movement. Becoming a true Muslim was the purpose, and only the movement could define what constituted such a person. Though it was never said, I did not doubt that the model was Said Nursi himself. The New Said, not the Old.


BY THE TIME we reached Emirdag, a small agricultural town on the western edge of the Anatolian steppe, a place even more desolate and lonely than Isparta, metallic gray clouds had covered the sky. There was a whiff of winter in the cold wind that whirled dust down streets where the only traffic was an occasional farm tractor.

We had come here to meet a small man in his early sixties with bright black eyes and a thin mustache who had a story to tell. He was waiting at the Nur headquarters.

Mahmut Çaliskan was his name; he had met and been befriended by Said Nursi in 1944, when he was a six-year-old. Bediuzzaman had come to Emirdag in late August of that year. While in Barla, he had been tried and sentenced repeatedly for offenses under Article 163 of the Criminal Code, the catch-all clause that prohibited exploitation of religion or religious feelings that might damage state security, a concept of wildly variable geometry. After serving a prison term of several months, he had been exiled to the town of Kastamonu, high in the mountains south of the Black Sea coast, where he spent seven years, cultivating once again a flourishing garden of followers.

When he finally reached Emirdag, he had just won acquittal on charges of sedition. Buoyed by optimism, Said and his pupils and followers began to expand the scope of their activities. "I was amazed to see him, wearing Ottoman dress and a turban, which was then illegal, even though he was accompanied by two soldiers," Mr. Çaliskan said, through Kerem, whose endurance and linguistic skills had been sorely tried, but not defeated, by the last 36 hours of intense, almost non-stop question-and-answer.

"It was fascinating for me, as a young boy, to see him praying in public, which was illegal. We were a family of believers, but we had heard nothing of this strange man. My older brother visited him at his hotel and offered to help. He was pleased, and asked us to rent a house for him. We found a place, on the main street right across from the police station. He insisted on paying the rent, otherwise he would not accept the kindness. They agreed—what could they do?—and he moved in. Then the writing and copying of the *Risale-i Nur* began again. We kept it a secret."

Said's activities may have been a secret in the eyes of the young Çaliskan, but they were no secret to the police. Alarmed by the quickening pace of a religious revival that was unfolding, all quite legally, beneath their very noses, and stimulated by the widespread indignation the last round of trials had stirred up and the relief the acquittal of Bediuzzaman had generated, the Ankara government had resolved to crack down, hard. Despite his protestations of indifference to the political world, Said, now armed with machine-duplicated copies of his work, "put the case of the *Risale-i Nur* directly to the authorities,"[176] by sending off copies to government ministries.

It was not a move calculated to appease. In the years since Atatürk's death in 1938, his successor Ismet Inönü had strengthened his iron-fingered grip on the state. Said's biographer Sükran Vahide claims that two of his leading ministers—precisely those who had instigated the earlier arrest and trial of Bediuzzaman—were communists who enjoyed close connections to the Soviet Union. As the Cold War began and the Truman Doctrine was proclaimed, Inönü was forced to choose between the West and the USSR, and permit political liberalization in sub-homeopathic doses as a condition of aid. This apparently further infuriated the still-influential atheists, who redoubled their attempts to silence the indomitable exile of Emirdag.[177]

In late 1947, police, seconded by officials from the dreaded Public Prosecutor's headquarters, came knocking on his door, and on several occasions, actually broke it down and searched the premises for subversive material. They found only copies of the *Risale-i Nur*, which they duly seized. In late January the other shoe dropped; Said and dozens of his supporters were arrested on charges of exploiting religious feelings and inciting people against the government.

The fury of the authorities zeroed in, with the accuracy of a latter-day NATO smart bomb, on Said's *Fifth Ray*, a lengthy commentary on the Qur'anic verses and commentaries that deal with the end of time. In it he quotes a Hadith that says: "A fearsome person at the end of time will rise in the morning and on his forehead will be written, 'This is a disbeliever.'" Said interpreted the saying thus: "The Sufyan [this fearsome person] will wear the headgear of non-believers, and make everyone else wear it.

However, since it will be generally adopted under compulsion ... those who wear it—unwillingly—will not become unbelievers."[178]

If the zealots in the Public Prosecutor's office immediately identified the Sufyan as none other than Atatürk, the author of the "hat laws," what were they to make of a later passage in which Said writes that the Sufyan who will emerge as a leader in the Islamic world "will be a leading politician who is extremely capable, intelligent, and active, does not like ostentation and gives no importance to personal rank and glory; he will be a military leader who is extremely bold, forceful, energetic and resolute, and does not condescend to fame-seeking, and he will captivate the Muslims"?[179] This leader will have it said that he possesses "wondrous and extraordinary power. [ ... ] He will attack religion and the sacred with a boldness and insolence arising from his absolute denial. But since the ordinary people will not know the truth of the matter, they will suppose it to be an extraordinary power and courage." A more accurate description of the irresistible ascension of the Father of the Turks could not easily have been written. It was all the more prescient for having been composed in 1907.

The accused conspirators were transported to Afyon, a city not far from Emirdag whose peculiar microclimate makes it one of the coldest places in Turkey. There they were thrown into an unheated wing of the prison, itself considered the worst in the country.

In his defense, Said noted that because the controversial reference to the Sufyan was so plain he had suppressed the commentary, allowing it to be circulated only after it had been declared legal by a previous court decision. This time, the defense failed. Nearly a year after his arrest, the Afyon court found Bediuzzaman guilty under old reliable Article 163, and sentenced him to two years of penal servitude, shortened to 20 months because of age. He was then 70 years old, frail and ill. The students and followers were handed slightly shorter sentences. Despite acquittal by appeal courts, he was made to serve the entire term, but it was not until 1956 that his name was finally cleared.

When, in 1949, he had served his sentence, Said returned to Emirdag and took up residence in the same house. Four years later, in 1953, Mr. Çaliskan had a vivid dream. Stalin had come in person, to Emirdag, to kill Bediuzzaman. A group of Nur students were standing guard at the gate, but he pushed them aside and strode down the long, dark corridor. There, Bediuzzaman attacked him with a hammer, killing him instead. "When I woke up, I told my brothers. Said found out and called me to him. He was seated in his bed. When I'd finished, he said: 'The *Risale-i Nur* will break the back of communism.' As it turned out, Stalin had died on the day I had my dream."

Like the Pope, to quote the late Mr. Djugashvili, Bediuzzaman Said Nursi could command no battalions. Though he never wrote to Uncle Joe exhorting him to forsake the evils of communism as did Imam Khomeini to Gorbachev two decades later, he did in later life become something of a cold warrior, endorsing Turkey's entry into NATO and applauding its participation in the Korean War as a campaign against atheism. Veterans of the expeditionary force would never forget him for it and now number among his most devoted followers.

By then, 1953, Mr. Çaliskan had grown so attached to the elderly mollah that he followed Said—who in the meantime traveled to Istanbul to face further charges under the marvelously elastic Article 163—and finally back to the house in Isparta, where he became his driver.

"What I remember most was that, even though the government repressed him, Said Nursi never bowed his head. Instead, he gave us the *Risale-i Nur*. 'For this lone Said,' he used to say, 'thousands of Saids will be entering the world.' His life and manner were simple, he loved to talk, and enjoyed my brothers' jokes. One bowl of soup would last him for three days. But his work was great."

I decide to raise a question that the community appears most anxious to avoid, that of Ustad's relations with women. "He never allowed females in his house," Mr. Çaliskan assures me categorically. "But in spite of this, he had many women students, perhaps more than men. Everyone was drawn to him, physically and spiritually. When you were in his presence, you wanted to kiss his hand; women wanted to kiss his hand. But in the Shafi'i school of Islamic jurisprudence [to which Said subscribed], a woman's touch would destroy the effect of the ablutions. So the women could only kiss his elbow."

By now Mr. Çaliskan was being swept along by the momentum of his reminiscences. The other people in the room, Mustafa, Salih, and several Nur brothers from Emirdag were listening in rapt attention to a tale they must have heard many times before yet found endlessly fascinating, endlessly renewed. Later, in Istanbul, I once again witnessed the exceptional deference, even reverence, with which these companions of Said Nursi were treated. Though the distilled wisdom of age often consisted of an inability to describe his character, younger people in their company hung eagerly from their every word. They had sat at the feet of the master and that was enough.

"My tongue cannot describe him. I could only be his servant. He is like an ocean. I did not serve him because of something in me," he concludes. "It was a matter of destiny."

The hour is growing late. We must leave Emirdag for the return trip to Isparta. Mr. Çaliskan leads us back to the automobile, then hops into the front seat. Slowly, we wind through the narrow streets until we reach the public square, where we disembark. Our guide of an afternoon points to a tumble-down building a few doors from where we are standing at the edge of the sidewalk. "There was the house that Bediuzzaman lived in for so many years here in Emirdag. After the death of the master, I took up business. First I had a clothing store, then I sold jewelry. This is my shop," he says, pointing to a small store window bright with the gleam of silver and gold. "Now, I devote my life to building *dershanes*."

THE ISTANBUL BUS leaves at midnight, giving us time enough for one last visit. "We think you will find it interesting," says Mustafa with an enigmatic smile. Soon the Toyota is winding upward through the streets of Isparta and into the brush-covered foothills among which the town is nestled.

The night is crystal cold. Under a near-full moon, the ground-hugging coal smoke has drawn a wispy veil over pine groves, mosques and minarets, and low-built houses. Soon Isparta lies beneath us, distant, ghostly in its mantle of haze and dim yellow streetlights. The car comes to a stop, we get out. A fresh breeze has sprung up. Here the air is clean, pungent with the scent of dry weeds. Pocketing the flashlight he'd brought along but does not need in the moonlight, Mustafa leads us down a short flight of steps through a stone gate.

The place is a cemetery, a remote, mountain cemetery, a final resting place for the bones of the poor. In the brilliant moonlight we pick our way between gravestones and the bushes that have overgrown several of the plots, until we come to a halt in front of a depression in the ground.

Several years ago, some people from Isparta had come to bury a family member who had just died, explains Mustafa. As they dug, their shovels hit metal. They dug some more and came upon a casket. Without opening it, they knew it held the remains of Said Nursi. Everybody in the town was aware of the circumstances of his death and burial, and of how his body had been removed from the grave in Urfa and hidden in these parts by the army. For nine years, the coffin had lain buried here, in this graveyard. Immediately they alerted the local Nur community. Some of the brothers dug up the coffin and carried it to a secret location for reburial. Now, only a handful of people know where he is buried, and they will never tell.

It was a fitting end for Said Nursi, who had always insisted that his place of burial not be known, that his sole monument should be his life's work, the *Risale-i Nur*. Perhaps the delirium of illness had driven him to Urfa, to die. Perhaps, in a final act of truly monumental irony, the State had become the unwitting executor of his often expressed will. No one will ever know.

For several minutes we stood there, shivering in the cold moonlight. The cemetery on the hillside above Isparta was a fitting end, too, for my journey into the hidden Turkey. I had come as far as I could come. Old Said had effaced himself, vanished into the memories of his aging pupils, been transformed into a saintly legend whose name was now invoked by young men in ritual prayers. He had become a living text. What that text would become was now in the hands of millions.

# XIV

# Epilogue

MY VOYAGE INTO ANATOLIA traced a long, looping trajectory that carried me from Istanbul into the wild mountains of Kurdistan, across the arid plains of the southeast, to the empty grave in Urfa and into the rolling steppes that stretched from Konya west to Isparta. As I went I encountered pious men and religious communities, the mute clamor of deserted battlefields and the ghosts of vanished peoples. But Bediuzzaman Said Nursi, the man whose footsteps I'd set out to follow, remained illusive and complex.

As I progressed, all I had seen, all I had heard and read drove me toward the conclusion that, if one word could sum up the career of Bediuzzaman Said Nursi as an Islamic militant, failure would be that word. His attempts to salvage the Ottoman Empire as the standard-bearer of Islam had been in vain. His combat against the despotism of the Sultan, cynically exploited by the Young Turks, had come to naught. His dash and courage as field commander of the Felt Hat militia could not stem the onrush of the Russian army. His dream of a new educational institution in far Anatolia which would reconcile the two Muslim brother peoples, Turks and Kurds, and infuse Islamic traditionalism with the technical genius of the

West, remained only a dream. By 1925 his world lay shattered, fragmented.

The collapse of that world, a process that reached its lowest ebb in the aftermath of the final, bitter confrontation with Mustafa Kemal in Ankara, had been as protracted as it was agonizing. Never a man to be swayed by sentiment, Kemal wielded certainty like a bludgeon, supreme authority like a bulldozer. What feeble arms could the man of faith muster, what disputation against the overweening argument of Might?

Turkey's future, Atatürk concluded, belonged to him. Across the Caucasus frontier, the Ottoman Empire's ancient Russian antagonist was now governed by a vanguard party that claimed to have harnessed the dynamic of historical inevitability. In the new Republic, that same dynamic would sweep along an entire society. As there would be a New Soviet Man, whose being would be shaped by the productive forces, so too there would be a New Turkish Man, whose identity would be remodeled along racial lines, liberated from the multiethnic and religious fetters of the past.

(While the victorious Bolsheviks could argue that they were acting in the interests of those whom they claimed to represent, the working class, the claims of Kemal and his followers were more ambiguous. They appeared to have cast the encumbrances of the old regime aside, but they had in fact seized control of its authoritarian heart.)

In the 1930s, as Kemal's CHP consolidated its control over the state, the race to the West took on even more bizarre overtones. A national opera and theatre, decreed the supreme leader, would lay the foundations of a modern, Western high culture. Few in power would have considered it odd that such once-powerful cultural influences as Ottoman, Arabic and Persian literature, art and music would be proscribed while the linguistic and esthetic models imported from the West would be imposed. Those that dared voice such objections were silenced.

Only one obstacle remained to be overcome: that of Islam. Though Mustafa Kemal moved quickly to disestablish, then assert control over the once-mighty Sunni religious establishment through the Directory of Religious Affairs, and outlawed the Sufi orders, no national opera, no national theater, no compulsory educational system nor military service could break the ties that bound the subjects of the new regime to their ancestral faith.

Around the bright islands of enlightened despotism that blazed in Istanbul and Ankara lay the vast sea of what the Kemalist jargoneers called reaction and darkness, the small towns, villages, hamlets of Anatolia, the communities who had declined to replace their belief in a system of divine order with worship of the Turkish national State, and Atatürk as its prophet.

ON THE NAQSHBANDI PATH, Said wrote during his darkest hours, one must abandon four things: the world, the hereafter, existence, and abandonment itself. Though his path was not that of the Sufis, Bediuzzaman knew it well, and marshaled its peculiar, paradoxical power. "On the way of impotence," he added, reformulating as he went, "four things are necessary: absolute poverty, absolute impotence, absolute thanks and absolute ardor."[180] In Barla these four things were given to him in an abundance of what must have seemed divine generosity. Alone, in the treehouses atop Pine Mountain or in the great plane tree of Barla, he either intuited the path he must follow, or that path was revealed to him in a burst of illumination.

There, among the devout peasants, fisherfolk and poor provincial religious intellectuals, the failure of political activism metamorphosed into a non-political religious rebirth. Through his encounters with the republican regime in Ankara, Said had concluded that traditional religious politics would encounter nothing but stern, unrelenting repression. To openly challenge the new state, with its powerful security apparatus and dictatorial command structure, would play into the hands of the westernizing forces who now ruled the country with an iron hand and would reduce him to a docile court mollah.

Even before exile and repression were thrust upon him, he had adopted the strategy of exile and cunning as his defense. Abandoning the temptation to change the world, he would devote his life and resources to changing the eye that sees the world. The instrument for bringing this about was the *Risale-i Nur*.

Within 25 years this curious document, at once an ever-expanding work in progress and compendium of essays and Qur'anic commentary that dwell in greatest length on those verses which concern what he called the truths of belief, had insinuated itself deep into the fabric of Turkish society. Perhaps it would be more accurate to say that the concerns it addressed had always been alive and active, that Bediuzzaman had found the words and the syntax that would awaken ancient resonances and make them fresh and new.

"Unlike other works," Said wrote, "the *Risale-i Nur* was not taken from the sciences and branches of learning or from other books; it has no source other than the Qur'an; it has no master other than the Qur'an; it has no authority other than the Qur'an. Its author had no other book with him when it was written."[181]

Success, a concept proper to the acquisitive society of the West, was a term foreign to Said Nursi. Still, the paradox of his life and career was this: only in failure did he attain his ultimate triumph. Where action had failed to rouse and mobilize the faithful, inaction that was stunning in its disinterestedness and self-denial would not. Where politics had attempted and failed to use religion to reach its ends, beneath his pen religion would abjure politics to recreate, in microcosm, a society that had been rent asunder by reform in the name of progress and inevitability.

\* \* \*

EVERY SATURDAY THE DUSTY COMPOUND beneath the interchange that funnels traffic from the main Istanbul ring road down into the city comes alive with birds. Pigeons, to be precise: homing pigeons, masterpieces of the pigeon breeder's art, sleek, powerful-looking creatures secured by a length of string; and decorative pigeons too, multi-hued hybrids with lustrous feather coats the color of alabaster or September dawn, held protectively in cloth-draped cages.

I had not, however, come here to peruse and covet the pigeons. In fact, I had been momentarily waylaid by them. Just beyond the bird market, atop a landscaped hillock overlooking the motorway, stands the granite monument that was my destination. Illuminated by floodlights at night, sculpted by raw sunlight at the meridian, the massive structure had caught my eye on my first entry into the city. It shelters the remains of Adnan Menderes, Turkey's first democratically elected prime minister—he who died swinging from the end of a rope in September 1961 more than a year after being toppled by a military *coup d'état*. Menderes' trial and summary execution had taken place on Yassiada, a prison island in the Sea of Marmara, a venue that was later echoed by the choice of Imrali for the show trial and death sentence of Abdullah Öcalan.

The monument is set in a no-man's land shoehorned between the densely populated slums that butt up against the inside of the Byzantine walls not far from the spot, marked by a Turkish flag, where Mehmet II's Janissaries had breached them, and the industrial suburbs that march off across the western hills. Leaving behind me the pigeon market, I was now moving up the esplanade where the man beloved of many, hated by many, now lies in an uneasy prominence that is studiously ignored, as if even his memory were impolite company.

Few in Turkey, when pressed, would not admit familiarity with the rise and tragic fall of the "the elected dictator." Most people I met had at least a grudging respect for the man who not only brought a semblance of democracy after decades of republican totalitarianism, but restored Islam to public legitimacy.

Unlike Atatürk, whose image today is as omnipresent as was Mao Ze-dong's during the wildest years of China's Cultural Revolution and who can, like Mao, be soon expected to become an object of irony, Adnan Menderes remains a man without a face. His memory, rehabilitated by the late Turgut Özal (whose tomb, coincidentally, is being built next to the Menderes memorial) has been amputated of all the other appurtenances of existence. There is no suggestion of the parabolic trajectory of his career: the politician's smile, the heroic pose, the grim-lipped acceptance of the death sentence, the swinging corpse. Menderes is a man, and a memory, encased in granite.

No firebrand and no revolutionary, Menderes was brilliant, charismatic and ambitious. Born in 1899 into the wealthy land-owning class in Aydin province, one of Turkey's richest agricultural regions, he assumed the leadership of the country's democratic forces in 1946. The Republic had observed strict neutrality throughout the war, but the cost of maintaining a force powerful enough to dissuade the Germans from crossing the Bulgarian border had proved crippling. As the United States began to assert itself not only as the prime mover of European reconstruction but as the leader in the struggle against Soviet communism, then-dictator Ismet Inönü was faced with a dilemma. In order to reap the full harvest of Yankee largesse, Turkey would have to democratize—superficially at least.

The Democrat Party, the first overt challenge to the ruling Republican People's Party (CHP), had been conceived as a lightning rod, to funnel the widespread pent-up hatred of the republican state and its gendarmes into the structures of parliamentary legitimacy. After all, its leadership was drawn from the same narrow class of landowners, traders, industrialists and military men that made up the CHP. On July 11, 1947, Inönü publicly declared that the Democrat Party was not a subversive organization. By purest coincidence, the Turkish-American Agreement on Aid was signed the following day. [182]

Another condition of American support was the fight against what was then known as the Red Menace. Though the Turkish bureaucracy sheltered many holdovers from the Kemalist bad old days of regimentation and heavy-handed state control in the name of secularism, few could have been mistaken for socialists. Those who dared to demonstrate sympathy for socialist ideas were now mutated into potential traitors and driven mercilessly from public life, a necessity on which the Democrats and Republicans saw eye to eye. In fact, argues historian Feroz Ahmad, the parties agreed that the status quo must be maintained, and that the changes needed for Turkey to carry through with its westernizing reforms would have to take place within the capitalist framework. [183]

On paper, it seemed like a fine idea. But the strategic planners in Ankara and Washington miscalculated. Menderes may have been a venal, greedy man, a true tribute to his class. But he was sensitive enough to the subterranean rumblings working their way through Turkish society to know that if he could ride the tiger of popular discontent with westernization, greater power would be his. He knew too that his ability to manipulate the symbols of Islam, which remained deeply rooted in the hearts of the Turks, would provide him the key.

In May, 1950, Menderes' Democrat Party won a stunning victory over the CHP, bringing 27 years of Kemalist rule to an end. One of the first acts of the new government was to lift the ban on the use of Arabic in the *azan*. As the introduction of Turkish in the call to prayer had shocked Turks, so the reversal of the edict galvanized them.

The Qur'an, goes the Turkish proverb, was revealed in the Hijaz, written in Egypt, and recited in Turkey. On that day, people fell to the ground, weeping, when they heard the sweet, lilting, slightly nasal cadences ring out once again from the minarets. In villages and towns, in Istanbul and in the capital, sacrificial lambs were slaughtered.

Moving rapidly, Menderes instituted state funding for religious high schools. Though he and his party were committed to Atatürkian secularism, the new prime minister had made it clear from the beginning that while the People's Party had exploited secularism as a weapon against Islam, his regime was determined to protect religion against state intervention. [184]

"The policy of the DP" writes Pakistani historian Mohammad Feroze, "was conducive to the development of a renewed interest in the study of Islam and its application to the daily life of the people. It resulted in the emergence of a new generation of young men and women who began to take a keen interest in Islam, and became proud of their Islamic heritage." [185]

Menderes' ten-year term of office coincided exactly with the return of Bediuzzaman Said Nursi to that activity which for the 27 hard years of the Kemalist dictatorship he had cursed and abhorred: politics. For all his saintly reserve, for all the rigors of house arrest, exile and prison, Said had remained extremely well-informed about developments in Turkish society. The same "postmen" who carried the latest hand-copied letters and essays to his followers and pupils around the country would return to Barla, Emirdag, Kastamonu and Isparta with news from Istanbul, the capital, provincial centers, the villages and the countryside. His repeated court appearances had kept him apprised of the disposition of the state, just as his uncompromising stand had exposed its contradictions and weaknesses.

"Do not call me to the world," he had admonished those friends who had attempted to persuade him to participate in active politics. Now the world itself was calling him to it. Said, after years of silent withdrawal, responded. While he served the last months of his prison sentence behind the cold walls of Afyon prison, he had written that he "surmised" that a Third Said, after the Old and the New Saids, would likely emerge. [186] His surmise was well-founded. Despite the repression, trials and imprisonments, the fervor with which millions of Turks had taken up the *Risale-i Nur* had become one of the forces that had led to the emergence of the Democrat Party. This too Said knew, and intended to exploit.

Never straying too close to the precipice of direct partisan involvement, he described the Democrats as the lesser of two evils, and lent the party both support and guidance. By now, many of his followers had gained influential positions, which they wielded to encourage DP deputies to adopt policies based on or favorable to Islamic principles.

If they were successful, Said reasoned, the gap that had been opened between Turkey and the rest of the Islamic world could be narrowed. The true nation of the Turks, as was that of the Arabs, he had long argued, was Islam. Closer relations with the other Islamic countries would revitalize Islamic brotherhood, itself the key to Islamic nationhood. Eagerly, he endorsed the Baghdad Pact as a step toward peace and unity among Muslim peoples. The alliance between Turkey and Iraq would strike a blow against what he called "racialism" but can be more easily identified as nationalism, both still in the ascendant today in Turkey and the Arab world.

For Bediuzzaman, those were heady years. Suddenly he had emerged from obscurity and into the spotlight of events, had become a force in public debate, a protagonist in the struggle. No longer the bandoliered firebrand ready to ride off at the head of a cavalry regiment, he fired off letters of exhortation and counsel to Menderes; his followers lobbied ceaselessly for the *Risale-i Nur* to be included in the educational curriculum.

Whether Bediuzzaman was acting out of conscious awareness or not, his attempts to influence the country's political life revealed how stubbornly the conflict between the traditional and the modern remained latent in the undercurrents of Turkish political life. Suddenly emerging to the surface, it took a sharp turn. In a series of messages to Menderes, Bediuzzaman explained how the socio-political ills of the land derived, ultimately, from their origin in Western philosophy, and offered remedies drawn from the ultimate countervailing source, the Qur'an itself, or the Hadith, the reports of a saying or action of the Prophet.

In his exhortations to the prime minister, Said often invoked what he called the "fundamental law" contained in the Qur'anic verse: "No bearer of burdens can bear the burden of another." Skulking beneath the catastrophes of the twentieth century, the wars and the campaigns of extermination, he detected the "human law" that had replaced divine prescription: that individuals may be sacrificed for the good of the nation and society. This perverse law, he argued, had "overturned a thousand years of human progress."[187]

Ostensibly referring to the domineering secularists who had been appointed to government and administrative positions during the Kemalist dictatorship, Bediuzzaman cautioned that "a nation's ruler is its servant." But the warning was meant for the prime minister. While the officials loyal to the secular regime remained encrusted in the state apparatus, awaiting the moment to attack the Democrats, Menderes himself had begun to display all the signs of a downfall foretold.

Elected with high hopes, not only for releasing Turks from the bondage of doctrinaire secularism but for improving the hard lot of the poor, Menderes was unable to make good on his implied promises. The riots that wracked Istanbul in 1955, touched off by public discontent over the Cyprus imbroglio, revealed a deep and virulent sense of economic dispossession and political estrangement.

Armed with the full powers granted to it under the Kemalist constitution, the Grand National Assembly became the ruling Democrat Party's wrecker's ball for the demolition of democratic institutions. After being triumphantly returned to power in 1954, Menderes began to resemble the dictator he had democratically defeated in 1950. His reasons were unimpeachable: Inönü and his supporters had never accepted their defeat, and, from their positions of power within the state machinery, had continued to undermine the new government's work. They saw Menderes' efforts to open a broader public space for Islam as a betrayal of the secular principles of Atatürkism.

Responding to these pressures, Menderes, in 1953 had commissioned the Anit Kabir in Ankara, the grandiloquent funerary monument to Atatürk. But no good-will gestures would ever assuage his enemies, driven as they were by a thirst for "philosophical" revenge. Using the considerable powers of his parliamentary majority, Menderes cracked down on the opposition;

on all who opposed him, for whatever reason. Newspapers were closed, journalists imprisoned. In an atmosphere of growing crisis, Turkey went to the polls in 1957.

This time, far from staying aloof from the bitter partisan struggle, Said Nursi weighed in with the full force of his influence, openly delivering his vote to the Democrat Party and calling upon his followers to do the same. The CHP had expected to win the elections. Now they held Bediuzzaman responsible for their defeat.

In February, 1959, Menderes survived the crash of his plane at Gatwick, near London. He attributed his miraculous survival to divine intervention. From there it was but a small step for the Democrat Party machine to depict their leader as a man chosen by God.

The year, writes Feroz Ahmad, was a tragic one for Turkish democracy. "For the press, which was considered the conscience and guardian of the democratic regime, it was a year of trial and tribulation during which more newspapers were closed down and journalists imprisoned than in any other year."

In April, 1960, a Committee of Investigation had been set up to investigate Democrat charges that the CHP opposition had transgressed legal limits. Soon after, it approved legislation empowering the Committee to censor the press, to suppress newspapers, to issue subpoenas, and to impose sentences. [188] By May, a military plot to overthrow the government was so well under way that it had advanced to the public rumor stage. In early May, the special Committee announced that it would extend its probe to the military establishment.

On May 21, a demonstration by cadets at the War College in Ankara struck a heavy blow to the government's authority and prestige. Martial law was declared and Ankara was placed under a state of siege. The military conspirators were not the creation of Menderes' imagination; they were real and they were deadly. They knew, too, that an investigation would uncover their subversive program. On May 27, officers of the Turkish armed forces transformed their threats into action and overthrew the Menderes government.

Over the radio crackled the message: "Honorable fellow countrymen! During the crisis into which our democracy has fallen, in view of the recent sad incidents and in order to avert fratricide, the Turkish Armed Forces have taken over the administration of the country." It was read out by Colonel Alparslan Türkes, head of the ultra-nationalist faction. The colonel would go on to lead the Gray Wolves militia, which was to distinguish itself as a street-fighting force and, latterly, in those very special assignments too delicate for the state to undertake directly, a strategic and political relationship that was laid bare decades later in the crash at Susurluk. The party Türkes founded, the MHP (National Movement Party), would become the junior partner in the ruling coalition in the aftermath of the April, 1999, election.

Menderes and his colleagues were tried by a military tribunal which brought down the expected guilty verdict in September of the following year. Of the fifteen death sentences, only those of the former prime minister and his two closest colleagues were not commuted. The army, more superstitious than its religious adversaries, desired at all costs to destroy the aura of invincibility and immortality that had come to surround Menderes. Immortal no more, the elected dictator now swung from a rope on a lonely island gallows. Though his greatest sin may have been excessive conviction of his own righteousness, he was also republican Turkey's first public figure to acknowledge the hidden Islamic undercurrent in the life of the country. For this, above all, he had to die.

It was too late for Bediuzzaman Said Nursi to intervene. The fiery old holy warrior had died and been buried in Urfa two months before the *coup d'état*. His faithful students had long before been neutralized, anesthetized by respect for the democratic principles that their tormentors would honor only in the breach. But even had they weighed into the sharpening conflict with only their strength of numbers and the legitimacy of their cause, they could not have overcome the guns and tanks of the army, nor Menderes' betrayal of the democratic principles he had first espoused.

The military dictators quickly proclaimed their intentions: Turkey was to return to Kemalist orthodoxy, which was to be forever after guaranteed by the armed forces. Article 111 of the new Constitution, adopted in 1961, established a National Security Council consisting of key government ministers, the chief of the General Staff and representatives of the Armed Forces. Its function was to "assist the cabinet in the making of decisions related to national security and coordination."[189] It was to become the true locus of state power.

Since 1961, Turkey's armed forces have been more than the disinterested guardian of the Kemalist heritage. In the aftermath of the coup, an agency called the Army Mutual Assistance Association (OYAK) was set up. Under its regulations, all regular officers of the Turkish Armed Forces are obliged to invest 10% of their salaries in the fund, to be reimbursed at a later date. Today, OYAK is the country's third-largest financial holding company, with connections to banks, industrial complexes and the lucrative national armament industry. With such a large stake not only in the economy, but in the perpetuation of the dominant economic system of huge private holding companies that control the country's banks, media conglomerates and industrial establishment, the Armed Forces cannot afford to remain neutral or above politics. And as the Susurluk incident and the February 28, 1997 coup showed, though the men in uniform could well tolerate a Mafia presence at the uppermost reaches of the State, they could not abide the presence of even a weak and docile parliamentary Islamist political party.

Against them, Bediuzzaman's followers have returned to the example of the New Said.

Throughout the Islamic world, for the last century, a debate has raged on how to halt and reverse the decline of a once dominant order in its confrontation with the West. Twenty years ago, the forces of Islamic revival, stimulated by the rise of Ayatollah

Khomeini in Iran, and driven by the theoretical brilliance of Ali Shariati, seemed flush with revolutionary promise.

That tide has ebbed. Islamic revolutionary movements have been defeated militarily, outmaneuvered politically or purchased by the World Superpower. In Turkey, the brave but flawed experiment of Dr. Erbakan's Refah Partisi illustrated the limits of parliamentary democracy in a crypto-military national security state.

The Nur community, aloof from the cut and thrust of partisan politics, is often accused of practicing a quietism that can only benefit the regime. It believes, I ultimately concluded, that it is simply emulating its namesake and refusing to allow politics to use religion, by building a stronger, more durable edifice.

High among the traditional values Turks hold precious rank the qualities of patience, stubbornness, frugality and honor. These, too, were the personal qualities of Bediuzzaman Said Nursi, the renewer of belief whose teachings are subtly, in strange and unchartable ways, renewing and reshaping hidden Turkey.

As I traveled from town to town across Anatolia, I never caught up with the elusive Said. His shadow was always disappearing around the next corner, his footprint blurred by the erosion of time. Yet his absence shone like a lodestar. As a man of proud humility who would not be bought, the Bediuzzaman I had come to know swam against the current, abominated the arrogance of the powerful, and braved the mean spirit of the times. I knew a friend when I saw one. And for that alone I would have shaken his hand.

# Notes

1.  The Shi'a, who make up perhaps ten percent of the world's estimated one billion Muslims, trace their spiritual difference with the majority Sunnis to the dispute over the succession of the Prophet Mohammad as head of the community of believers. Before his death, Mohammad had favored his cousin and son-in-law Ali as successor. Ali's claim was rejected by a majority of the community, which selected Abu Bakr, an early convert to Islam and prestigious military commander. Ali became the fourth Caliph, but was assassinated by doctrinal adversaries. His followers became known as the *shi'a*, or party, of Ali, who, by virtue of his blood ties to Mohammad, became the first Imam of Shi'a tradition, in which greater weight is given to the Prophet's descendants.

    The Sunnis, who form the vast majority of Muslims, derive their name from the *Sunna*, or the words and deeds of Mohammad as recorded in the *Hadith*, which lends weight to their claim to be following the example of the Prophet.

2.  The Sufi, writes Laleh Bakhtiar (*Sufi: Expressions of the Mystic Quest*, [London: Thames & Hudson, 1976]) "remembers and invokes the Divine order as it resides in a hidden state within all forms. [...] ... the Sufi-to-be reaches toward the Divine centre through the mystic Quest." Sufis, all of whom trace their spiritual antecedents back to Ali (see endnote 1 above), brought an inner spirituality to a religion which had become excessively concerned with the outward forms of worship. In a world obsessed with pursuit of wealth and political power, they stood for piety and asceticism.

3.  Muhmmad Rashid Feroze, *Islam and Secularism in Kemalist Turkey* (Islamabad: Islamic Research Institute, 1976), 2-3.

4.  See Jean-Daniel Lafond, *Le temps des barbares*, a film produced by Alter-Ciné, 1999.

5.  Herman Hesse, *Steppenwolf*, translated from the German by Basil Creighton (New York: Frederick Ungar Publishing Co., 1957), 300-301.

6.  Sükran Vahide, *Bediuzzaman Said Nursi: The Author of the Risale-i Nur* (Istanbul: Sözler Publications, 1992), 373. In reconstituting the life and times of Bediuzzaman Saïd Nursi, I have relied extensively on Sükran Vahide's painstaking and devout biography.

7.  Ibid., 374.

8.  Serif Mardin, *Religion and Social Change in Modern Turkey: The Case of Bediuzzaman Saïd Nursi* (Albany: State University of New York Press, 1989), 3.

9.  Laleh Bahktiar, *Sufi: Expressions of the Mystic Quest* (London: Thames & Hudson, 1976), 24.

10. Aziz Nesin, *Böyle Gelmis, Böyle Gitmez* (Ankara: 1972), translated and reprinted in Yasar Nuri Öztürk, *The Eye of the Heart: An Introduction to Sufism and the Major Tariqats of Anatolia and the Balkans*, translated by Richard Blakeny (Istanbul: Redhouse Press, 1988).

11. Vahide, 119.

12. Christopher J. Walker, *Armenia: The Survival of a Nation* (London: Croom Helm, 1980), 215.

13. Ibid., 197-198.

14. Mardin, 223.

15. Alan Palmer, *The Decline and Fall of the Ottoman Empire* (London: John Murray, 1992), 249.

16. Quoted in A. A. Vasilisev, *History of the Byzantine Empire 324-1453* (Madison: University of Wisconsin Press, 1958), 357.

17. International Helsinki Federation for Human Rights, *Annual Report, 1997: Human Rights Developments in 1996* (Vienna: International Helsinki Federation for Human Rights, 1997), and Greek Helsinki Committee, *1998 Press Freedom Review* (Athens: 1998). The precise number of journalists imprisoned for their writings in Turkey has been a topic of hot debate for some time. When Mesut Yilmaz took over as Prime Minister in July 1997, 78

journalists were behind bars, according to count kept by the international Committee to Protect Journalists. On leaving office in November 1998, that number had fallen to 25. Article 8 of the Anti-Terror Law provides for prosecution of "written and oral propaganda and assemblies, meetings and demonstrations with the aim of damaging the unity of the State of the Republic of Turkey, the nation ... regardless of the method, intention and ideas thereof." The Report goes on to note that "numerous journalists, academics and human rights defenders were still being arrested and prosecuted in significant numbers under this provision."

18.  Greek Helsinki Committee, *1998 Press Freedom Review* (Athens: 1998). Though based in "arch enemy" Greece, the Greek Helsinki Committee's human rights monitoring in the Balkans is widely recognized as rigorous and even-handed. The GHC has repeatedly distinguished itself by its spirited defense of Greece's embattled Turkish minority.

19.  Lynne Emily Webb, *Fetullah Gülen: Is There More to Him Than Meets the Eye?* (Istanbul: Mercury International Publishing, n.d), 40. This curious little book presents a detailed defense of Fetullah Gülen against his numerous detractors. Although it is written "for the purpose of presenting to the Western public information regarding the recent controversies around radical secularism and fundamentalism in Turkey," (iv) it presupposes a specialist's grasp of contemporary Turkish religious politics. Given the poor quality of its English, this book must be considered as at best a translated assemblage of ill-identified documents, and at worst as a crude polemic verging on imposture. Certainly it will do nothing to dissipate the cloud of ambiguity that surrounds Mr. Gülen.

20.  Palmer, 254.

21.  Bediuzzaman Saïd Nursi, *Letters 1928-1932* (Istanbul: Sözler Publications, 1997), 504.

22.  Muhammad Rashid Feroze, *Islam and Secularism in Kemalist Turkey* (Islamabad, Islamic Research Institute, 1976), 5.

23.  Yasar Nuri Öztürk, *The Eye of the Heart: An Introduction to Sufism and the Major Tariqats of Anatolia and the Balkans*, translated by Richard Blakeny (Istanbul: Redhouse Press, 1988), 15.

24.  Ibid., 63.

25.  Ibid., 21.

26. Hugh Poulton, *Top Hat, Grey Wolf and Crescent: Turkish Nationalism and the Turkish Republic* (New York: New York University Press, 1997), 208.

27. Ibid., 217.

28. Ibid., 213.

29. Vahide, 5.

30. Ibid., 3.

31. Ibid., 5-6.

32. Mardin, 43.

33. Ibid., 42.

34. Ibid., 45.

35. Walker, 126.

36. Vahide, 15.

37. Mardin, 64.

38. Walker, 154-155.

39. Mardin, 167.

40. Mardin, 13.

41. Vahide, 9.

42. Ibid., 9.

43. Mardin, 70.

44. Öztürk, 103.

45. Vahide, 15.

46. Ibid., 16.

47. Mardin, 75.

48. Vahide, 23.

49. Mardin, 76.

50. Ibid., 77.

51. Vasiliev, 461.

52. Lord Kinross (John Patrick Douglas Balfour), *The Ottoman Centuries, The Rise and Fall of the Turkish Empire* (New York: Morrow, 1977), 321.

53. Resat Kasaba, *The Ottoman Empire and the World Economy: The 19th Century* (Albany: State University of New York, 1988), 110.

54. Vahide, 29.

55. Quoted in Ibid., 30.

56. Kinross, 562.

57. Vahide, 34.

58. Palmer, 149.

59. Vahide, 38.

60. Palmer, 144.

61. Walker, 107.

62. Vahide, 34-35.

63. Poulton, 59.

64. Vahide, 41.

65. Mardin, 80.

66. Vahide, 47.

67. Quoted in Vahide, 51-52.

68. See: Fred A. Reed, *Salonica Terminus: Travels Into the Balkan Nightmare* (Vancouver: Talonbooks, 1996).

69. Ibid., 58.

70. Palmer, 201.

71. Ibid., 141-142.

72. Ibid., 208.

73. Vahide, 76-77.

74. Quoted in Vahide, 85.

75. Poulton, 77.

76. Quoted in Vahide, 93-95.

77. Ibid., 87.

78. Bediuzzaman Saïd Nursi, *The Damascus Sermon*, translated by Sükran Vahide (Istanbul: Sözler Nesriyat, 1989), 26-27.

79. Ibid., 35-36.

80. Ibid., 54.

81. Cf. Fred A. Reed, *Salonica Terminus.*

82. Mardin, 87.

83. Ibid., 169.

84. Vahide, 26.

85. Ibid., 114.

86. *La civilisation iranienne* (Paris: Payot, 1952), 212-213.

87. Kinross, 166-167.

88. Walker, 206.

89. Vahide, 120.

90. Ibid., 128.

91. Ibid., 42-43.

92. Hamid Algar, "A Brief History of the Naqshbandi Order," in *Naqshbandis. Cheminements et situation actuelle d'un ordre mystique musulman*, Actes de la Table Ronde de Sèvres, 2-4 mai, 1985 (Istanbul: Institut Français d'Études Anatoliennes, 1990), 3.

93. Ibid., 5.

94. Ibid., 15.

95. Ibid., 137.

96. Quoted in Vahide, 257.

97. Ibid., 256.

98. *Le Monde Diplomatique*, mars, 1998.

99. Quoted in Mardin, 196-197.

100. Hakan Aslaneli, "Hurrah for the Criminals' Day" in *Turkish Daily News*, November 4, 1997. Mr. Aslaneki, an outspoken and courageous reporter for the country's only English newspaper, encouraged me to explore the ramifications of the Susurluk Incident. This account draws on a lengthy interview with him, as well as on articles under his byline published on the anniversary of the event.

101. *Turkish Daily News*, April 6, 1998.

102. Poulton, 48.

103. Ibid., 62.

104. Ibid., 84.

105. Ibid., 138.

106. Edward Mead Earle, *Turkey, the Great Powers and the Baghdad Railway: A Study in Imperialism* (New York: Macmillan, 1935), 3-4.

107. Palmer, 192.

108. Op. cit., 65.

109. Vahide, 110.

110. Ibid., 116.

111. Palmer, 226-227.

112. Yerasimon, Stéphane, "Dix Jours en Méditerranée," in *Istanbul 1914-1923*, les éditions Autrement, Série Mémoires, N° 14 (Paris, mars, 1992): 43-60.

113. Vahide, 21.

114. Ibid., 22.

115. Walker, 211.

116. Ibid., 222.

117. Philip K. Hitti, *History of the Arabs* (New York, St. Martin's Press, 1970), 397-399.

118. Özturk, 27.

119. Ibid., 37.

120. Vahide, 18.

121. Hitti, 751.

122. Malise Ruthven, *Islam in the World* (New York: Oxford University Press, 1984), 302-307.

123. Ibid., 305.

124. Hitti, 437.

125. Ibid., 78-79.

126. Ibid., 153.

127. Quoted in Autremont, *Istanbul 1914-1923*, 144.

128. Vahide, 116.

129. Ibid., 117.

130. Ibid., 137.

131. Palmer, 248.

132. Ibid., 252.

133. Quoted in Vahide, 150-151.

134. Ibid., 172.

135. Ibid., 165.

136. Mardin, 93.

137. Vahide, 159.

138. Ibid., 160.

139. Georgios S. Mastropoulos, "Ecumenical Patriarchate of Constantinople," in *Motion: The Magazine of Olympic Airways* (Athens, 1991), 18.

140. Poulton, 88.

141. Ibid., 102.

142. Ibid., 117.

143. Ahmad, Feroz, *The Turkish Experiment in Democracy 1950-1975* (London: C. Hurst & Co., 1977), 54.

144. Anonymous, *Ta Tourkika Englemata tes Konstantinouleos ten 6en kai 7en Septembriou 1955* (Athenai: Etaireia Thrakikon Meleton, 1956).

145. Grégoire Cassimatis, *Esquisse d'une sociologie du Phariotisme in Symposium l'Époque phanariote 21-25 octobre 1970* (Thessaloniki: Institute for Balkan Studies, 1974), 160.

146. Ibid., 164.

147. Kinross, 405.

148. Quoted in Nicolas Iorga, *Byzance après Byzance* (Paris: Éditions Balland, 1992), 247.

149. Vahide, 178.

150. Ibid., 180.

151. Mardin, 95.

152. Qur'an II: 258, *The Meaning of the Glorious Qur'an*, text and explanatory translation by Marmaduke Pickthall (Tehran: Salehi Publications, n.d.)

153. Qur'an XXI: 52-69, Ibid.

154. Mardin, 177.

155. John L. Esposito, *Islam and Politics* (Syracuse: Syracuse University Press, 1984), 1.

156. Bernard Lewis, *The Muslim Discovery of Europe* (New York: Norton, 1982), 223.

157. The Janissaries, from the Turkish "Yeni Ceri"—"New Troops"— were chosen from among the finest physical and intellectual specimens of their villages, and drawn exclusively from Christian families. Though forcible recruitment of their youths into the Corps underlined the inferior status of the Christian communities, families chosen enjoyed favored status in a society where proximity to the ruler was the sole avenue of social promotion. After being forcibly converted, the recruits were initiated into the arcana of Janissary doctrine and discipline. The practice, unique to the Ottoman state, had no visible Qur'anic justification. Selective rather than all-inclusive, this particular institution, known as the *devsirme* ("gathering"), was instituted by Sultan Beyazit I, the survivor and victor of the battle of Kosova, at the end of the fourteenth century. In theory, the converted adolescents would prove devoted servants and protectors of their sole benefactor, the Sultan. In practice, after several centuries, they formed a dissolute, domineering praetorian guard that successfully overthrew several rulers.

158. Öztürk, 63.

159. Kinross, 48.

160. Ibid., 82.

161. Melikoff, Irène, "Le problème Kizilbas" in *Turcica*, Vol. VI (1975): 65.

162. Bakhtiar, 95.

163. Bediuzzaman Saïd Nursi, *The Flashes Collection*, translated from the Turkish by Sukhran Vahide (Istanbul: Sözler Nesriyat, 1995), 43.

164. Vahide, 184. I have relied extensively on Sükran Vahide's biography in this account of Bediuzzaman's voyage into exile and his years in western Anatolia.

165. Poulton, 98.

166. Op. cit., 193.

167. Poulton, 98.

168. Mardin, 147-155.

169. Vasiliev, 428-430.

170. Op cit., 156.

171. Vahide, 219.

172. Op. cit., 157.

173. Bediuzzaman Saïd Nursi, *The Words*, translated from the Turkish by Sükran Vahide (Istanbul: Sözler Nesriyat, 1992), 9.

174. Bediuzzaman Saïd Nursi, *The Damascus Sermon*, 11.

175. Mardin, 199.

176. Vahide, 302.

177. Ibid., 301.

178. Bediuzzaman Saïd Nursi, *The Rays Collection*, translated by Sükran Vahide (Istanbul: Sözler Nesriyat, 1998), 103.

179. Ibid., 116.

180. Quoted in Vahide, 212.

181. Quoted in Vahide, 205.

182. Feroz Ahmad, *The Turkish Experiment in Democracy 1950-1975* (London: C. Hurst & Co., 1977), 24.

183. Ibid., 40-42.

184. Feroze, 121.

185. Ibid., 124.

186. Vahide, 329.

187. Quoted in Vahide, 357.

188. Ibid., 62.

189. Ibid., 181.

# Index

Akyürek, Akeman, 174-175
Al-Afghani, Jamal al-Din, 196-197
Alevis, 155, 156, 174, 251, 257-258
    ablution technique of, 259
    mixed worship, 251, 259
    percentage of population, 260
Al-Khalil (Abraham, Prophet),
    230-231
Alliance Israélite Universelle, 118
Armenians of Anatolia, 53-54,
    103, 104, 114
    battle for Van, 52, 156-158
    lone survivor in Diyarbakir,
    190-191
    victims of violence, 104-105,
    125
American Protestant missionaries,
    102-104
Ankara, 21, 22, 152, 173
Army Mutual Assistance
    Association (OYAK), 301
Arslan, Alp, 61-62
Atatürk, Mustafa Kemal, 23, 127,
    209, 268
    Bektashis and, 256-257

cultism and, 110, 161, 163,
    218
death of, 235
disorder in eastern provinces
    and, 58-59, 207
founder of secular state, 21
head of CUP force, 139
lack of freedom and, 23, 24,
    110-111, 219
legacy of, 22, 34, 42, 162,
    290-291
policy of Westernization of,
    78, 153, 275
residence in Erzurum, 58, 59
resistance to Allied
    occupation by, 212
seen as national savior, 29, 75,
    226
Aymaz, Abdullah, 65-66
    encounter with Nur
    movement, 66-67
Arzan-ar-Rum, see Erzurum

Balkans, 16, 17, 154, 178
Barla, 269, 270, 273, 276
Bartholomeos I, 79, 214, 215, 218,
    222

Beyoglu, 119, 167, 169, 203
Bitlis, 106, 108, 184-185
    repression of Armenians in,
    186
Bir, Cevik, 70
Blair, Anthony, 125
Bulut, Faik, 72-73, 75, 87

Çaliskan, Mahmut, 282, 285-286
Çatli, Abdullah, 172-173, 174,
    175, 177
census of 1889, 102
Chaldiran, battle of, 90, 154
Committee of Union and Progress
    (CUP), 53, 127, 133-135,
    138-139, 144, 179
    dictating national policy 143
    hidden objective 144
    see also Young Turk movement
Communist Manifesto, 21
conscription, 263, 264
Crusade, Fourth, 120-121

Declaration of Independence, 58
Dede, Abdülhalim, 63, 64-65
Demirci, Yasir, 162, 165
    views on Said Nursi, 162-163
Demirel, Suleiman, 68, 177
Dergah see Halilürahman Dergah
Deyrul Zafaran monastery, 198-
    200, 201
Dimitras, Panayote, 64
Diyarbakir, 183, 188-189
    main mosque in, 191
    ruins of Armenian cathedral
    in, 190-191

social equality in, 191
tekke in, 191-192

Emirdag, 279, 281-282, 283
Enver Pasha, 134, 177, 178, 180
    offensive against Russia and,
    53-54
    support of Libyan expedition,
    207
Erbakan, Necmettin, 38, 68
    difference between Gülen
    and, 76
    political humiliation of, 40,
    141
    Refah Partisi founded by, 20,
    163
    see also Fazilet Partisi
    see also Refah Partisi
    see also Welfare Party
Erzurum, 46, 57-58, 158
    history of, 48-49
    Turkish coffee in, 54-55
Evren, Kenan, 59-60

Fazilet Partisi, 20-21, 38, 39, 41,
    128
    see also Erbakan, Necmettin
    see also Refah Partisi
    see also Welfare Party

Galata, 119-120, 122, 123, 124
    patrolled by Allied police, 204
Gladstone, William, 125
Gökalp, Ziya, 136, 144
Golden Generation, 21, 75-77, 88
    see also Gülen, Fetullah
Great Anatolia Project (GAP),
    188-189

Grand National Assembly, 226,
298
exchange between Said Nursi
and Atatürk, 226-227
Greece, 16, 17, 63
expansionism of, 178-180
defeat of, 213
Greeks of Instanbul, 213, 214,
220-221
*see also Rum Millet*
Gülen, Fetullah, 21, 39, 128, 141
charisma of, 87
comparison between Said
Nursi's followers and, 87
concern for minorities by, 78-
80
interview with, 79-86
media empire of 65-66, 67-68
political strategy of, 75-76,
78, 88
ruling on women and hijab by,
245, 248
school run by, 161
*see also* Golden Generation

Hajji Bektash Vali, 49, 83, 255,
260
followers of, 255-257
Halilürahman Dergah, 33, 238
Halilürahman Dergah (Photo),
14, 27
Hanafi School, 191
Harbiye, 253, 256
Hasim, Ahmet, 170
Hizan, 92, 104
Hoca Effendi *see* Gülen, Fetullah
Homel, David, 169

Horhor *medrese*, 115, 158, 159-
160
destruction of, 212
houses of reading *see* Nur
movement: *dershane*

intercity transport, 60-61, 183
Illuminist school, 111
Imam Ali, 83, 86
Iran, 38, 57, 65, 84
refugees from, 160
twenty years after the Islamic
revolution, 43, 47
Iraqi Kurdistan, 46, 48
Islam, 17, 18, 43
heterodoxies, 260
renewal movment, 15, 16, 28,
25, 35, 64, 143
resistance to Westernization
by, 18
tolerance of religious
communities, 83-84
Turkish repression of, 249-
250
Westernization of, 18, 19, 20
*see also* Political Islam
*see also* Shi'ism
*see also* Sunnis
Islamic fundamentalism *see* Islam:
renewal movement
Isparta, 30, 32, 269, 277
Israel, 47
Istanbul, 18, 107
Ottoman seat of power, 115
railway system, 71-72
Istanbul Foundation for Science
and Culture, 36, 38
Istiklal Caddesi, 23, 167-168, 171

Janissary Corps, 254, 255-256, 260
*jihad fetva*, 180-181, 205
journalists *see* media
Journalists' and Writers' Foundation, 65, 68, 79, 87

Kamondo, Comte Moïse de, 118
Kavakci, Merve, 21
Kemal, Namik, 126
Kemal, Mustafa *see* Atatürk
Kemal, Yashar, 69
Kemalism, 136, 138, 219
Kemalist regime, 59-60
Koutan, Recai, 21
Kurdish Intellectuals for Peace, 73
Kurdish Worker's Party (PKK), 47, 73, 93, 173, 189
    legitimacy of, 95
    reputation for ruthlessness of, 109
    Turkish perception of, 95
Kurds, 90
    denied rights of, 74-75, 94
    Ottoman reform and, 101
    Parliament and, 95

Lewis, Bernard, 153, 253-254
Lausanne Treaty, 217, 219, 221, 225, 267

Mahcupyan, Etyen, 77-78, 87
Maradonna, Diego, 66
March 31 Incident, 138-140, 142-143
Mardin, 194, 195-196, 201, 237

media, 22
    personalities in, 37
    political constraints on, 21, 69-70
    propagating Gülen, 87
Mehmet VI Vahideddin, 203-204, 206, 225
Menderes, Adnan, 31, 33, 292-294, 295-296, 297, 298-300
*millet* system, 64, 78, 79, 175-176, 214, 219
monophysites, 200-201
Mürsel, Safa, 42
    thesis on Said Nursi, 42
*murshid*, 87, 192
Mustafa Pasha, 112-113, 185
Myriokephalon, battle of, 272

Naqshband, Baha ad-Din, 163
Naqshbandis, 163, 165, 256
    resistance to Westernization and, 87, 104
    Said Nursi and, 278, 291
    *tekke* and, 192-193
National Movement Party, 175, 177, 300
National Pact, 59, 209
National Security Council, 23, 40
    *coup d'etat* of February 28, 1997, 40, 84-85
    proclamation of, 301
NATO, 24, 47, 59, 178, 285
National Unity Council, 177
New Bosnia *see* Yeni Bosna
Nur movement, 36, 66, 171
    absence of racial barriers in, 193

debating Western science by,
56-57
*dershane*, 92, 110, 151, 195,
202, 234, 280-281
women and, 242-243,
246-247
leader in Urfa of, 230
masculine universe of, 185,
241, 277
political Islam anathema to,
246, 302
political objectives of, 39-40,
41-42, 150-151
recruiting efforts by, 280
*Risale-i Nur* and, 202
source of success of, 146-147
women followers of, 243
*see also* Said Nursi: followers of
Nurcus *see* Nur movement
Nurs, 96, 99, 100, 105, 184
author's journey to, 91-93,
95-99

Öcalan, Abdullah, 40, 46, 47, 189,
267, 293
extradition of, 93
PKK founded by, 94
Ömer Pasha, 184, 185
Ottoman Empire, collapse of,
206-207
Ottoman Special Service, 205
Ottoman Reform Movement,
102-103, 124, 135, 176
dissidents of, 126
Özal, Turgut, 141, 243-244, 294

Palestine Liberation
Organization, 73

Pan-Turkism, 175, 177
Phanariotes, 213-225
Pipes, Daniel, 40
Political Islam, 38, 40, 42, 85, 88,
138
*see also* Islam
Pomaks, 63
Public Debt Administration
(PDA), 124
Poulton, Hugh, 94, 130, 175, 177,
219, 266
power politics, 47-48

Qizilbash *see* Alevis

Refah Partisi, 39, 68, 128, 163
difference between Gülen
and, 75-76, 85
election victories of, 38
removal from office, 66, 302
*see also* Erbakan, Necmettin
*see also* Fazilet Partisi
*see also* Welfare Party
Rifa'i dervishes, 49-50
Republican People's Party (CHP),
31, 275, 290, 294, 299
*Risale-i Nur*, 272, 277, 282-283,
285, 287
as instrument of change, 34,
292, 296, 279
first collection of essays of,
278-279
first printing of, 274-275
source of, 292
*Rum Millet*, 205, 214, 217
*see also* Greeks of Istanbul

**Said Nursi, Bediuzzaman,** 36, 39, 42, 54, 140, 163
Address to Freedom, 134
Adnan Menderes and, 296-297, 299
arrest and conviction under Article 163, 283, 284
audience with Sultan Abdülhamid, 131, 132
birth of, 91
birthplace of, 96, 99
call for tolerance by, 75, 145
campaign against atheism by, 57, 138, 145-146, 271, 285
court-martial of, 142
    acquittal of, 142, 145
Damascus sermon by, 145-146
emblematic of Islam, 26, 57, 289-290
encounter with Ömer Pasha, 184
espouses Pan-Islamism, 180, 225-226
*fetva* drafted by, 180
first school of, 96
followers of, 36-37, 38-39, 73, 93, 151, 189, 286
    *see also* Nur movement
imprisonment in Russia, 164, 186, 208
legacy of, 291-292, 296-297
Libyan expedition by, 182, 205-206
mission to open educational institution by, 125, 129, 130, 147-148, 154, 162
nationalism and, 75, 297
personal qualities of, 285, 302
place of internment of, 29, 34, 45, 201, 239, 265, 287, 289, 300
refuge on Pine Mountain, 272, 291
refusal to support Sheikh Said revolt, 267, 268
residence in Barla, 270-271, 272, 273
residence in Emirdag, 279, 282, 286
residence in Isparta, 269, 277
residence in Istanbul, 128-129
role in WWI by, 51-52, 156, 158-159, 203
    casualty of war, 186
Safa Mürsel views on, 42-43
similarity with Khomeini, 197, 285
spiritual crisis of, 210-211
St.Sophia sermon by, 138
upbringing of, 99-101
    gains in stature, 130-131, 132
    geographical journey, 107-108, 111-113, 164
    spiritual progress, 114-115, 125-126, 196, 198
    years of exile, 30-33, 265-269, 270-271, 273-274, 279, 283
**Said Nursi, Bediuzzaman** (Photo), 97, 116
**Salahuddin, Ahmet,** 19-20
**Salonica,** 133, 134, 135
*Selam,* 21
*semahane,* 251-152, 258-260
**Shafi'i School,** 191
**Shah Ismail,** 154-155
**Sheikh Said revolt,** 266-267

Shi'ism, 17, 154, 257
  Naqshbandi hostility to, 163
  *see also* Islam
*Signs of Miraculousness*, 54, 208
Society of Islamic Unity, 138, 140
Special Emergency Rule Zone,
  183
STV, 67-68
Sufis, Sufism *see tariqat*
Sultan Abdülhamid, 104, 114,
  115, 125
  aftermath of Russian offensive
  and, 126-127
  fall from power, 133, 135,
  179, 180
  personality and career, 129-
  130
  promoting Pan-Islamism,
  176, 179, 197
  rise to the throne, 137
  Sheikh Emin Effendi and,
  108
Sultan Abdülassiz, 136-137
Sultan Mahmut II, 20
  burial place of, 128
Sultan Selim I, 73, 155
Sun Language Theory, 219
Sunnis, 18, 101
  suspicion of Alevis, 260-261
  *see also* Islam
Supreme Board of Higher
  Education (YÖK), 22, 23
Susurluk incident, 172-174

Tahir Pasha, 152, 154
*Tanzimat*, 114, 176, 253
*tariqat*, 163, 198,

banned by Atatürk, 268, 269,
  275
  Gülen and, 87
  Nur movement and, 36, 87,
  242
  Rifa'i and, 49
  Said Nursi and, 39
thought crimes, 23, 24, 172
Tokak, Harun, 68-69
Treaty of Sèvres, 74-75, 205
Türkes, Alparslan, 177
Turkish Grand National
  Assembly, 93
Turkish Kurdistan, 183
Turkish Mafia, 172, 174, 245, 301

*ulama*, 111, 131, 210, 274
  advice to rulers, 122-123, 185,
  struggle against
  Westernization, 20
United Nations, 47
Urfa, 30, 229, 236-237

Vahide, Sükran, 283
Van, 62, 89-91, 114, 149-150
  citadel of 156-157
Virillio, Paul, 169

Water and Irrigation Authority,
  187, 188, 194
Welfare Party, 41, 68, 73, 136, 141
  rise of, 244
  *see also* Erbakan, Necmettin
  *see also* Fazilet Partisi
  *see also* Refah Partisi

Yeni Bosna, 36, 37, 65

YÖK *see* Supreme Board of
  Higher Education
Young Ottomans, 126, 127, 176
Young Turk movement, 127, 133,
  134, 136, 138, 143-144, 177-
  178, 179
  government of, 207
  Pan-Islamism espoused by,
  180
  opposition to, 138, 181
  *see also* CUP

*Zaman*, 65, 67-68, 70
Zionist movement, 47, 118